REFLECTIVE TEACHING IN THE POSTMODERN WORLD

REFLECTIVE TEACHING IN THE POSTMODERN WORLD
A MANIFESTO FOR EDUCATION IN POSTMODERNITY

Stuart Parker

Open University Press
Buckingham · Philadelphia

Open University Press
Celtic Court
22 Ballmoor
Buckingham
MK18 1XW

and

1900 Frost Road, Suite 101
Bristol, PA 19007, USA

First Published 1997

A catalogue record of this book is available from the British Library

ISBN 0 335 19586 5 (hbk)   0 335 19585 7 (pbk)

Library of Congress Cataloging-in-Publication Data
Parker, Stuart. 1954–
    Reflective teaching in the postmodern world: a manifesto for
education in postmodernity / Stuart Parker.
       p.   cm.
    Includes bibliographical references and index.
    ISBN 0–335–19586–5. — ISBN 0–335–19585–7 (pbk.)
    1. Education—Philosophy. 2. Teaching. 3. Reflection
(Philosophy) 4. Postmodernism and education. I. Title.
LB14.7.P356 1997
370′.1—dc20   96–28699
                                                  CIP

Typeset by Graphicraft Typesetters Ltd, Hong Kong
Printed in Great Britain by Biddles Ltd, Guildford and Kings Lynn

Dedicated to
Val
and
Pete and Tim.
Diamonds

CONTENTS

ACKNOWLEDGEMENTS

My thanks to:

My wife Val for more than I can say.

My parents; they know why.

BEd and BA students at South Bank University: especially those taking the philosophy options.

Pam Ray and Chris Costa for taking the strain.

Shona Mullen of Open University Press.

Numerous friends with whom I have been able to discuss and develop these ideas: Gaby Weiner, Sally Mitchell, Alan Parkinson, Roger Gibson, Chris Sweet, Stuart Deval, John White, Pat White, Reynold Jones, Graham Haydon, Terry Moore, David and Mollie Louth, George Lowe, John Turner, Peter Roy and Peter Gilroy.

Their trace is apparent on every page.

CONVENTIONS

References to the writings of Wittgenstein follow convention by citing sections except where a page number is specified. I have used the following abbreviations for his books: *Philosophical Investigations* (PI); *On Certainty* (OC); *Remarks on the Foundations of Mathematics* (RFM). References to Kemp-Smith's translation of Kant's *Critique of Pure Reason* use his convention of referring to the two editions as A and B followed by the page number. Full details of these texts are included in the bibliography.

PART I

THE SCENE OF MODERN EDUCATIONAL THEORY AND PRACTICE

1

THE OPENING

Perhaps our sense of belonging more to a world
held together by networks of ephemeral confidences
(such as philosophies and stock markets) rather
than permanent certainties, predisposes us to
embrace the pleasures of our most primitive, un-
langued sense. Being mystified doesn't frighten us
as much as it used to. And the point for me is not
to expect perfumery to take its place in some nice,
reliable, rational world order, but to expect
everything else to become like it: the future will be
like perfume.

(Brian Eno, *Guardian Weekend*,
11 March 1995: 53)

The book of the stories

This is about two stories of education. In one there is a vocabulary of means,
efficiency, universals, law-like generalization and bureaucracy; in the other,
one of autonomy, emancipation, uniqueness, democracy, ends and values.
The stories have different characters. The former's stars include the detached
academic researcher, the manager, the scientist, the bureaucrat, the inspector
and the therapist; the latter's champion is the autonomous, reflective teacher-
researcher who is committed to the improvement and emancipation of her
work-context. The first story's heroes are lone operators at the top of distinctive hierarchies; each charged with the responsibility of administrating over the
discrete domain of their expertise and authority. Their institutions are *man-
aged*, hierarchical. In the second story the heroine is a member of a reflexive
community where hierarchies are flattened or eliminated under democratic
commitments.

Each tale contains an irony. Although the first story's heroes operate dis-
cretely, their rule over their hierarchies is guaranteed only by appeal to the
higher authority of natural and universal laws which it is the hero's job to
apply scrupulously in regulating his domain; while the heroine of the second
story defends collectivist, democratic ideals, she also champions the unique
distinctiveness of each collective. People who subscribe to one of these stories tend not to understand anyone else's preferring the other. This is not

just an intellectual or aesthetic disagreement; it is a difference in entire world views.

To talk about itself, the second story uses names like 'reflective teaching', 'action-research' and 'critical thinking'; to talk about the other story it uses names like 'positivism', 'scientism' and 'technical-rationality'. Reflective teaching has widespread appeal among a large group of educationalists and teachers. However, it is probably true that positivism or technical-rationalism is today's dominant philosophy. Not only does it have a long history, it offers something which the story of reflective teaching does not: a way of justifying a bureaucracy and one's place within it. Indeed, there is, within education, a rising tide of bellicose managerialism manifested in hierarchical lines of command and decision-making, centralization of power, massively increased bureaucracy, a management-oriented vocabulary of pedagogy and, in England and Wales, a National Curriculum dreamed up by politicians and an inspection service run as an enforcement organization. The bureaucracy runs to a belief that in education there is a single right answer, and that managers know it, and precipitates a lack of trust of the underlings which necessitates a strong police force of inspectors and an intolerance of pluralism except where alternatives can be purchased by those rich enough to afford the privilege.

In such times, when governmental discourse employs a language of *bureaucracy* rather than *democracy* or *reflection*, we can expect positivism's story to flourish through its constant re-telling and confirmation, while other stories will be forced to borrow its vocabulary as the only means of telling their narrative meaningfully. As a result, what *gets* expressed by alternatives is something quite different from what was intended, some thin surrogate which does not convey faithfully the original's meaning but always finishes up being a distortion of it. The story's heroine has to display herself as some version of one or more of the dominant story's heroes and inevitably is left disgraced and inadequate to the role.

But those who see the bureaucratization of education as a grave mistake, those for whom reflective teaching seems to offer a promising alternative, are confronted by the dilemma of providing encouragement to pluralism while preventing the *descent* into a relativism where what is true, or good, varies between one culture and another. Managerialism, with its *one right answer*, has no such relativistic worries; it simply doesn't tolerate difference. This makes reflective teaching vulnerable to the charge of relativism since, from the managerialist's perspective, pluralism is simply a polite expression masking an anything-goes relativism.

Sub-plot and supplement

Relativism arises as a subplot to reflection's story in the question of the limits of liberal tolerance. What, for example, makes it OK to *tolerate* a Muslim's ritual slaughter of animals, a Jew's ritual GBH of a boy's genitals, but not human sacrifice as practised by extinct Aztec cultures and, for all I know, today's suburban witches? What is there, in other words, to prevent liberal tolerance from spontaneously collapsing into a relativism in which *anything goes*? These questions are worrying to liberals, since if relativism is the inevitable end of reason's process then how can we make a justified stand on any issue?

Supplementary to this is the vocabulary of *postmodernism, poststructuralism* and *deconstruction* which peppers the conversations that today's culture has with itself in magazines, newspapers, Sunday supplements, cyber-talk, films, architecture, education etc. The words are used as slogans which serve to identify the writer's credentials at the 'cutting edge' of discourse fashion; but in most cases they could safely be omitted without doing serious harm to the quality of the writer's message. The titles are worn as accessories by writers wishing to be thought of as *avant garde*. Few such writers, however, get to be thought of as having anything to say. What separates the many sloganizers from the few authentic postmodernists is the reluctance or inability of the former to countenance the consequences of living a conversation in which the words bite; of facing, among other things, the consequences of relativism.

The story of the book

The purpose of this book is to perform a deconstruction of the stories of reflective teaching, action-research, critical theory and liberal philosophies of education. Between these there is sufficient intellectual, methodological and political overlap – especially at the points where deconstruction penetrates – for them to be considered as one; though of course, as with any family, there are detail differences in the views of writers who would nevertheless be happy to be identified with the general thrust of these positions. The text I have deconstructed belongs, therefore, to no one in particular. It is as yet unwritten. But what it consists in are the exemplary theses and arguments of a character, whom I have called *the reflective teacher*, whose views are expressed through a number of writers, none of whom, I take it, would find themselves greatly at odds with my mutation.

I begin by identifying the culture of positivism; the hostile theoretical background against which reflective teaching must be viewed and against which it reacts. I end by showing how many of the commitments of reflective teaching may be preserved, albeit in distorted forms, within a different, deconstructively styled fashion of writing. In between I argue that reflective teaching is insufficiently divorced from the traditions it rejects for it to be capable of expressing the things that it *feels* or realizing its declared emancipatory purpose. I situate its historical importance in evolutionary and strategic terms. In evolutionary terms its method of rejecting traditional conceptions of the nature and purpose of educational theory provides clues to novel ways of thinking which could not be grasped in traditional vocabulary but which cannot be approached through reflective teaching's own criteria. Strategically it is crucial in that it provides the cognitive and linguistic stepping stone for understanding and expressing the stylistic innovations which surpass it. In the present context it is therefore employed as a pedagogic tool with which to ease the way from tradition to avant garde.

Part I of this book unfurls the account of the struggle between positivism's story and the cluster of narratives anthologized around reflective teaching. In Chapters 2 and 3 I describe the main principles and consequences of positivism: its commitment to objectivity, its technical-rationalist account of value-free notions of efficiency and effectiveness, and its desire for ultimate convergence of all rational views. Positivism's story is incompatible with a vocabulary of pluralism in education and, consequently, predisposes the system to suppress differences of pedagogy and culture. Chapter 4 sets the idea of reflective teaching against this backdrop to show how it differs from its opponent and what attractions it offers. I examine key aspects of its shifted vocabulary: concern with ends and values, uniqueness, action research, emancipation, autonomy, rationality and democracy.

The character of the reflective teacher embodies an optimistic vision of human potential within a pessimistic picture of its present realization. Those committed to its ideals, and who wish to place reflectiveness at the centre of our conception of what it is to be a professional educator, share a hope that this will nurture certain social, democratic and emancipatory commitments as well as pedagogic effectiveness. Such reflective professionals differ from positivism's blueprint of the teacher in a number of ways; most importantly in terms of their attitudes to the social, moral and dynamic dimensions of education. Reflective professionals would be conscious of the social implications of educational practices and policy. They would be adaptive, but not passively, celebrating change and taking the initiative in its promotion.

In Chapter 5 I argue that reflective teaching requires the philosophical foundation provided by the kind of critical theory developed by Habermas and applied within educational contexts by Carr and Kemmis (among others). I argue further that at a deep, fundamental level reflective teaching and positivism share a common set of terms, commitments, forms and strategies which are the common genetic inheritance – *realism* – out of which spring their distinctive, oppositional stories.

Part II of the book introduces and then applies the manoeuvres of deconstruction and initiates the stylistic shift away from the realist conventions of academia to the literary play of postmodernism. The story which develops does not attempt to defend reflective teaching against positivism; nor does it emplot a synthesis of the two stories and their disputed vocabularies. It provides no translation manual for expressing the central expressions of positivism within reflective teaching's vocabulary. It is not even an attempt to move beyond these stories; not, at least, in the sense of providing a reasoned, dialectical critique of their arguments to move to a *more rational, more enlightened truth*.

It is more an attempt, as Rorty puts it, to change the subject; to stop playing this game and do something else. It is a suggestion that we begin to talk in a different way, not because the old vocabulary was wrong or that it is inadequate to the task of representing how things are, but because it has become passé and there might be a more useful, more exciting way for us to talk about the affairs of the early twenty-first century.

In Chapter 6 I prepare readers for the arguments which follow. This chapter can stand independently as a guide to the strategies of deconstruction.

I explain the technicalities of deconstruction: the role of binary conceptual hierarchies, the strategy of reversal and displacement, *différance*, writing and metaphor, presence and trace, *sous rature*, marginality and the supplement. The story situates deconstruction as a strategy, not a position; a strategy which is a device of style, of *textualism*, whose appropriate attitude is one of irony. The strategy is employed in Chapters 7 and 8 to displace the realist concepts of reason, truth, reality and autonomy that are structurally necessary for the narrative coherence of reflective teaching's philosophy.

I attempt to open the space in which a new fashion of writing can emerge by borrowing rhetorical manoeuvres from Richard Rorty, Ludwig Wittgenstein and Jacques Derrida to show how the required fracture is already inevitably present within the vocabulary of the old story styles. This fracture is the opening of the story of postmodernism. In Part III I write a preface for the story of postmodern education. The postmodern world is more *style* than *thing*. It is a world in which old vocabularies and old oppositions of true/false, good/ evil, theory/practice, heaven/hell get junked or refashioned to serve new purposes and new styles of inventing others and creating ourselves.

2

TECHNICAL-RATIONALITY

Reflection

To state, first, the obvious, *reflective teaching* involves reflecting on one's teaching. This reflection can take place before the event of teaching and manifest itself as planning, after the event as evaluation and simultaneous to the teaching as reflection in action involving adjustments to or accommodation of some of the contingencies which arise. At a very general level, reflective teaching involves *thinking about one's teaching,* an account of which will include use of such cognate terms as 'reasoning' and 'reasons', 'critical thinking' and 'analysis' as well as the previously mentioned 'planning' and 'evaluating'.

But if this is to state the obvious it is hardly less obvious that the vocabulary of reason, critical thinking and so on was not *invented* by the reflective teaching movement; nor is it dependent for its meaning on the existence of something called reflective teaching. The inevitable conclusion is sometimes missed: reflective teaching is not identical with 'reasoning about teaching' or 'analysing and evaluating one's teaching'. It does not mean the same thing as either of these expressions. Reflective teaching, if it involves the terms 'reason' or 'analysis' at all, involves a particular conception of the terms and their legitimate range of application; a conception which, among other things, will serve to differentiate genuine examples of reflective teaching from just any old example of *thinking about what one is doing.*

From this, two important conclusions follow. First, reflective teaching is a technical term with a quite particular meaning which cannot be assumed straightforwardly to emerge from everyday notions of thinking and reasoning. Consequently, this technical concept presupposes a theory of rationality which will at least enable the distinction to be drawn between reflective teaching and rational teaching that does not qualify as *reflective.*

Means–ends reasoning

The requisite view of rationality is examined in Chapter 4. An understanding of its force, however, presupposes grasp of the nature of an earlier culture whose view of rationality is what genuine cases of reflective teaching are differentiated from: *'earlier'* because the reflective teaching movement can, with some justification, be characterized as a reaction against what it takes to be an impoverished notion of reason. But 'earlier' must not be taken to mean 'superseded'.

This earlier culture is one in which rationality is construed entirely as a process of divining the most efficient means of achieving some pre-established result or end. The teacher is seen as essentially a means–ends broker and teaching is conceived as a technical exercise, an applied science, concerned with, and judged according to, the criteria of means–ends efficiency. Rational teaching, on this view, relies upon a range of means-enhancing devices such as 'psychometric analyses, isolated technical competence, linear thinking and instrumental reason' (Beyer 1987: 19). Education is a technical 'delivery system' within which the worth of teacher-operatives is defined entirely in terms of their possession of a prescribed set of skills or competences and professional beliefs require justification by technical-rational procedures of investigation (cf. Carr 1980; Carr and Kemmis 1986: 62).

As Siegel has observed, far from being superseded, this *technical-rationalist* picture is easily the most prevalent one on the market today. It is, crucially, a conception of rationality which takes ends as given, outside the scope of rational scrutiny; judging rationality 'solely in terms of the efficiency of means in achieving ends' (Siegel 1988: 130). Rational choice becomes entirely a matter of choosing 'so as to achieve most efficiently those ends, or to maximize utility or the satisfaction of preference' (Siegel 1988: 129).

Positivism

The cultural framework within which the technical model of rationality is embedded implicitly, and sometimes explicitly, embraces the philosophy of *positivism*. Its modes of discourse are shot through with the assumption that the description and explanation of anything – including social phenomena – must employ the procedural and justificatory standards of the natural sciences; or, more accurately, *this* coupled with the belief that the arguments, theories and practices of such discourses as philosophy, ethics, sociology and politics must take as their premises some statement(s) of natural science, the truth of statements about social phenomena – including educational practices – being dependent upon the truth of some class of statements of natural science. Knowledge, consequently, is only achievable through the objective, experimental, inductive activities of science. *Facts* – as revealed by the methodology of science – are the only possible content of true statements. The only guarantee that moral or sociological statements contain *facts* is that they have been arrived at through methods which are essentially those of natural science.

Positivism is thus reductive of a range of discourses or modes of theorizing; rendering all their statements into expressions of the language of science and their candidate referring terms as constructions out of the referring terms of science's foundational vocabulary. Through this methodological parsimony of observation and experiment positivism promises to reveal the fundamental natural laws – expressible as universal, non-analytic generalizations – which govern the cause and effect relations of social and institutional phenomena. This parsimony extends to the nomological formulations themselves, which may contain only terms that refer to observable phenomena or terms that have been defined operationally.

The hierarchical relationship by which referring, observational terms contitute the epistemological foundations of the laws of nature, and, in turn, of the theories ultimately derived, is the mirror of positivism's metaphysical atomism which takes it as axiomatic that the simple components of the universe are more fundamental than the complex ones. Consequently, the truth of singular referring statements is independent of the truth of any particular general law, and the truth of a general law is similarly independent of the truth of any particular theory. The relation of *truth-value dependency* works from complex to simple. The truth of any theory is dependent upon the truth of a range of particular, referring sentences; the reverse does not hold. The whole system of theory, law and reference is brought together under a tightly defined formal logic in which ontological commitment is embodied in the terms which happen to be taken as the values of its bound variables (Quine 1948: 15).

The consequences of positivism for the way in which we represent or theorize social reality are massive. Positivism continues the narrative of the enlightenment, telling a story of cultural progress in which modernity is depicted as the epoch when science finally replaces religion and custom as the foundation for social organization. In this modern, positivist world the law-like generalizations of science form the foundations of any claims to expertise. The expert becomes one who has grasp of a certain set of law-like generalizations with which to inform and justify his or her decisions. Moreover, the requirement that putative fact-stating expressions should be capable of being brought under the regimentation of a quantificational logic ensures that any statements concerning moral principles or ends, and those which contain intensional terms such as beliefs or wishes, *can no longer be regarded as expressing facts*. Value – insofar as value statements are capable of being true or false – becomes definable solely as a function of a means–end relation; the value of item x is expressible entirely in terms of its contribution to the efficient realization of some particular end y. When that end is some social situation – personal, institutional or bureaucratic – the value of the individual person is simply his or her instrumental value to the process of bringing about that end. Rationality is the process by which the most efficient route from wherever we are now to the desired end can be determined. To behave rationally is to act on that information. Rational teaching, on this model, is the application of the methods of science – systematic quantitative methods involving observation and collection of data, classification, analysis, generalization, concern to generate predictions and achieve control – in the efficient realization of education's prespecified ends.

Technical-rationalism enacts the positivist principle that ends themselves are *outside the rational sphere*. Disputes about ends cannot be conducted by appeal to facts. As Hume (1740: 415) puts it, reason is the slave of the passions. The technical-rationalist teacher adopts this *teleological* view of education; that is, her actions are to be judged or valued according to the extent to which they are effective in bringing about whatever are taken to be education's proper ends. She is opposed to a *deontological* perspective, which would hold some actions – educational experiences, items of content – to be valuable or worthwhile in themselves. She sees life in an essentially game-theoretic way, in which the end goals, desirable outcomes, are unitary and given; the challenge for reason is how to find the most effective, efficient way of reaching the ends. This presupposes that the ends remain consistent across the range of possible means (and uncontaminated by them) and that life in general, and education in particular, is primarily a matter of realizing certain objectives (see Flew 1972).

The professionals

A crucial point of opposition between positivism's view of education and that embraced by the reflective teacher is over the question of whether individual human beings simply gain their moral, personal and social value in virtue of their role in helping to bring about certain ends, or whether, following Kant, the rights attaching to individuals-as-persons include, fundamentally, that of their unconditional worth; a right which carries as a moral imperative that no person should be treated simply as a means to someone else's end.

Positivism's construal of value-as-means is congruent with its conception of what it means to be a 'professional'. For positivism, professional activity in general 'consists in instrumental problem solving made rigorous by the application of scientific theory and technique' (Schön 1983: 21). In consequence, the foundations of professional status are to be found in 'the substantive field of knowledge that the specialist professes to command and . . . the technique of production or application of knowledge over which the specialist claims mastery' (Schön 1983: 22).

The implications for teaching and teacher *training* are clear. Indeed, once this picture of professionalism is accepted it becomes entirely natural to speak of teacher *training* and correspondingly perverse to use the vocabulary of teacher *education*. Whatever in the content of the term 'education' exceeds the scope of the meaning of 'training' is at best redundant, since what marks out the professional teacher from the lay person is the specialist training she has received in the techniques of bringing about learning in others. Any critical thinking which such trained professionals are required to bring to bear upon their activities can be fully characterized as a proficiency in finding efficient routes to the effective realization of prespecified teaching goals.

The moral authority or pedagogical legitimacy of the goals themselves is not an issue of professional concern. Professionals do their job, they don't define it (Schön 1983: 12). Indeed, it is the goals themselves – whether they be expressed in terms of a curriculum to be delivered, learning targets to be attained, truancy or withdrawal levels to be met – which serve, at least in part, to define the nature of the profession and provide the framework within which professional success and failure can be measured. Like industrialists, 'educational managers and workers must emphasize increased productivity, the maintenance of a higher quality "product", and gains in efficiency, through the adoption of new management systems, better incentives, and the use of new technologies' (Beyer 1987: 25). The imperatives of measurement consequent upon this picture – particularly those concerning questions of professional effectiveness and efficiency – ensure that the goals are required to be prespecified, fully determinate and unambiguous.

Can teaching be a profession?

Given this account of professional expertise, the question arises as to whether teaching can even be considered a profession. Schön has described how within this model a contrast can be drawn between major professions which are, as described above, disciplined by determinate ends and techniques of bringing about these ends, and the minor professions which 'suffer from shifting, ambiguous ends and from unstable institutional contexts of practice' (Schön 1983: 23). However, because of the corresponding difference in status likely to attach to this distinction, it would perhaps be more accurate to drop the prefix 'major' from what are, under positivism, the *true* professions and rename Schön's minor professions 'proto' or 'candidate' professions; activities which yet have some way to go to achieve the professional status they desire. It is certainly clear what these activities must become if they are to achieve the status of professions: they must express determinate goals that are recognizably achievable through the application of specific technical processes.

The message for education is no less clear: if education is to become a profession its practitioners must strive to achieve universal consensus about the ends of education and about the techniques necessary for bringing about these ends; all of this being grounded in a demonstrable knowledge base, which also commands universal, rational assent, and housed within institutions whose structure enables the techniques to be efficiently and effectively applied and the results to be accurately assessed. Given a technical-rationalist conception of professional expertise, it follows that insofar as teaching tolerates conflict over its aims or disagreement about its proper techniques it prohibits itself from entitlement to the status of *profession*.

This structure of the relations between professional status, aims and techniques provides strong contingent support for the supposition that the task of professionalizing teaching will lead to a hierarchical division of labour across its practitioners. The agents of the system, the workers, the teachers, cannot act as the guarantors of the truths of the system or profession. Their activities take place in contexts which are simply too various to assume immunity against idiosyncrasy. Heavily redolent of Plato's elevating of the role of the guardians in his *Republic*, the solution is a division of labour along the theory–practice divide, where the profound, general, universalizing questions of education are the exclusive concern of politicians or, possibly, of university-based curriculum designers (Carr and Kemmis 1986: 16).

This adds to *the transmission of techniques* a second essential requirement of the mission of teacher *training*. It is the initiation of students into the standardized, nationally uniform curriculum designs and practices devised and authorized by the politicians or university researchers, the guardians of the profession's *logos*. If teaching has to gain professional status on these grounds it will not have far to look to find theoretical perspectives and research which could support the required move to universal agreement. In what follows I sketch possible sources of such support.

Behaviourism originated in 1914 with the work of J. B. Watson. The rise of positivism ensured an intellectual climate that was especially welcoming to an approach to psychology which promised to replace the 'unscientific' pseudo-techniques of subjective introspection with properly empirical practices. Thus, the model for psychology would be physics: behaviour supplying the raw empirical material susceptible to exact measurement and objective verification, and supporting, ultimately, the control of the psychological realm to be afforded by rendering its phenomena predictable; an optimism nourished by the results of the experiments conducted by Pavlov. Psychological terms – thoughts, desires, intentions, feelings and so on – would be translated into expressions of behaviour or stimulus–response relations and dispositions; elements fit for the role of giving a value to logic's variables. The only significant question about this reduction of the psychological to the material was whether the reduction should take as its base the molar behaviour of human action or whether it should be pushed all the way through to the bedrock laws of physics itself.

Within education this latter reduction has not been carried through, but B.F. Skinner's explanation of the mind in terms of molar behaviour has been influential in supplying the conceptual framework within which modern reductions of the qualities constitutive of the teacher to sets of behaviourally verifiable competences could become articulated. Skinnerian behaviourism has also set the technical-rationalist conceptual agenda of a range of educational programmes, of which the National Curriculum itself is, arguably, but the latest evolution. Indeed, Skinner's 'methodology' – which rejects theory on the premise that the inductive process leads directly from observational data to generalizable conclusions – is itself prototypical for technical-rationalism's monopolization of the educational dialogue through its distrust of theory and its exclusive focus on means rather than ends.

Jean Piaget's *genetic epistemology* is another example of the way in which technical-rationalism impinges upon educational practice via psychological theory. It is, in one sense at least, even more of a testimony to the hegemony of the technical-rationalist conceptual framework than is the widespread cultural fallout of behaviourism, since the philosophical setting for Piaget's own thought is anything but technical-rationalist. Piaget's programme was essentially an attempt to describe the empirical concomitants of Kant's epistemology. In using Kant as the springboard for his own investigations, Piaget was bound to employ a mode of theorizing which appreciated the fundamental role our conceptual framework has in forming our perceptions of reality; a constructivism quite alien to the tenets of technical-rationalism. In spite of this, the public exchange of Piagetian doctrine represents the position as a set of experimentally grounded, inductive generalizations which describe the universal stages of child development. The philosophical setting of Piaget's epistemology is suppressed, the experimental foundations for his generalizations are emphasized and Piaget is repackaged as another icon of positivism whose scientific credentials lend their authority to the picture of learning's linearity.

The *macro-sociological surveys* which have abounded in educational research in recent decades, and which have variously attempted to throw light on the nature of school effectiveness, the effectiveness of teaching style or classroom organization, constitute another enactment of the values of technical-rationalism (see Bennett 1976; Galton *et al.* 1980; Mortimore *et al.* 1988). The predictive confidence of these forms of research is premised on the assumption – common to all incarnations of technical-rationalism – that social reality is essentially uniform, that large samples are therefore necessarily representative and that the effects of uniqueness and contingency are substantially less prevalent than are the regularities and similarities which the law-like generalizations of the research adequately describe.

The philosophy of education has not escaped the domination of technical-rationalism. Paul Hirst's (1965) enormously influential account of the *forms of knowledge* argues that any genuine example of knowledge must fall within the domain of one of an exhaustive set of several discrete epistemological categories or forms of knowledge. The technical-rationalism of this account is evident in the criteria Hirst invokes to individuate each form, which generalize the practices of physical science to all other modes of experience. Thus knowledge in art or philosophy, history or mathematics, is, like the knowledge falling within the domain of natural science, identified in virtue of its *representation* – through a discrete set of structurally related central concepts that are unique to the form – and its *linguistic expression* in the form's distinctive statements, which are testable against experience using methods peculiar to the form.

It is the testability against experience which is the most obvious mark of technical-rationalism's generalization of science; but the discrete regimentation of the forms is enough in itself to fit the technical-rationalist model of knowledge as a set of statements, the logical relations between which are determinately ordered. What Hirst's analysis bequeaths to us is a model of the curriculum consisting of discrete subjects, the logic of whose structures implies a programmatic teaching and learning regime, and a rationale of truth-testing which is entirely instrumental, *even in ethics and philosophy*. Despite Hirst's intention to provide an epistemological foundation for liberal education, critics have noted the anti-liberal consequences of his *distribution across the forms* of the technical epistemology supplied by the model of science.[1]

The hunger for technique

The dominance which technical-rationalism has enjoyed over large regions of the beliefs and practices of the West throughout the twentieth century is evident, arguably increasingly so, across the spectrum of educational practice, design and organization. In 1983 Schön observed that there is no more vivid sign of the persistence of the ideas of technical-rationality and its underpinning of the claims of professionals to social mandate, autonomy and licence 'than the hunger for technique which is so characteristic of students of the professions in this decade' (Schön 1983: 288). In education, at least in the UK, Schön's observation is if anything even more apposite to the 1990s, when the government-imposed minimum competency vocabulary of courses awarding qualified teacher status reinforces the idea that teaching is simply the technical mastery of a set of discrete procedures, achievement of which is readily manifested as a corresponding set of discrete behaviours.

And students do not escape the confines of this picture on graduation, but are subject to its systematic reinforcement as, under the slogans of technical efficiency and effectiveness which mark out the technical-rational view of educational processes, in-service courses 'have become predominantly short-burst, 'quick fix' one-day events concerned with curriculum implementation' (Day 1993: 84). These 'quick fixes' are premised upon the technical-rationalist assumption that the techniques by which the problems of teaching are to be solved are universally applicable to *any* teaching and learning context: to any child, by any teacher, in any school whatsoever. The power which technical-rationalism exerts over teachers and teaching in Great Britain can be judged by the extent to which a vocabulary of discrete competences defines the concept of the professional, while minimum-competency testing constitutes the measure of student achievement, teacher accreditation requirements and professional expertise.

Metaphors of technical-rationalism

For technical-rationalists, the curriculum is seen through the metaphor of a delivery system; teachers becoming operatives in education's factory (Carr and Kemmis 1986: 15–16). Knowledge – of whatever kind – is seen as a commodity to be packaged, and transmitted or sold to others. The commodity metaphor supports and is reinforced by a network of other metaphors which picture knowledge as something that can be assembled and acquired in a purely linear, additive manner. The power of such metaphors has consequences for the way in which we must describe the teaching and learning process. Knowledge becomes an atomic system of epistemic building blocks which get additively combined into larger epistemic molecules. This knowledge packaging enterprise finds expression in the modularized courses which abound today, the components of which are defined and differentiated in terms of discrete sets of *learning outcomes* or competences that the delivery system works to distribute. Knowledge, because its movement, through learning, from the simple to the complex is a process which is entirely additive, brooks no anomaly or contradiction; a picture which leads naturally to the legitimization of a 'pick-and-mix' type of curriculum where coherence is guaranteed entirely by the principle that the addition of one unit of knowledge to another cannot but precipitate a coherent result.

The *characters* of technical-rationalism: managers and therapists

Alasdair MacIntyre has extended the analysis of the metaphors of positivism in a direction which throws further light upon the form that education has taken in the modern world. Symptomatic of the immanence of technical-rationality within modernity is the rise to cultural prominence of certain kinds of social roles or *characters* which serve to define for modern culture its morality and its social norms (MacIntyre 1985: 27ff). MacIntyre uses *'character'* precisely because it fuses the dramatic demands of *role* with the term's positive moral connotations. A culture's *characters* serve as models or socio-moral icons in terms of which the rest of its members are able to define and describe themselves. The actions of the wider public have meaning and are judged for their value against a set of criteria and within a vocabulary made available by the typical comings and goings of the *characters* in the enactment of their functions.

Characters are the 'moral representatives of their culture . . . because of the way in which moral and metaphysical ideas and theories assume through them an embodied existence in the social world. *Characters* are the masks worn by moral philosophies' (MacIntyre 1985: 28). Indeed, the pervasiveness of the power of the *characters* to define the subjective and social lives of others is such that although universal assent to the moral principles which they embody may be lacking, moral disagreement will still be expressed with reference to the *characters*, whose styles of criteria and vocabulary will continue to form the focal point for the consideration and resolution of moral conflicts (MacIntyre 1985: 31).

It is inevitable that one of the *characters* of technical-rationalism should be the *manager*. The manager is the embodiment of bureaucratic rationality, the rationality of the efficient and economical matching of means to pre-determined ends (MacIntyre 1985: 25). The manager's defining responsibility is to marshal human and other resources in the service of achieving those ends. His expertise in this role is underwritten by his grasp of the law-like generalizations of management theory and is manifested in the application of this knowledge to the control of bureaucratic processes and the prediction of the results which his interventions will achieve.[2] As MacIntyre points out, this sets a particular agenda for the way in which social relationships and interactions can be conceived; for it becomes impossible, or at least difficult, to develop a narrative in which individual persons constitute moral ends in themselves without departing from the vocabulary and criteria embodied in the *character* of the manager. And if, as MacIntyre insists, this technical-rationalist vocabulary is the vocabulary of modernity, then any account of the in-trinsic moral worth of individuals is going to seem odd or quaint, since it will, of necessity, have to be expressed in a language which is alien to that employed by the dominant culture. The manager is the embodiment of a morality which sees the value of others only in terms of their potential as means to an end that lies outside of the individual's own interests.[3] Thus emotivism, the name of the moral theory of technical-rationalism, effectively obliterates the distinction between manipulative and non-manipulative social relations (MacIntyre 1985: 23).

Given this bureaucratic court of legitimation, it is unsurprising that the ends of any activity become divorced from the practice of value-setting or moral evaluation. Ends are removed from the game of rational appraisal. The only notion of rationality available is one in which means to ends are assessed in terms of the bureaucracy's own notions of effectiveness. What is rational, therefore, is whatever stands the best chance of effectively achieving predetermined ends as efficiently as possible. The ends themselves are not suitable objects for rational scrutiny.

MacIntyre's other *character* of modernity is the *therapist*.[4] What the manager does for social relations the therapist does for personal, subjective life; that is, he obliterates the distinction between manipulative and non-manipulative interactions. The therapist employs technique in the service of predetermined ends – the establishment of cures, normalities, states of well-adjustedness – whose value is not questioned. The effectiveness of the therapist lies, like that of the manager, in the effective and efficient realization of these ends, and requires no reference to the recipient's own claim to be, in herself, a moral end.

And inspectors

MacIntyre's thesis is that positivism is the dominant culture of modernity and that its self-conception is embodied in its metaphors and, in particular, the metaphors which are the *characters* of the manager and the therapist. One way in which the thesis is made visible is through current fashions of educational inspection, the practices of which are easily accommodated within the vocabulary described above. Three observations should be sufficient to demonstrate the case that educational inspection – such as that presently carried out in the UK by HMI and Ofsted in schools, colleges and univer-sities – is grounded in a technical-rationalist framework whose values are those of the bureaucracy and whose cultural *characters* are the manager and the therapist.

1   Inspection is algorithmic, depending on the use of standardized pro-cedures and even set wordings for comment and analysis. Popper's (1959: 99) view that 'any empirical scientific statement can be presented in such a way that anyone who has learned the relevant technique can test it' is given exag-gerated extension into the sphere of social exchange, to engender in technical-rationalist educators a desire for readily applicable *scientific* techniques of

testing statements about educational quality. This enables lay (non-expert) inspectors to be rapidly trained to carry out inspections. They are able to do this because the operations of inspection are essentially mechanical. This mechanism is constructed out of predetermined criteria which are employed in forming judgments. The criteria are couched in a vocabulary which obliterates unwanted or unvalued features of distinctiveness to seize upon elements susceptible to description under some universalized generalities. This results in an emaciated representation of the institution which rigorously and systematically works to eliminate rich descriptions capable of accommodating diversity. Judging educational practices against universalizable, quantifiable elements mirrors the universals of business bureaucracy, where profit is the universal concept by means of which companies engaged in radically different enterprises can unfailingly be compared (see Handy 1984: 135ff).

The positivistic restriction on reality – that if something is *genuinely real* it must be possible to quantify it – is over-stretched into the presumption that whatever can be easily quantified must be closer to the essential truth of some region of experience. Consequently, while 'good teaching' is reduced to a set of behavioural competences and such observable 'qualities' as 'reliability; punctuality; co-operation; and willingness to take on essential tasks' (Tickle 1992: 93), universities find themselves assessed for their research *quality* on the basis of the *quantity* of publications produced by their staff over a given period. Funding becomes linked to this number in such a way as to distort the timetable of research, as academics struggle to publish before the research census deadline, delay publication deliberately to register on the next census or rehash a piece of research into several forms to facilitate multiple publication.

2   These criteria are not simply universal. They embody the values of bureaucratic efficiency: ease of application and determinateness of interpretation. The criteria are to be applied without regard to the peculiarities of context. Inspectors themselves are explicit that it is not their job to question the criteria or the ends of inspection but simply to apply them. Issues of their value are consequently outside the scope of inspection. The implementation of such a bureaucratic rationality supports the realization of a further bureaucratic value: that of *efficiency*. The predetermined values are carried by a predetermined, set vocabulary for assessment and reporting, such that rapid turnaround of inspections is facilitated. A school can be inspected in four days, a university in eight. The set vocabulary is designed to eliminate interpretive disputes. Its language is intended to be easily digested and understood. And all the while the call is for clearer competences, objectively verifiable targets, national standards.

3   Inspection enacts the positivistic application of the methodologies of the natural sciences to social phenomena in an experimental cycle of testing, manipulating and retesting. In protecting the integrity of the experimental cycle from contamination by subjective judgement or partiality, the practices of inspection and advice are separated in a way which mirrors the characteristic operations of management and therapy. The inspection process precipitates a purportedly value-free description of the quality of an institution's

performance judged in terms of the extent to which it is efficient and effective in achieving a set of predetermined ends. There is, in the reporting of
inspections, a radical separation of fact and judgement in which only the
factual statements can be questioned by the institution under inspection; a
separation which builds into the inspection process the assumption that its
judgements emerge straightforwardly from the objective facts observed by
the inspectors. Indeed, these judgements *pretend not to be judgements* at all,
since the entire process is set up to ensure that the judgements of inspection
will themselves be facts which are rendered immune to any polluting effects
of interpretation by the algorithmic application of objective performance
criteria to the data. These facts of judgement emerge as conclusions in the
application of deductive logic to premises supplied by the agreed, objective
facts of the data. While the facts of data may be questioned, the unswerving,
deductive rigour by which inspection derives its facts of judgement from the
premises so defined cannot be questioned. Its expertise has the infallibility
of deductive logic.

This conception of inspection as a rational and objective assessment of
bureaucratic performance entails that systems of advice and support will
necessarily embody a vocabulary of therapy, since their *raison d'être* will be to
make good the failure of educational institutions to achieve the ends which
have been determined as their proper concern. The therapeutic dimension
is strengthened by the climate of suspicion which cloaks the inspection process; members of educational institutions are implicitly assumed to have a
pathological desire to cheat the bureaucratic enterprise.

Notes

1 Martin argues that Hirst's position on liberal education represents an atomistic
ideology within which people become 'asocial', lacking 'other-directed feelings
and emotions', and see themselves 'not as mutually dependent, cooperating
members of a society, but as self-sustaining atoms' (Martin 1994: 182). Martin's
view is that the output population of Hirst's liberal education is primed to take
up its place in a society whose values are those of technical-rationalism and the
value of others is a function of their capacity for providing effective means to
another's end.
2 The masculine pronoun is deliberate. The *character* of the manager, as distinct
from particular human actors in the role, carries with it a galaxy of masculine-
valued metaphors.
3 As many philosophers have pointed out, treating someone as a moral end
involves, at least, a kind of respect for them which carries with it an entitlement that they should be given reasons for one's actions, insofar as they affect
others, and that they should be free to evaluate the validity of those reasons
(see Peters 1966; Dearden 1968, 1975; MacIntyre 1985; Siegel 1988, 1991). In
each case, their arguments depend heavily upon a theory of reasons and rationality, an issue which I take up in discussion of the philosophical setting of
reflective teaching.
4 MacIntyre completes his list of modern *characters* with the *rich aesthete*: one

who removes moral ends from the rational sphere by seeing the value of others solely in terms of their potential for feeding his or her desire for pleasure. I have not elaborated on the activities of this *character* because I believe that any aesthete operating within educational contexts would do so by taking the form of the manager or the therapist; roles which the aesthete fuses most strikingly in the creation of the *educational management consultant* – especially if the prefix *rich* is insisted upon.

3

REALISM

If any assumption provides the foundation for what we regard as our common-sense intuitions it is probably the belief that the world exists independently of our lives, our minds and our social and cultural practices. However exquisite our investigations in science or philosophy, they must, it seems, remain tied to common sense by the fundamental belief that the world exists around us, *out there*, extended in space and time, indifferent to whatever we happen to believe about it at any particular moment. Indeed, this inscrutable, recalcitrant *world* constitutes the independent yardstick against which we must measure our beliefs in establishing their truth or falsity. Thus we make discoveries about it – about the exploits of Caesar, the behaviour of sub-atomic particles, the level at which Kate is reading, the quality of Joseph's social interactions in the nursery – and our knowledge increases the more such discoveries we make.

When common sense does philosophy it dons the mantle of *realism;* the thesis that the world exists independently of the perceptions, actions and statements of this or that group, culture or individual, and that our descriptions of this unique, singular world are testable for their veracity against the standards supplied *by* the world in virtue of its independence. And realism is pervasive: the technical-rationalist faith in the efficacy of science and technology, for example, has its deep foundations in the philosophy of realism.

The general features of realism sketched below constitute the conceptual framework presupposed by the theories of positivism and the practices of technical-rationalism. It is a metaphysical framework which often passes unnoticed by common sense and theory alike, so omnipresent, so innocuous, are the assumptions it embodies and so seemingly inevitable are its implications. Nevertheless, although it pretends merely to be the refinement of common sense, realism *is a metaphysical thesis;* and the boundary of the range of things on which it has something to say far exceeds the limits of common-sense intuition.

Objectivity

When happily surrounded by our common-sense assumptions, reinforced as they are by the normal discourse and furniture of everyday life, it is easy to forget how parochial common sense can be. *My* common-sense assumptions are likely to be quite different from those of a Christian, or Muslim, across a range of situations. My common-sense assumptions are not identical with those of the Borgias, or even those of my parents. What establishes the authority of common sense is its *commonality* within a social context and not its veracity; and we slip in and out of social contexts day by day. Realism is partly to be characterized as common sense's attempt to theorize *ultimate commonality* by showing that at a certain basic level its assumptions do bottom out in universal truth. It is an attempt to give metaphysical underpinning to a picture of objectivity.

Consequently realism characteristically represents itself as a metaphysical or ontological theory about the fundamental nature of the universe and the inventory of its basic contents.[1] It carries a view of what kinds of things exist; a view which claims contiguity with common sense. Because of this it is natural to find realists urging that disputes over realism have nothing to do with semantic theories of truth and meaning (see Popper 1974: 17ff; Devitt 1984: 215). Accordingly realists entreat us to settle metaphysical or ontological questions first before moving to consider those of semantics or epistemology.

The priority of metaphysics is simply an expression of the priority given by realism to the independent world. It exists outside us. It existed before we were born and continues to exist beyond where our senses can reach in time and space. Its network of causes and effects are similarly independent and reach far beyond the limits of our possible experience. The job of semantics is to account for how we manage to say meaningful things about this unitary reality; and it is epistemology's duty to explain how we can gain knowledge about it. But both of these activities are parasitic upon the fact of the world's prior, independent existence and its *being there* for us to describe and make discoveries about.

This metaphysical priority has remarkably extensive cultural fallout. It is a small step from metaphysics to the received wisdom of the school staffroom, where tacit obedience to the realist metaphysic manifests itself in the widespread use of expressions such as 'the reality of the classroom' or 'real teachers' to close down theory, debate and speculation, and to engineer a sharp divide between action and *mere* talk, practice and theory, the practicalities of 'getting on with the job' and the ephemeral luxury of 'idle' discourse. Commitment to realism facilitates this 'small step'. The world's independence is the very essence of the view of objectivity shared by common sense, science and technical-rationalism in which the world is the ultimate arbiter of disputes about what is real or what is true.[2] As one realist describes it,

> Different languages such as French, English, Swedish or any other, or even different types of language, such as scientific language and religious

language, do not refer to a different world. They all refer in their different ways to the same world, and at times they may misdescribe it. This must be so whenever there is a conflict about what is the case, since in any disagreement both sides cannot be equally right. For instance it cannot both be raining and not raining, and the world cannot both be God's creation and the result of a totally random process of evolution.

(Trigg 1973: 154)

On this view truth is achieved through the application of the appropriate, rationally grounded techniques which enable discoveries to be made about the world. The thesis guarantees that once a statement has been found to be true it is true absolutely, for everyone. This metaphysical stance underwrites the idea that for any region of experience – like, for example, the particular regions marked out as the concern of the various professions – there will be one true description of the world which, in virtue of this, ought to command universal assent among the cognoscenti. Indeed, should this agreement be lacking to any significant degree it is taken as symptomatic of the fact either that the means of exploring the region of experience in question are not yet sufficiently refined to be worthy of the status of a true science, or that, like mythology and superstition, *there is in fact nothing in the world for the supposed experience to be experience of.* The technical-rationalist requirement of uniformity of judgement in the *true* professions and the demands which this makes on educational practice are a natural, inevitable extension of the realist view of objectivity.

Additional pressure on professionals to conform with the requirements of technical-rationality comes with the recognition, crucial to realism, that once a question has been answered, a discovery made, a problem solved, then it is by virtue of that fact unassailable. In terms of educational thinking and practice, this translates, as theorists of reflective teaching point out, into an institutionalized reluctance of the professional to raise questions about the ends of education as opposed to questions about the means by which prespecified educational ends are to be achieved. In such a situation the inertia of beliefs trades on an image of truth where the *inertia is a result of the beliefs being true and not vice versa.*

Given that in its position on truth realism is the metaphysical expression of common sense, there is obviously enormous pressure on the professions, including education, to align themselves with the metaphysic and swallow the technical-rationalist consequences. Indeed, so powerful is this realist picture that even if faith in the efficacy of science and technology were imposed on operatives by means of coercion, the methods of imposition and the rhetoric in which they were dressed would yet employ the vocabulary of realism and its account of the singular truth discoverable only through rationally warranted investigation of ratification-independent reality. The problem of persuasion which greets the reflective teacher, consequently, is that in rejecting technical-rationality she will reject or revise at least some fragment of the edifice of realism and, to a greater or lesser degree, offend common sense.

Science and progress: convergence and commensurability

The realist disregards the limitations of the capacities of the speakers of a language for verifying the truth of their statements; crediting them with a grasp of the meanings of sentences which far exceeds the possibilities of their capacity for recognizing whether the statements are true or false. Thus I can describe the conditions which obtain on a distant planet or in the remote past or future, a description the truth or falsehood of which I may never be in a position to determine. Nevertheless, in understanding each description I am certain, at least, that either it is true or it is false; that I shall never know *which* is simply a contingent fact of my own physical limitations. Similarly, our thinking on education will be informed by regulative ideals such as *the best teaching method*, or *the best reading scheme*, or *the most effective curriculum* which actually exist, in some conceptual reality, even though we may not yet have discovered them. Truth, for the realist, is 'radically non-epistemic' (Putnam 1976: 125): the world exists independently of ourselves and of our efforts to know it; truth is, in general, verification-transcendent and our best efforts to throw light on the true nature of reality may fall short of absolute correctness.

Given this separation between belief and language and the reality which is their object, realism claims to supply us with the best explanation of how and why we manage to be able to refer to and have knowledge of the world. Common-sense realism is thus taken as explaining the surface flux and the deeper uniformity of experience on the ground that what it is for a theory positing the existence of *x*s to be successful is 'for it to be experientially *as if* there are *x*s' (Devitt 1984: 108).

But this notion of 'best explanation' needs further refining if it is to be capable of distinguishing between rival theories championing incompatible *as-if*s. Much of the necessary work has been done by philosophers of science. Realism holds that the independent world is *the* neutral standard against which our statements are rendered true or false; a conception that applies automatically to scientific statements which realism sees as better or worse attempts to describe the world and its contents. Realism thus maintains the point of science to be to bring us progressively closer to *the* true description of the world. It is the search for 'theories which are nearer than others to the truth – which correspond better to the facts' (Popper 1963: 226).

This portrayal of scientific progress as the approach to truth, when coupled with the independence thesis on which realism rests, requires that grasp of the relation between our theories, our understanding and the world be construed on the model of the 'external perspective' or through the omniscience metaphor of the 'God's eye point of view'. According to this metaphor, 'the world consists of some fixed totality of mind-independent objects. There is exactly one true and complete description of "the way the world is". Truth involves some sort of correspondence relation between words or thought-signs and external things and sets of things' (Putnam 1981: 49). The *presence* of reality determines, at every point, the nature of truth. *Presence* is thus central to realism as the censorial voice of nature, which places absolute restrictions on how the world may truthfully be described. The conception of science this maintains is seen as overcoming 'any systematic bias or distortion . . . in our representation of the world' (Williams 1978: 66).

Thus, embodied in realism is a picture of some universally correct standard of rationality operating according to its own determinate laws (see Winch 1958: 54). By gaining access to this standard, by whatever privileged means are available, we may achieve the capacity to 'extend our knowledge systematically'; nothing being admitted as knowledge which does not meet our ultimate criteria (Bernstein 1983: 117). Accordingly, while most realist philosophers doubt that we actually can discover a determinate procedure for advancing knowledge, they typically hold that there are ways of testing rival theories so that progress towards the truth is guaranteed. Most commonly it is held that there is a permanent neutral framework of scientific standards or a foundational observation language, grasp of which entitles us to assert, for example, that observational success over time gives us a framework-free standard for assessing and comparing styles of reasoning and descriptions of reality (Newton-Smith 1982: 122).

This thought lies behind Popper's falsificationist theory of scientific progress, which asserts that although we may never be in a position to recognize that we have reached *the truth*, there will nevertheless be cases when we are certain that we have not reached the truth; cases where our theories have run up against reality and reality has shown them to be mistaken (see Popper 1963: 226). This ensures that our latest theories are also our best theories, the ones closest to ultimate truth. Realism thus represents the history of science as a cumulative, linear progression (Kuhn 1970: 167), in which a relation of derivability obtains between theories of lesser and greater comprehensiveness; earlier theories being derivable from later, better ones which establish the source of the former's incompleteness and error (Bernstein 1983: 83–4).

It is this picture of progress from ignorance to knowledge – through the linear convergence of plural or conflicting beliefs on the singular truth – that is the metaphysical foundation of the technical-rationalist concept of the profession. The convergence of expert opinion that is seen as essential to the professions is not simply *any* consensus; it is a *rational* consensus around *the truth*. The consensus is *achieved* because a single truth is recognized; and not *created* out of contingent, *ad hoc* agreement. It is this picture that gives the technical-rationalist view of the profession its strength, for the consensus of a profession is taken as signifying the objective truth of the facts which make the consensus possible and rational. A teacher labouring under this picture will carry the belief that there is always, for any classroom situation, one *true* set of causes, one *correct* explanation and one *best* solution.

Realism and reference

The priority of *the world* over *our descriptions* of the world has immediate and powerful consequences for the philosophy of language, for, within the picture, the role of language is to be a transparent medium which enables the true reality of the world to be accurately represented, free from the distortions of interpretation, connotation or perspective. Indeed, the transparency require-ment entails that all sincerely meant uses of language must aspire to be literal, representational; metaphorical or figurative language being consigned to the linguistic periphery as merely contingent effects of language's physical mani-festation in writing or speech rather than genuine communication.

Realism sees language as being tied to the world via ostention by means of which relations of correspondence are set up between names and sen-tences of our language and objects and states of the world. The meaning of 'truth' is given by analysing sentences into the ostensive components which would make their truth apparent (Rorty 1980: 304). A corollary of this is that for the realist, genuinely rational agreement is only possible where there is correspondence with reality (Rorty 1980: 337). This involves a commitment to the objectivity of those statements that are construed realistically, and about and in terms of which rational agreement may ultimately be obtained. Realists thus hold

> the basic conviction that there is ... some permanent, ahistorical matrix or framework to which we can ultimately appeal in determining the na-ture of rationality, knowledge, truth, reality, goodness, or rightness. [They claim] that there is (or must be) such a matrix and that the primary task of the philosopher is to discover what it is and to support his or her claims to have discovered such a matrix with the strongest possible reasons ... [They maintain] that unless we can ground philosophy, knowledge, or language in a rigorous manner we cannot avoid radical scepticism.
>
> (Bernstein 1983: 8)

Rationality is seen not as an outcome of the norms of this or that society but rather after the manner of a natural kind; an ideal of rationality being one which would give the necessary and sufficient conditions for a belief to be rational (Putnam 1981: 104). Given ideal epistemic conditions, the applica-tion of rationality precipitates truth.

Truth and meaning

The tenet underpinning these beliefs may be expressed thus: realism requires that it be integral to our understanding of any statement of the realistically construed class that it is rendered determinately true or false independently of our knowledge, or means of knowing, by an objective reality whose exist-ence and constitution is itself independent of our knowledge (Dummett 1963: 146; 1981: 434). In consequence it is possible to characterize realism as a thesis about the appropriate notion of truth for a given class of statements and, as Dummett notes, because of the intimate connection between the notions of truth and meaning, it therefore constitutes a thesis about the kind of meaning those statements possess.

I have linked realism to an attitude towards classes of statements. This is because one can be a realist about some things and not about others. One's realism may apply to physical objects, space, time, the past or future, minds, theoretical entities such as quarks, sense-data, ethical principles, values and so on. It is possible to be a realist about various combinations of these classes and consequently there can be no single argument that can show realism to be correct for all classes of statements. An argument in support of realism in physical science, for example, will not compel us also to adopt realism for ethical statements or for statements about mental phenomena.

The realism of technical-rationality takes positivism's commitment to a fully determinate physical reality and sees human behaviour and its social, bureaucratic and educational manifestations as being just a special case of the behaviour of physical objects in general. Technical-rationalism is fully realistic therefore about the knowledge and the rationality possessed and applied by the manager and his ilk, but non-realist about ends and ethical principles which it sees as merely linguistic dressing for personal preferences or arbitrary taste.[3]

It is important to remember here that realism for a class of statements involves the belief that its members are capable of being *literally true* in virtue of their relation to the independent world. If this relation is to be tight enough to disallow relativism then the thesis that statements of the realistically construed class are determined as true or as false, independently of anyone's beliefs, in virtue of the relation in which they stand to conditions obtaining in the world has to be supplemented with the stronger thesis that the values *true* and *false* exhaust all possibilities. Without this caveat, the values *'undecidable'* or *'neither true nor false'* or *'true for x'* could encroach on the gap between absolute truth and absolute falsehood and thereby legitimize, among other things, the notion of a relativized plurality of incommensurable truths. For the realist 'true for x' and 'neither true nor false' have no meaning, all statements being determinately and absolutely either true or false, and 'undecidable' is an epistemological rather than a semantic or metaphysical property of a statement: we may not know whether the statement is true or false; we do know that it must be either true or false. Consequently, *'false'*, for a realist, is equivalent to *'not-true'*.

Disputes about realism have been distilled by Michael Dummett into a dispute about the circumstances under which we are 'entitled to assume the principle of bivalence for some class of statements' (1978: xxxi). Bivalence is the principle that every statement is determined as true or is determined as false.[4] *The world* provides the foundational, structural concept of reality; but what constitutes *the world* is given in the classes of statements for which we take a realist attitude; that is, in the classes for which bivalence holds. As Dummett notes, the only answer that would yield the unqualified correctness of a realist view would be one which assumes bivalence to hold for every class of statements whatever. Consequently the rejection of any form of realism – that is, the rejection of the thesis that facts of a particular kind determinately obtain independently of our knowledge as states of the world existing independently of ourselves, our language, thoughts and decisions – is tantamount to the rejection of bivalence for the corresponding class of statements. Conversely, if bivalence demonstrably fails for a class of statements, a realistic construal of that class will not be possible. This conclusion has potentially enormous consequences: if bivalence fails altogether then realism, and the common-sense view of the world it enshrines, must also collapse.

Notes

1 For the technical-rationalist this inventory will typically include such items as physical objects, their behaviour and their relations, but not mental objects or ethical principles; competences but not personal qualities or attitudes; learning outcomes but not learning processes; logic and rationality but not intuition or empathy; etc.

2 Common sense, science and, ultimately, technical-rationalism advertise their authority over other discourses by highlighting their commitment to truth through their submission to the impartial arbitration of the world. For technical-rationalism's version of realism, in which reality is physical and management is causally efficacious on human behaviour, this has the consequence that every discourse is construed as a more or less successful attempt to do or apply science. Thus religion becomes a failed or pseudo-science, ethics becomes an arcane literature which masks an account more properly couched in terms referring to base biological motivations, and education is a science of behaviour modification.

3 Realism maintains that each statement of the realistically construed class has a genuine reference. A fully fledged or naive realism would go still further to assert that 'the semantic role of a singular term occurring in a statement of the given class is to stand for some particular object within that domain' (Dummett 1981: 441). The statements of such a class are true, if they are true, through a direct correspondence with their referents; and we know them to be true, if at all, by having direct knowledge of the states of reality which render them true (see Dummett 1981: 446–9). Naive realism regarding mental capacities or states such as thinking, understanding or learning will resist the behaviourist's efforts to reduce statements about them to a sub-class of statements about molar physical displays. Nevertheless, accepting the reduction does not necessarily constitute an abandoning of realism, for the reduction might preserve, exactly, the logical structure of the disputed class of statements within some more fundamental class in which the former is embedded or, though realism may be abandoned for the disputed class as isomorphism fails, statements of the reductive class may yet be construed realistically. In the former case the conditions under which the statements of the disputed class are true or false exactly match those under which their counterparts in the reductive class are true or false. In the latter case this relation will, in general, fail, since some of the statements of the disputed class will lack truth conditions or will not have truth conditions which under translation into statements of the reductive class preserve their individuation.

4 Bivalence is the semantic principle related to the somewhat better known Law of Excluded Middle. While that logical law states that 'A or not-A' – anything must be either A (a man, red, beautiful, 100 kilos in weight etc.) or not-A (not a man, not red, not beautiful etc.) – bivalence is the principle that 'every statement is either true or false'; a principle which is often itself referred to as the Law of Excluded Middle. Thus while anti-realist logic may preserve excluded

middle it will reject the principle of bivalence and thus open a gap between *not-true* and *false*. Bivalence embodies the common-sense and realist commitment to the idea that *true* and *false* exhaust all possibilities and that, consequently, *not-true* and *false* are equivalent. It is only on the assumption of the principle of bivalence, *the assumption essential to realism*, that the Law of Excluded Middle can be claimed to determine a two-valued logic in which the negation of *true* is *false* and the double negation of *true* is *true*.

4

THE IDEA OF REFLECTIVE TEACHING

Central features of reflective teaching

When a philosophy is so dominant that it becomes absorbed into the fibres of the general world-view of a culture, its power can pass unnoticed since its agenda and its vocabulary define what will be regarded as normal, ordinary and what can be uncritically assumed in theory and politics as well as in the conversation of everyday humdrum life. One consequence of the cultural predominance of technical-rationalism is that any kind of *thinking about one's practice* tends to get described as *reflective*. This linguistic hegemony severely inhibits the potential for an analysis and critique of the reflective process to institute innovation in education. Wherever the dialogue of technical-rationality hijacks the term for itself, the linguistic currency of 'reflection' has become devalued beyond the point of usefulness in prompting innovation, thus enabling positivist practices and their traditional authority to be preserved in a revised linguistic package.[1] Through a semantic sleight of hand *all* teaching becomes reflective. The language of 'reflection' is rendered mute; lacking the vocabulary within which to signal the presence of an opposition to established practice, it loses its transformative power, making it difficult to initiate fundamental change or even to describe its motivating ideas.

Clearly it is vital that the essential features and underlying principles of reflective teaching are identified if it is to be sufficiently demarcated from its positivist rivals to stand as a coherent and viable alternative. If reflective practice is to assert an identity distinguishable from mere *thinking about practice*, then its theoretical foundations need to be exhibited and its central principles and their consequences made visible.

Reactive upon positivism's linguistic acquisitiveness, a rich and diverse literature has developed to provide the requisite distinctive vision. In what follows I summarize the general character of reflective teaching before tracing its genealogy and expanding upon the features which set it apart from its rivals and underpin its self-justification. The literature paints a picture of the reflective teacher as one who turns her attention to the wider issues of education – its aims, its social and personal consequences, its ethics, the rationale of its methods and its curricula – and to the intimate relationship between these and the immediate reality of her classroom practice. Reflective teaching is emancipatory. It is concerned to *improve* practice rather than *collect* knowledge and to foster the rationality and autonomy of the teachers and the taught within a setting of democratic and liberal values.

Each school, each classroom, is seen as unique by dint of its qualities, meanings and challenges. Consequently reflective teachers develop their practice through their own *action*-research performed in the actual context in which their teaching takes place, upon and with the specific population which it concerns. This ferment of practice and research is informed by a knowledge of theories of education; but reflective teachers retain a critical perspective on these, their meaning, their veracity and their applicability within their own classroom, with its *unique set* of interests and relationships. *Generalizing educational theory* is not rejected wholesale but its status is reconceptualized and placed in the service of the teacher who is struggling constantly to understand or come to terms with the unique conditions of her particular experiential context.

Practice, on this view, is constantly subject to a spiralling process of hypothesizing, investigation, reasoning, testing and evaluation, leading to modification and on, in turn, to further investigation (Dewey 1933: 107ff). This is no solitary enterprise: although *individuals* are urged continually to subject their own practice to rational interrogation, the principal means by which the appropriate critical perspective may be achieved will not be private but public. The public setting of such interrogations and the dialogue which surrounds them is essential to the notion of rationality upon which the distinctive character of reflective teaching depends. Any *private* investigation must therefore be at best provisional. Indeed, the image of the conversation, with its intimations of a public, social setting, is employed by Schön as a metaphor for the relationship which the reflective practitioner has with her context; an interaction which takes the form of a 'reflective conversation with the situation' (Schön 1983: 241–2).

Reflective teaching involves 'a willingness to engage in constant self-appraisal and development', which, among other things, 'implies flexibility, rigorous analysis and social awareness' (Pollard and Tann 1994: 9). Drawing on Dewey's (1933) blueprint, reflective teaching opposes 'routine action' which is guided by 'tradition, habit and authority and by institutional definitions and expectations' (Pollard and Tann 1994: 9). Consequently a reflective teacher has need of personal qualities of *open-mindedness* in entertaining the claims of a range of views or theories, *responsibility* in the readiness to submit to the authority of rationality and *wholeheartedness* of commitment (Pollard and Tann 1994: 13–15).

While one enemy of reflective teaching is the unreflective, uncritical following of tradition or habit – an enemy to be despatched by asserting the claims of reason and critical thinking – another is the particular kind of thinking-about-education which conceives rationality on a means–ends model and relies on the authority of a general, overarching theory with universalizing concerns which overlook or trivialize any features that might signal the essential uniqueness of the particular context. That enemy is positivism.

Parent traditions

An understanding of reflective teaching must locate its position at the intersection of a number of overlapping traditions in philosophy, theory, education and politics. These traditions each have distinctive concepts, structures, emphases, interests, fields of application and histories. But they do share a strong family resemblance in terms of those features which are constitutive of the theory and practice of reflective teaching. They share, at least, the following: commitment to the authority of reason; rejection of a means–end conception of rationality and of a technical-rationalist view of human worth; a commitment to personal autonomy and its rational components of honesty and sincerity; emancipatory concerns, liberal and democratic politics, an idea of genuine knowledge as essentially purposeful rather than inert; a transcendental justification. I list these traditions briefly now in order to draw upon them in the sections which follow:

- The reflective practice movement itself, which is generally viewed as arriving at the present day via Dewey and Schön.
- The falsificationism of Karl Popper, which grounds the distinctiveness of science in a concern for increasing verisimilitude and the constant desire to subject its truth claims to testing and interrogation; a practice central in the Dewey–Schön tradition of reflectiveness.
- The enlightenment project running through Kantian and Hegelian philosophy to the critical theory of Habermas and the Frankfurt school and finding application in education in the work of Carr and Kemmis (1986) and Young (1989, 1992) among others. The central concern here is with emancipation through the development of rational, autonomous persons in a democratic, dialogical society which protects the individual from the oppression of technical, bureaucratic means–ends conceptions of social organization.
- The democratic character of the enlightenment project is also found in the liberal philosophical and political traditions exemplified within British philosophy of education through the massively influential work of R.S. Peters and others such as Paul Hirst, Robert Dearden and John and Pat White; work which has been principally concerned to illuminate the logical, epistemological and ethical components of a rationally justifiable concept of education.
- It is further manifested in the emancipatory concerns of feminism and in the liberationist philosophies of Freire (1972a, b), Bowles and Gintis (1976) and McLaren (1995).
- The action research movement (e.g. Winter 1989; Elliott 1991) contributes a sensitivity to the richness and uniqueness of the particular practice-contexts of the classroom or educational institution and a corresponding awareness of the inadequacies of positivist generalizing theories for providing

guidance in educational planning. Action research constitutes the systematization of reflection in teaching.

- The critical thinking movement, exemplified in the work of Paul (1984), Lipman (1985) and Ennis (1996), explores methods of nurturing rationality in children and adults. Within philosophy a corresponding movement exemplified by the work of Peters and latterly by Harvey Siegel (1988) has attempted to establish the philosophical foundations of rationality.

These ingredients contribute to a recipe for a distinctive conception of reflection which is determinedly and recognizably anti-positivist, a position the distinctive features of which we are now ready to examine.

Concern with ends and values

With regard to *ends*, the cluster of philosophical positions and traditions associated with the reflective teaching movement oppose technical-rationalism on three main counts. The first is over the question of the availability of ends to rational scrutiny.

The rationality of ends

The means–end conception of rationality judges reasoning solely in terms of its contribution to the efficient realization of ends which are taken as given. But this conception of rationality is inadequate, since we also *need to be able to criticize ends rationally*. The necessity of taking this step beyond the limits of positivism's technical-rationality may be seen in the way that meaningful and legitimate questions arise spontaneously *within* positivism which its view of rationality prevents it from answering:

> If, for example, one takes the end of scientific inquiry to be the maximization of explanatory power, or the solving of problems, or the ability to predict or control nature, or the discovery of truth, then rational theory choice is a matter of choosing the theory that affords maximal explanatory power ... etc. But if these goals conflict, as they sometimes do, then the means–ends account will not help to determine the rationality of theory choice. Nor will it help settle disputes about the legitimacy of these several alternative putative goals of scientific inquiry. In short, the means–ends account of rationality, because of its inability to assess the rationality of ends, is inadequate for the resolution of outstanding questions regarding the rationality of science.
>
> (Siegel 1988: 130)

Positivism sees ends sometimes as arbitrarily given, sometimes as given in nature. Ethical positions on the value of justice or human freedom are examples of the former categorization while the operations and outcomes of science fit the latter. In each case ends are rendered immune from rational questioning either because the unitary, absolute nature of reality underwrites the truth of some class of statements – as in science – or, as in ethics, there literally is nothing there to be rational about.

The reflective teacher, however, reifies ends (and values) and is concerned to bring them within the remit of reason. She or he recognizes the central position occupied by particular ends and particular values in the determination of the meaning which a social context has for its actors. She or he will not take ends as given, as outside the scope of reason, but will raise her or his critical horizon beyond the narrow concerns of curriculum-delivery techniques to interrogate the global context within which technical notions of *efficiency* and *effectiveness* get their meaning. Paying close attention to the unique features of the particular context, the reflective teacher becomes a researcher in the teaching context (Schön 1983: 68). Instead of relying on established theories and techniques, she 'constructs a new theory of the unique case'. This inquiry 'is not limited to a deliberation about means which depends on a prior agreement about ends . . . but defines them interactively' within the teaching context (Schön 1983: 68).

This concern with ends and values serves to differentiate the kind of reflection characteristic of reflective teaching from the austere, technical process of reasoning recognized by positivism. For the latter, the concept of reflection implies no value commitment except in the minimal sense of obedience to the laws of logic and to a prior set of rules determining what, within the practice, will count as *a good reason,* or *good evidence*; it is entirely instrumental.

The values of reflective practice

Reflective teaching is not value-neutral. Not only does it hold ends to be available to rational scrutiny, it embodies a richly developed value system which it takes to be necessarily valued. Some of the features of this value system – the essentially Kantian, enlightenment, liberal view of human worth, with its concern for *persons,* for their autonomy, emancipation and the authority of reason – are explicated below. What this shows is that the vocabulary of reflective teaching cannot be taken as value-neutral. Reflection becomes, in this context, a technical term which no longer applies to just *any old example of thinking* but must be reserved for application only in cases which meet quite particular conditions.

Ends determine the nature of the context

The third point of opposition concerns the reflective teacher's awareness of the complex of relations obtaining between ends and values, contexts of practice and instrumental standards of rationality. Technical-rationalism tells a seriously emaciated story of practice, for practices cannot be characterized merely as problems to be solved. Outside of the artificially prescribed confines of the prepared experiment problematic situations – such as those presented in any classroom – are 'characterized by uncertainty, disorder, and indeterminacy' (Schön 1983: 15–16). This does not mean that the reflective teacher neglects to think about the means by which her intended ends are to be realized, nor that she is uninterested in exploring ways of making her methods more technically efficient. Rather, it suggests that reflection incorporates an awareness that concepts like *efficiency* and *effectiveness* are parasitic for their meaning upon the role prepared for them by a framework of particular ends and particular values.

These ends and values (involving human perceptions of, beliefs about, attitudes towards and interpretations of their social and cultural context) will vary from context to context; and in moving from one context of ends and values to another we will experience a corresponding change in the criteria governing judgements of efficiency and effectiveness. Indeed, failure to recognize the strength of the link between the concepts of efficiency and effectiveness and the particular ends/values context within which they are employed will result in the misapplication of the standards appropriate to one context to the practices of another. The warping effects of such misapplications may be bizarre; as if we were to apply the criteria of success in poker to a game of chess or the criteria of efficiency in Olympic sprinting to sex. The shock of the bizarre, however, can be dangerously lost if familiarity enables the preposterous to come to be seen as the normal. This, according to reflective teachers, is precisely the circumstance which technical-rationalism has precipitated: school effectiveness is viewed according to the standards by which we normally judge the effectiveness of a car engine; questions of religious faith as assessable by the techniques and standards of physics; all aspects of human relationships as essentially economic, or power based, or manipulative; classroom interactions as cases of management, counselling or therapy.

This is not to see contexts as necessarily sovereign. Reflective teaching is not relativism.[2] Its pluralism is not a product of the arbitrary selection of ends nor is it eliminable by a reduction to some fundamental, universal class of statements or criteria. Rather, its pluralism chimes the hermeneutic point that in order to understand a social situation it is not sufficient to apply – from some detached position – ready-made criteria or descriptions to the situation that confronts us; as if we were to understand political debate or democratic practices by applying a game-theoretical description on the naive assumption that everyone in politics shares identical motivations, the same agenda, the same view of what counts as success, that a 'win' is unequivocal. This is not the relativist's point that different practices with different values and ends will have different criteria for what is to count as instrumentally rational, for the authority of rationality remains, as we shall see, constant over contexts. It is rather that the differences in material circumstances – in resources, staffing levels, children's age-range, gender and ability mix, geography, inner-city or rural, socio-cultural setting, local employment situation and job prospects, crime levels, personnel, talents and qualities of staff, interests, hopes and ambitions of pupils and parents, amount and kind of external participation in school, school's relationship with its governors, prevailing and minority regional customs, religions and values etc. – will determine that what it is rational to do, think or value in each context will not be able to be settled by the application of one, neutral, universal theory.

The uniqueness of contexts of practice

The reflective teacher is one who attempts to bring about improvement in her practice by applying critical thinking to her situation; an approach which is modulated by her appreciation of that situation's uniqueness and its resistance to ready-made descriptions and interpretations.

Each educational context – that complex of ends, values, rational standards and instrumental means – is seen by reflective teachers as unique and therefore inscrutable to description and analysis under some universal theory (Schön 1983: 129). From the reflective teaching standpoint the universalizing tendencies of positivistic theories look like manifestations of the fallacies of accident and converse accident. While positivism appears too ready to apply its generalizations to all contexts, it is also, paradoxically, over-hasty in its desire to universalize from a limited range of data. This effectively obliterates the distinctive features of each context under imperatives of similarity or identity. General theory is incapable of making all the adjustments which would be necessary to ensure its smooth and accurate application to the particular case. For reflective teachers the uniqueness of the local context and the claims to generality of theory constitute a contradictory stand-off which precludes the straightforward application of such theory.[3]

By highlighting the manner in which contexts are resistant to ready generalizations the reflective teacher sets severe limits to the extent to which positivist theories can help in the description, categorization and analysis of the contexts and problems of teaching. Educational contexts are simply too rich to fall readily under the kind of universal laws which enable predictions to be employed to such useful effect in natural science, car manufacturing and pharmacy. The introduction of a general theory to such different and unique situations as my attempts to develop critical thinking in my students or your coming to terms with the nuances and protocols of a new relationship is likely to obscure at least as much as it enlightens. Consequently generalization over similarities is replaced by the particularized rational art of reflection by which those involved deal with situations of uncertainty and value conflict (Schön 1983: 50).

For the reflective teacher uniqueness is further underlined by the way in which the static accounts of context available to positivism are replaced by ones which involve change as a necessary ingredient. Each context is viewed as fundamentally *dynamic,* enacting a unique process of change, balanced between the contradictory opposition of its unity, externally perceived, and its internal disunity or individuation (Winter 1989: 49). This dynamism enables the concepts of *progress* and *improvement* to be drawn into the theory–practice framework as senior partners to *description* and *explanation.* Progress may be achieved through a dialectical process in which the theoretical or conceptual oppositions, generally referred to as thesis and antithesis, are reconciled in a synthesis which moves beyond present oppositions to a further dynamic of new oppositions. The preference for dialectic over the application of general laws is symptomatic of reflective teaching's commitment to the uniqueness of each educational context.

Reflexivity

Winter (1989: 39) discusses the assertion: 'Martin and Rosie in my class know the rules for multiplication.' At first glance this appears straightfor-wardly objective and context-independent. Winter, however, points out the reflexivity of the assertion: that it inevitably refers back upon the teacher's own interpretations, assumptions and concerns, factors which are themselves further contextualized through the influences upon his prior framework of interpretation; his recent reading of a novel or a policy document, for example (Winter 1989: 40).

Reflexivity insists upon *modest claims* where 'making judgments depends on *examples* from various personal experiences (not on representative samples of universally agreed categories)' (Winter 1989: 42). Although, for the prac-tical purposes of getting on with business, reflexivity must be 'forgotten' within normal professional life, it is important, nevertheless, that it forms the focus of the research stance so that it may be appraised and its validity increased 'by showing more fully its foundations' (Winter 1989: 42). Through *questioning*, any claim is related 'more closely to the experiences in which it is grounded' (Winter 1989: 43). By making explicit the reflexive basis of judgements in 'personal interpretive systems' we establish that 'the basis of the account is *not* simply factual (and thus indisputable) *nor* a universal law derived from an agreed body of knowledge (and thus necessarily true)' (Winter 1989: 44).

Action research

The professional students of education, as distinguished from the practi-tioners, have taken over the scientific method and are disposed to guard research activities closely as their province.

(Corey 1953: 1)

Such is the power of positivism that Corey's concerns of 1953 have been restated by many others to the present day. Action research may be seen as reflective teaching's systematized attempt to overturn this hierarchy, to eman-cipate the teacher-researcher from the oppression of the positivist's division of theory and practice labour by exhibiting the interdependency of theory and practice within a rational process of change (Winter 1989: 66).

Research in unique contexts

Attention to the uniqueness of the particular case has consequences for the kind of research which can legitimately be seen as providing an illumination of that context. Action research, *research-in-action*, is research which studies a particular, *actual* population instead of one which is theoretically constructed as 'random' or 'representative' (Corey 1953: 14). Action research constitutes systematic and public reflection on practice which recognizes and celebrates the uniqueness of the situations it investigates, situations which 'do not lend themselves to the application of theories and techniques derived from science developed in the mode of technical-rationality' (Schön 1983: 319).

Because each situation is seen as unique – and therefore resistant to the explanatory ambitions of traditionally construed universalizing theories – the reflective teacher must construct her own *new* theories in attempting to understand, evaluate and bring about change in each unique case. In rejecting the creed of positivism her construction of the localized theories will include consideration of the ends or values inherent in that context and as seen from within it (Winter 1989: 27). The values which define the ends of a practice should not however 'be viewed as concrete objectives or targets which can be perfectly realized at some future point in time' or 'technical ends which can be clearly specified in advance of practice' (Elliott 1991: 51). For the reflective teacher engaged in action research, 'Values as ends cannot be clearly defined independently of and prior to practice ... The ends are defined in the practice and not in advance of it' (Elliott 1991: 51).

Consequently inquiry will not be 'limited to a deliberation about means which depends on a prior agreement about ends', for means and ends can no longer be seen as separate (Schön 1983: 68). It is the particular set of ends or values that are found or constructed in each particular case which partly – at least – determine its uniqueness and which, therefore, cannot be ignored in any attempt to understand the processes and relations which obtain in that context.

The action research imperative: change and improve

Reflective teaching has the aim of *transforming* education, a factor which entails revision to the traditionally dominant scientific aims of explanation and understanding which instead become placed in the service of the transformative process itself (Carr and Kemmis 1986: 156). It is not that traditional, academy-based researchers in education have been unconcerned about practice and its improvement. It is rather that they have seen their job as gathering and publishing knowledge which, through the process of its being digested and applied by others, would, in due course, bring about change for the better (Corey 1953: 5). In this the detachment and practice-independence of the researcher is cited as a virtue; involvement being denigrated as a possible source of contamination of the data or the research method.

For the action researcher this detached, scientific and technical purity, symptomatic of the fear of contamination, is the principal reason why traditional research has proved to be an inadequate springboard for change and improvement. Reflective teaching, systematized in action research through a process of 'review, diagnosis, planning, implementation, [and] monitoring' (Elliott cited in Winter 1989: 3), attempts to remedy this failure by replacing a perspective which values research for the 'amount of dependable knowledge' it adds to the collection in some university library with one which sees the value of research as 'determined primarily by the extent to which findings lead to improvement in the practices of the people engaged in the research' (Corey 1953: 13). Action research replaces university-based, context-independent researchers with teacher-researchers who reflect and act upon the context in which they are working. Doubts are raised about the validity of externally generated educational theories, since the appropriate knowledge

> cannot be of a law-like, general nature, but will always be intimately related to specific contexts ... can never be based on 'pure' observation, but will always be bound up with contextual, here-and-now judgments (concerning the interpretation of particular data) ... can never be established, finalized, and codified in abstract theories, because it will always be developing alongside and within professional practice.
>
> (Winter 1989: 29–30)

Unlike traditional theorizing, the dialogue generated makes no claim to universality or permanence. Its motives are not to be found in a desire to describe or provide mere explanation but in a *concern to bring about change*. Its interests are not those of the university, with its imperatives of generalization and publication, but those which arise within the specific, idiosyncratic context of *this* school or *that* classroom. Its motivation is not the increase of knowledge of how children learn but the improvement of the reading in these particular children in this particular class. The kind of generalizations action research precipitates are not in the positivist, 'lateral' mould of being *across* contexts but are instead 'vertical', concerned to guide the self-understanding of *this* population through the dynamics of *its* changes into *its* future (Corey 1953: 14).

This fundamental concern with the improvement of practice rather than the accumulation of knowledge distinguishes action research from positivist forms of investigation. Action research is thus the means by which reflective teaching can become properly *critical*. On the premise that knowledge frees the knower from taken-for-granted constraints (Groundwater-Smith 1988: 258), action research is the process through which critical reflection becomes a principal causal factor in bringing about change and, crucially, the emancipation of teachers, the agents of reflection, and their pupils.

Action research and the generation of theory

Action research is concerned with the ends – the value-framework – of education and the problem-setting menu which such ends embody. Explanation and description are therefore of value to the reflective teacher only insofar as they throw light upon the processes which support the maintenance and realization of educational ends *and* their conceptualization.

Action research represents a radical reversal of the hierarchy which has traditionally characterized the theory–practice relation in terms favouring theory-generation over theory-application. This also represents a rejection of a major plank in positivism's realist metaphysics; its belief in fundamental underlying regularities of social reality which constitute the truth conditions for its law-like generalizations. Positivism's deification of the directionality of the general to the particular – of the universalizing theory to each and every particular case – is replaced by a picture in which theory is generated and legitimized only by its immediate derivation from and application to the local situation.

Action research 'resists the temptation to simplify cases by theoretical abstraction' (Elliott 1991: 53). The characteristics which render a situation or context unique – the elements in terms of which it differs from other concrete cases – are not obliterated by theory as unworthy of consideration because they do not fit into some previously defined universal category; instead they are given prominence. Their significance for action research stems from the requirement that theory should begin with reflection upon the local context, since that context is manifestly different from and similar to other local contexts in ways that cannot be determinately and finally settled by the blind application of a universal description favouring some given set of criteria for judging sameness.

This epistemological and methodological shift from universalization towards particularization requires new forms of writing which are not restricted by the positivistic academic codes that issue in the research report form of: literature review, methodology, data collection, conclusion. Suggested developments in this area include narrative writing and autobiography, each of which attempts to articulate stories that are faithful to the uniqueness, the rich particularity, of each educational context (see Winter 1989: 72–4).

Problem-setting

While preserving the problem-solving authority of reason, reflective teaching extends reason's compass to include consideration of the context-setting educational ends in reference to which any problem-solving must take place. Action research is the working out of this problem-setting (see Schön 1983: 40). For the reflective teacher problems do not exist 'out there', ready made, well defined and waiting to be solved. Instead, a problem is seen as a human construct which arises out of a particular perception or interpretation formed about a unique educational context with its values and ends; the values, interests and actions of its inhabitants; and, crucially, the particular relation of these features to a theoretical perspective which describes and explains them and their interrelations.

It is this theoretical perspective which links elements of the social context to some perceived problem. Indeed, it is only because of the adoption of a particular theory that one is able to describe some aspect of the manifold relations obtaining between the elements of the unique context as anomalous or problematic. The problem gets its significance *qua problem* only by virtue of the role which a prior theory has prepared for it. Only against this rich background of description and interpretation, of human perceptions and interests, can a phenomenon, a situation, an event or a state of affairs be *seen as* a problem.

Problem-setting, then, is the construction of a perspective on a situation the description of which precipitates anomalies. Problems, in turn, are parasitic for their existence on the chosen descriptions; they are, we might say, theory relative; and the adoption of a different theory – a different paradigm – will have the result of some problems being dissolved while others are created (see Schön 1983: 314). This process of choosing between competing paradigms is not an entirely arbitrary process. It only looks arbitrary if one holds to positivism's denuded view of reason as essentially and exhaustively connected to processes of solving ready-made problems.

Emancipation

Emancipation involves establishing the material conditions for the rational conduct of life. Emancipation represents a freeing of the mind from the distortions of ignorance, ideology, irrationality, tradition and habit so that the beneficiary is able to become properly rational and see the world right. It entails commitment to individual autonomy and democratic principles of equality and justice. It embodies the liberal, meliorist sense of the infinite perfectibility – through the application of reason – of humans and their institutions (see Gray 1995), and a vision of the kind of persons and institutions that are the ideal objects of rational convergence. The emancipated form of life which is both the goal and the essence of reflective teaching is seen by Habermas and other bearers of the enlightenment tradition to be inherent in the very notion of truth itself and 'anticipated in every act of communication' (McCarthy in Habermas 1976: xviii). The claimed relations of necessity between ethical, epistemological, metaphysical and semantic concerns provide the philosophical foundation for reflective practice in an *ideal speech situation* (see Chapter 5).

Emancipation from anti-rational traditions

Reflective teaching is centrally concerned with emancipation through enlightenment, through the activity of securing improvement in rationality (in the rigour of thought and methodology, in the clarity and accuracy of accounts of reality) and in ethics; the justice of a particular situation being intimately linked with the accuracy of representation of its rationality. The reason why emancipation is *the* moral imperative of reflective teaching lies partly in the conviction that while self-critical reflection is essential to bring about improvements in practices and in persons, the processes of reflection are constantly under threat from the *distorting influences of ideological forces and institutional imperatives*. Consequently it is crucial to the integrity of the process of critical reflection that it goes beyond merely 'informed practical judgement' to enable systematically distorted practices to be identified, analysed, *then* eliminated through social and educational action (Carr and Kemmis 1986: 31).

Action research is seen as an emancipatory strategy which empowers participants by enabling and encouraging them to engage in 'a continuous, relentless interrogation of sedimented social practices with the intention of changing those which result in inequality and injustice' (Groundwater-Smith 1988: 257).

The kind of anti-rational traditions which cause such sedimentation of practice may be seen exerting their influence across the entire spectrum of educational contexts, from staffroom 'justifications' like 'We've always done it this way' to non-consultative, politically expedient curriculum decisions.

As an example of the need for emancipation from oppressive political and cultural values, consider the fertile potential of curriculum history for the transmission of externally determined ideology. A cabinet of values are implicit in the construction of history as a curriculum subject. The activity of construction, of selection and organization, involves prior decisions about the range of events and characters that will be regarded as the proper concern of history and the laying down of rules for what historical explanation can consist in: placing limitations on what may count as a possible item of evidence in explaining events, giving reasons, plotting motives, balancing the contingencies of chance with intended outcomes, tracking responsibility and cause etc. Through this process there is ample opportunity for the construction of history to be achieved entirely within a narrowly selective European perspective – one which excludes the voice of black people, losers, the working class, women, the local and provincial – precipitating a curriculum which tells history's story through imperatives of emplotment and characterization which eulogize the influence of Great White Men and normalize assumptions of the march of progress in science, politics, morality and social organization; plotting the ascent of man from primitive origins to the triumph of the West. Emancipation here is the struggle to break out of a code of historical narrative which is elitist, ethnocentric, phallocentric, imperialist and Whiggish (see Claire 1996: 5–19).

Once again the necessary logical links between *rationality* and *liberal principles* presupposed in the realization of emancipation from the distorting oppression of tradition, habit, authority and institutional hegemony must be stressed. This is not simply a conceptual issue, however, for as McLaren has argued, 'Before undistorted communication can occur, an ethical culture must be created in which there exist communities of understanding related to realized material structures of equality' (McLaren 1995: 190). This suggests that the reflective teacher must also take up an 'activist' role in the sense of attempting to secure the emancipation of *institutions* which can provide the 'materially equal circumstances necessary for rational discussion' (McLaren 1995: 190). Emancipation is thus a matter of teachers acquiring both the *rational* and the *material* resources which will make critical, reflective teaching possible.

Emancipation from technical-rationalism

The tyranny of technical-rationalism, with its oppressive generalizations, its positivistic division of labour between *expert* and *practitioner*, and its austere view of the precinct of reason, is the predominant tradition against which reflective teachers seeking enlightenment and emancipation must struggle. The restrictive potency of technical-rationalism is manifested through its insistence that all social, moral and educational questions are *technical* questions which require answers supplied by technical means. Against this picture, Habermas argues that even a scientific, technical civilization

> is not granted dispensation from practical questions; therefore a peculiar danger arises when the process of scientification transgresses the limit of technical questions, without, however, departing from the level of reflection of a rationality confined to the technological horizon. For then no attempt is made to attain a rational consensus on the part of citizens concerning the practical control of their destiny. Its place is taken by the attempt to attain technical control over history by perfecting the administration of society, an attempt that is just as impractical as it is unhistorical.
>
> (Habermas 1973: 255)

By securing a place for the principles outlined in this chapter, the reflective teacher can fight this oppression and establish a context within which democratic, rational discourse is possible. This will involve her in articulating an account of social phenomena which refuses to describe them in the vocabulary of universalized cause and effect or to evaluate them through context-free concepts of effectiveness or efficiency.

Given the positivist's reliance on grasp of law-like generalizations to license claims to professional expertise, this emancipatory stance will involve necessary revisions to the notion of the *expert* and the *professional*. Reflective teaching will seek to mount a critical attack upon the mystique of the professional and undermine the technical source of her authority. Expertise, now visible as the generation of mystique, is able to be exhibited for what it has been: an instrument for the 'social control of the have-nots – the poor, the dispossessed, ethnic and racial minorities, women – by a social elite' (Schön 1983: 288). The emancipatory thrust of reflective teaching is to establish a situation in which experts and clients, teachers and pupils, lecturers and students alike can develop and exercise their rational autonomy within an institutional framework of participatory democracy.

Autonomy

Autonomy and reason

The concept of *autonomy* is inextricably bound up with the concepts of *reflective teaching* and its constituents: *rationality, emancipation* and *democracy*. Autonomy is essential to reflection as both a logical and a material condition, since reflection is possible only for an individual who is free and able to think rationally and to act upon her rationally conceived decisions.

But this relation is not simply one way; the capacity for reflection is also a necessary condition of autonomy. Rationality – the ability and inclination to look for reasons – is an essential feature of one who is capable of seeing the world right, of discovering truth, or of recognizing when one line of argument is better than, one way of life is preferable to, another.

Autonomy thus involves what Dewey called 'intellectual *responsibility*'; submission to the consequences of the rule of reason. Responsibility commits the reflective teacher to acting in accord with a range of values clustered around the notions of fidelity to the processes of reason, commitment to the integrity of its results and confidence in the limitlessness of its jurisdiction. Because of the intimate connection between reasoning and the public principles by which reasons may be judged, the kind of critical thinking which results from these commitments is, argues Siegel, *principled thinking*. Because *principles* involve *consistency*, the kind of critical thinking embodied in the notion of reflective teaching must be 'impartial, consistent and non-arbitrary'. The properly critical thinker

> thinks and acts in accordance with, and values, consistency, fairness, and impartiality of judgment and action. Principled, critical judgment, in its rejection of arbitrariness, inconsistency, and partiality, thus presupposes a recognition of the binding force of standards, taken to be universal and objective, in accordance with which judgments are to be made.
>
> (Siegel 1988: 34)

Thus, intellectual responsibility compels the reflective teacher 'to consider the consequences of a projected step [and] to be willing to adopt these consequences when they follow reasonably' (Dewey 1933: 32). Such intellectual responsibility 'secures integrity'; the integrity of a willingness to commit oneself to the results of reasoning and to the principles which underpin reason, make it possible, and enable its use to be justified. The thinking and actions of the autonomous individual are independent of the prescriptions or arbitrary directions of authorities 'and based instead on reason' (Dearden 1968: 46).

Persons

Even this is not sufficient for autonomy, however; the autonomous individual must be able to turn this responsibility inward upon herself to achieve *integrity* through the rational self-knowledge which enables a *person* to determine his or her true nature, genuine self and real interests, and to keep faith with them. If acting freely involves acting according to one's own will then autonomy requires not only a capacity to think rationally about situations obtaining in the objective, public realm but also an ability to bring the same, publicly warranted criteria to bear upon one's judgements of one's own real nature, interests, motives and so on. Autonomous free will is, in other words, a will that is rationally conceived.[4]

It is in the person, so construed, that autonomy finds its clearest embodiment. A person is more than an individual. Persons act on principles, choose for themselves, are held responsible for their actions, participate in the determination of their own destiny and, crucially, have respect for other persons in treating them, *seriously*, as commanding identical authority over *themselves* (Peters 1966: 209–12). Indeed, having the concept of a person is to see one as an 'object of respect in a form of life which is conducted on the basis of those principles which are presuppositions of the use of practical reason'

(p. 215); it is to recognize 'that it matters that individuals represent distinct assertive points of view' (p. 213). Autonomy attaches to persons, not individuals. Reflective teaching aims to develop rational persons by rational processes. This is not simply a matter of the teacher laying down the rules of how to reason but involves also the initiation of children into the rational way of life with its associated principles of autonomy and democracy (see Dewey 1916; Peters 1966; Carr and Kemmis 1986; Siegel 1988). It thus sets the liberal, value framework for the institutions within which authentic education can take place.

Initiation

Reflective teaching seeks to initiate children into the rational way of life so that they may become passionately committed to reason and come to possess rational dispositions: a love of 'clarity, accuracy and fair-mindedness', a 'devotion to truth' and the seeking out of evidence, and a corresponding aversion to 'contradiction, sloppy thinking' and inconsistency (Paul 1984; cited in Siegel 1988: 40). Becoming rational involves, for many liberal philosophers of education, mastery not simply of the general, context-independent, universal principles exemplified by formal and informal logic through principles such as 'consider all relevant evidence' and 'avoid fallacies', and principles governing proper inductive and deductive inference (Siegel 1988: 34–50). Such philosophers maintain that there are, additionally, rational principles specific to certain epistemological contexts which govern the assessment of reasons within those contexts (Siegel 1988: 34). Probably the most famous proposal of this kind is Hirst's *forms of knowledge* thesis, in which he claims that each distinct form has its own central concepts and criteria which compose a coherent system that is both constitutive and individuative of the form. A genuinely liberal education must, for Hirst, enable its beneficiaries to become fully immersed in each of the distinctive forms which reason can take. Any process which falls short of such initiation constitutes an unjustified impediment to an individual's development into an autonomous, rational person (Hirst 1965, 1974; cf. White 1973).

The reflective teacher and her pupils will strive to become properly critical thinkers who both are 'appropriately moved by reasons' and have an 'ability properly to assess the force of reasons in the many contexts in which reasons play a role' (Siegel 1988: 23). The practice of initiation, *education*, is held to be rational in its aims, in its teaching methods and in the justification of its general conception (Peters 1966) and its particular processes. Reflective teaching – by dint of its entire constitution being tied to reason – is also necessarily *teaching for autonomy*. Its emancipatory process is the dual one of the teacher seeking to achieve autonomy for her pupils and for herself.

Self-knowledge

I have noted that an essential component of the reflective teacher's conception of autonomy is a view of a person's rationality. Rationality is a necessary condition of autonomy. Consequently autonomy is not manifested in behaviour which is 'free' in the sense of being idiosyncratic or rule-breaking, for rational behaviour is not arbitrary. It is crucial therefore that the autonomous person should *know herself* (Siegel 1988: 13; McLaren 1995: 23), her true motives, her real nature and interests. Autonomy involves acting in fidelity to one's own real nature; and reflective teaching holds it as axiomatic that this real nature is rational in its constitution and in its proper functions.

Reflective teaching's emancipatory remit thus traverses the public *and* the subjective realms and has material consequences as well as logical ones (Martin 1994: 181). Reflective teaching seeks to liberate teacher and taught from restrictions to their freedom, whether these are externally produced – such as restrictive institutional practices, resource limitations, technical-rationalist pedagogies – or the outcome of internal psychological, epistemological or conceptual phenomena which distort a person's self-reflections and inhibit her capacity for seeing herself right. In the latter enterprise its concern is to free the person from self-delusion or self-distortion; a necessary exercise for those who wish to enter a culture which is based on the traditional hopes of democratic liberalism. Such people must have 'the courage to examine themselves honestly' (Arcilla 1995: 154).

Within reflective teaching, the autonomous individual becomes another ingredient contributing to the uniqueness of each particular educational context. This has provoked the fashion for prefacing or inseminating action research narratives with autobiography on the ground that 'the declaration of "self" add[s] to the honest and authentic qualities of the research' (Dadds 1995: 172). Its value presupposes the earlier point: that reflective teaching holds the self to have a real nature which, in its fundamental constitution, is rational. It presupposes that there is a unique, true story of that self which is rich in narrative content and irreducible to the 'algebraic and bureaucratic paradigms of thought' that misleadingly simplify, reduce and alienate (Dadds 1995: 166). It presupposes that understanding the person right, and true self-understanding, are crucial to the understanding of the research. An example makes the point:

> Understanding Vicki as a person was essential if the impact of her research and learning on her school was to be understood ... Vicki's hopes, motivations, biography, personal and interpersonal qualities were significant. They were related to her effectiveness as action researcher and agent of change in her school. They had a bearing on her choice of action research topics as well as on her effectiveness in changing practice in her school through them.
>
> (Dadds 1995: 168. Other examples include Abbs 1974;
> Weiner 1994; Thomas 1995)

Of course, the process of achieving a story of the self which overcomes the distortions of one's own passions, prejudices and preconceptions is not simply a private exercise but one which involves the application of public criteria through a dialogue with others (see Dadds 1995: 172). Contrary to technical-rationalist practice, this social dimension is not viewed as optional.

If the individual is to develop as a properly rational being then her social development as a person – as a member of a community who also sees herself and other members in terms of a shared framework of rights, responsibilities and roles – is essential (see Langford 1985). What should be noted is the realism, or *naturalism*, which underpins this. It is a naturalism about each individual self and its constitution. It is also a naturalism about the human condition and our place in the world such that 'An adequate theory of education needs to go beyond a conception of persons as autonomous individuals not simply because education ought to bind human beings to one another, but because it should bind us to the natural order of which we are a part' (Martin 1994: 182).[5]

The rational, public framework within which this naturalism is worked out is marked by the concepts of dialogue, community and democracy.

Community and communication

In its rejection of positivism's technical-rationality, reflective teaching also rejects the idea that rationality is a psychological state attainable by the unconnected individual through mental processes entirely private to himself. Reflective teaching instead sees *becoming rational* as identical with developing as a *social person*. Rationality is conceived not simply as a skill which can be privately enacted but as a practice which, like the exercise of good manners, is embodied in and developed and refined through interaction with fellow members of a community.

The standards which determine what it is to be rational are intimately bound up with the standards appropriate to genuine communication and, indeed, to the foundation of the liberal democracy. As I discuss in Chapter 5, these philosophical foundations run deep to provide a unification of the ethics, epistemology and metaphysics of reflective teaching. At the surface of practice this philosophy is manifested in a cluster of attitudes – towards openmindedness and progress, communication and objectivity, rational responsibility, theory and the expert–client relationship – to which I now turn.

Open-mindedness and progress

The reflective teacher attempts to achieve 'freedom from prejudice, partisanship, and such other habits as close the mind and make it unwilling to consider new problems and entertain new ideas' (Dewey 1933: 30). She thus opposes conservative traditions, with their inherent reliance on unexamined commitments to hierarchy and order, authority and loyalty, which issue in an epistemology licensing the professional, in virtue of his technical expertise, to impose his theories, generalizations, categories and techniques on whatever situation confronts him while ignoring or trivializing any features which are anomalous to his ready-made theory-generated descriptions and explanations (Schön 1983: 345–6).

The exclusivity of personnel and focus underwritten by this philosophy is rejected outright by the reflective teacher. Reflectiveness takes possession of the technical skills of reasoning and embeds them within a set of attitudes which include the tendency to exercise the skills and see them as valuable, the tendency to be well informed, to demand appropriate precision and so on (Siegel 1988: 7). They include also the disposition to be open-minded in Dewey's sense of having 'an active desire to listen to more sides than one, to give heed to facts from whatever source they come, to give full attention to alternative possibilities, to recognise the possibility of error even in the beliefs which are dearest to us' (Dewey 1933: 30). Open-mindedness involves consideration of all the relevant evidence and different perspectives that are available, abhorring conclusions drawn from partial, incomplete evidence.

Open-mindedness also involves subjecting one's own beliefs and conclusions to rigorous, rational public interrogation as a means of increasing their validity (Winter 1989: 42–3). This willingness to constantly subject one's most cherished beliefs to interrogation has, after Karl Popper, become a hallmark of post-positivist philosophy of science (see Winter 1989: 60–2). According to Popper, what distinguishes the practice of science from non-science or pseudo-science is the testability and, potentially, the falsifiability of its theories (Popper 1963: 33–59). Knowledge is increased through the researcher's willingness to subject her beliefs to the risk of refutation. Confirmations of one's beliefs, argues Popper, 'should count only if they are the result of *risky predictions*; that is to say, if, unenlightened by the theory in question, we should have expected an event which was incompatible with the theory – an event which would have refuted the theory' (p. 36). Consequently, 'every genuine *test* of a theory is an attempt to falsify it' (p. 36). It is this aspect of Popper's view of *true* science – this willingness to subject one's own position to rigorous interrogation – that embodies the open-minded spirit of reflective teaching.

Community, democracy and objectivity

As a necessary condition of such open-mindedness the reflective teacher must commit herself to the *public* context of investigation and shun any putative conception of research which views the enterprise as essentially a private matter between the solitary researcher and his rational judgement. A reflective teacher submits her work to *systematic examination* within *critical communities of enquirers* (Carr and Kemmis 1986: 40), thus ensuring 'that the conclusions of the work are broadly based, balanced, and comprehensively grounded in the perceptions of a variety of others' (Winter 1989: 23–4). This communal setting is essential to reflective teaching because of its commitment to a concept of rationality which is intimately tied to the concept of democracy. Any *rational* consideration, of any school situation, must take into account the views of all those involved in that situation – pupils, teachers, parents – as well as relevant external agencies such as inspectors and advisors, industry and business, and university researchers. Conventional status-hierarchies are suspended and all viewpoints are treated 'as potentially of equal significance' (Winter 1989: 56–7). This democratic view of rationality has its roots in the Kantian, enlightenment philosophy of *respect for persons*, where a condition of rational discourse is seen to be the 'reciprocal recognition by each participant of the other as an autonomous source of both claims which have initial plausibility and demands for justification which must be addressed' (White 1988: 56).

Putting aside for the moment potentially serious questions concerning the status of the criteria which can serve to demarcate the domain over which the democratic franchise must range in order to preserve the rationality of our dialogue, it is clear that, given the communal commitment, failure to take into consideration the arguments and views of the franchised must result in partiality and a consequent loss of rationality of any account of that context. The intersubjective judgements of the members of a dialogical community thus become the source of our recognition of objectivity and provide the setting within which the idea of objectivity finds currency. Knowledge and belief is not susceptible to purely subjective testing and ratification. The necessary framework within which we can recognize when our subjective judgements go right and when they are in error is the framework provided by our fellow inquirers, whose opinions and arguments must be given the same kind of respect we give to our own.

This leaves open the question of what role is left for *theory* in the promotion of reflective practice. The summary answer is that general theory will become one voice in the open, democratic dialogue which reflective teachers have within and about their practice; one voice, that is, rather than the last word on the matter. The collaborative, social enterprise that is reflective teaching dissolves the traditional division of labour between theorists and practitioners, replacing it with a generalized critical attitude towards practice and its theories; an attitude that is grounded firmly within the framework of rational values outlined in this chapter.

The democratic, communal setting of these values is crucial; reflection, as an essentially public, dialogical enterprise, is the criterion by which the notion of the reflective teacher is distinguishable from the thinking-but-privative teacher available to positivism. Indeed, for Griffiths and Tann, the choice for teachers is between submitting their personal theories to public, reflective dialogue or allowing themselves 'to be turned into low level operatives, content with carrying out their tasks more and more efficiently, while remaining blind to large issues of the underlying purposes and results of schooling' (Griffiths and Tann 1991: 100). Reflective teaching constitutes an attempt to pursue a commitment to rationality which avoids the universalism and naked instrumentalism of positivism on the one hand and subjectivism or arbitrariness on the other. It steers this course not by throwing in its lot with relativist assertions of the incommensurability of sovereign social contexts but by seeing knowledge of the particular context and participation in its dialogues as essential components in the process of mediation between general theory and particular practice. The product of this interaction of general theory and unique context, and of the application of reason within public, democratic dialogue, is nothing other than objectivity itself (see Winter 1989: 55–9).

'The client'

Such considerations issue in a more democratic relationship between the professional and her client. This revision may be characterized in terms of a shift from a theatre in which the professional's warrant stems from her expertise in applying the general principles of her 'science' to the particular context – a situation which leaves 'the client' peripheral to the process, as the mere recipient of the benefits which result from the professional dispensing her expertise – to an interactive, democratic discourse in which the professional engages with the client in a context of uncertainty, equality and openness. The metaphor of discourse is central in replacing the mechanical, technical conception of professional expertise that is characteristic of positivism with an image of expertise as constantly undergoing a process of negotiation, renewal, reconceptualization and revision. Like a conversation, its directionality is non-linear, its end is not always apparent at the outset, its criteria of success are not necessarily clear and stable. Like a conversation, the expert's understanding of the meanings inherent in her context of practice cannot be derived through the application of a general law but must instead grow out of her immersion within that context and its manifold interactions and exchanges.

Whereas by tradition the 'expert' is presumed to possess knowledge which, at least in the area of her expertise, prohibits uncertainty, presumptions about the knowledge and expertise of the reflective teacher do not exclude the knowledge of others – including the client, *whoever that happens to be* – nor is the claim to expertise employed to mask areas of uncertainty. The ideal of *detachment* characteristic of positivistically construed expert–client relations is replaced by one of *immersion* in the practice-research context, where the reflective teacher seeks to construct a dialogue with the client enabling connections to to be made with the client's own thoughts and feelings. Consequently there arises a different kind of 'contract' between practitioner and client in which each party shares a responsibility for bringing about improvement. The client no longer surrenders herself and her judgement to the expert in an act of faith, but instead becomes directly involved in the forming of judgements and in the making of decisions (see Schön 1983: 300–3). Through immersion, commitment and responsibility, the reflective teacher softens or dissolves altogether the boundary between expert and client. Indeed, this entails that the reflective teacher is always primarily *her own client*.

With the outline of the democratic framework of reflective teaching we complete the inventory of its central features. It exhibits itself as an approach to the theorizing of educational practice which differs from positivist traditions in several important ways. Its concern with ends and values opposes it to positivism's technical, means-driven perspective on the role of theory; its concern for an open-minded mode of questioning gives it a reflexive dimension which is missing from the earlier tradition; its concept of rationality stretches traditional limitations on the domain of reason to include consideration of ends and a commitment to a democratic value-system; in contrast to its positivist opponent it celebrates rather than suppresses the uniqueness of educational and professional contexts and suggests a view of knowledge which accommodates this uniqueness (and the limits of generalization) and provides a justification of the practice of action research. Finally, reflective teaching embodies a view of the teleology of research and knowledge which is emancipatory; its purpose is to free *persons* from the social control inherent in perspectives which are distorted in their representation of reality.

Notes

1 It is interesting that in 1989 John Elliott needed to write that the term 'action research' had become hijacked into the service of technical-rationality and that facilitators of *reflective practice* should stop using that vocabulary! Also see Winter (1989: 31–4) on the difficulties of establishing a role for reflection that is free of positivism.
2 In stressing the distinctiveness of each practice-context some defenders of reflective teaching do appear to flirt with some form of relativism. Young criticizes Carr and Kemmis (1986) for placing too much emphasis on the particular context and understating the importance of the wider, interactive collection of external agents who exercise an interest on the practice (Young 1989: 158–60). In most cases an insistence on an absolute conception of rationality provides the inter-contextual bridgehead which avoids relativism. Concerning Carr and Kemmis, Young is, I think, simply wrong (cf. Carr and Kemmis 1986: 9).
3 In his pioneering of the cause of action research Stephen Corey (1953: 13) notes an additional tension in the positivist approach, between the need to provide samples which are *representative* of large populations and the requirement of *random* sampling to avoid bias in selection. Like the other tensions, this one arises out of the positivist need to both demonstrate and assume regularities in nature.
4 The rich, value encrusted notion of autonomy manifested in the discourse of reflective teaching thus differs from the thin construal of the concept of personal freedom as non-interference typical of forms of liberalism that are compatible with technical-rationalism (see Gray 1995: 56–60).
5 It is also a naturalism about the kinds of rights which attach to the individual (e.g. see Nozick 1974).

5

PHILOSOPHICAL
FOUNDATIONS

The absolute conception of rationality

The main conflict between the world-views of reflective teaching and positivism concerns the range and quality of rationality rather than its authority. The number of classes of statements to which it is possible to take a rational approach is massively increased by the reflective teacher as ends and values and moral considerations are brought within reason's compass. The reductive tendencies of positivism are resisted. Reasoning about human enterprises, for example, is protected from expression within positivism's austere, physicalist logic. This increase in rationality's range is complemented by a similarly motivated increase in the complexity of its structure as the easy application of general rules across situations *similar under one mode of classification* is rejected in favour of a perspective in which the various ways in which contexts are *dissimilar* and resistant to generalization are recognized. The result of this approbation of the uniqueness of contexts is a kind of epistemological pluralism in which reason takes a different yet compatible form in each epistemic context.

Nevertheless, positivism's fully realistic view of rationality continues to be taken. The concept of rationality is seen as embodying absolute standards against which particular cases of reasoning must be judged; standards such as consistency, avoidance of fallacy, commitment to the 'laws of thought' and to bivalence. Relativism is rejected outright.[1] The absolutist commitments in the reflective teacher's concept of rationality can recognize the virtues – both philosophical and pedagogical – of exposure to the variety of theories and methods of investigation which pluralism accommodates. This open-mindedness about diversity does not extend to relativism's 'anything goes' view, which holds rational choice between rival ideas and approaches to be impossible (Siegel 1988: 108). Although a pluralism of practices and contexts of meaning is presaged in the assertion of the uniqueness of particular cases, this does not mean that rationality's determination of what good reasons look like is itself relative to this or that context, society, culture or practice.

Unlike relativists, reflective teachers hold reason to be unimpeachable and the unitary coherence of its absolute laws to include all contexts within its precinct. Indeed, certain kinds of relativism – moral relativism, for example – are resisted even more firmly by reflective teachers than by positivists, since unlike the latter they believe that ends and values *are* open to rational scrutiny and that the selection of a morality, therefore, does not automatically determine a context which is immune to rational appraisal.

Thus rationality generates the standards by which ends as well as means may be judged; an ideal embodying determinate and absolute notions of validity in the relations of premises to conclusions, reasons to actions and evidence to hypotheses. This ideal, which for reflective teaching is an essential component in the decision-making process of the liberal, democratic society, is given metaphysical expression and philosophical justification in Habermas's conception of the ideal speech situation.[2]

Ideal speech situation

Rationality as a reflection of ideology?

Relativist writers have called into question the authority and cultural independence of the ideals of rationality, arguing that Western rational practices are just another ideological stance which has no special claim to universal assent (e.g. see Winch 1958; Barnes and Bloor 1982; Feyerabend 1982). Such philosophers deny that there is an ideologically neutral standpoint from which to mount a rational critique of alternative ideologies.

Philosophers of the enlightenment tradition, however, those whose concern is to defend the universal authority of reason, of critical thinking and reflective teaching, argue in response that an 'enlightened rationalism ... which takes rationality and critical thinking to be fundamental intellectual ideals' is presupposed by the very study of ideology and cannot, therefore, 'be regarded as just another ideology' (Siegel 1988: 75). Clearly the cogency of the picture of 'enlightened rationalism' is crucial to the entire critical-reflective enterprise if it is to steer a course between positivism and relativism and enshrine rationality as *the* meta-dialogue through which all ideologies can be critically appraised.

In recent years a number of educators have argued that the *ideal speech situation* posited by Jurgen Habermas provides the metaphysical foundation required by the idea of the reflective teacher to underpin the kind of critical practices necessary for emancipation. It is the dialogical context which comprises the conditions necessary for rational, critical and reflective activity to take place. Its authority is taken by Habermas to be necessarily presupposed in all attempts to engage in reflective activity. One attraction of the ideal speech situation is that it appears to capture the essence of the ideally rational context which is constantly employed in the internationally influential liberal, democratic philosophy of education practised since the 1960s by British philosophers such as R.S. Peters, whose own arguments point to the kind of foundational rational framework which Habermas describes.

Because of its foundational role in facilitating discourse of undistorted rational clarity, the realization of such an ideal speech situation is viewed as a necessary condition of the establishment of any critical social science capable of differentiating between those ideas, interpretations and self-understandings which are ideologically distorted and those which are not (Carr and Kemmis 1986: 149).

Distortion and its elimination

The need to eliminate distortion in the form of subjective biases or inherited ideological baggage is acutely felt by researchers committed to the reflective critical style (e.g. Dadds 1995: 6, 121). Interpretations, together with one's own self-reflections and self-understandings, are, it is argued, vulnerable to the distorting effects of ideology, custom, habit, tradition, coercion, authority and institutionally imposed and maintained definitions and expectations; the very forces which result in the kind of anti-critical turn of mind whose symptoms include routinized and unresponsive behaviour (Pollard and Tann 1994: 8–9). However, breaking the grip of distortion to free oneself from the stultifying thoughtlessness of routinized action and achieve a self-conscious, reflective grasp of one's situation, one's own potentialities and the potentialities of others is no easy thing given the power of the forces of distortion. Indeed, it requires a special, refined, method for,

> if self-reflection and self-understanding may be distorted by social conditions, then the rational capabilities of human beings for self-emancipation will only be realized by a critical social science that can elucidate these conditions and reveal how they can be eliminated. Hence, a critical social science will seek to offer individuals an awareness of how their aims and purposes may have become distorted or repressed and to specify how these can be eradicated so that the rational pursuit of their real goals can be undertaken.
>
> (Carr and Kemmis 1986: 136)

The emancipatory operations of Habermas's critical theory may be seen as a kind of psychoanalysis performed upon contexts of distortion. The subject is freed from self-delusion by grasping the illusions which feed its distortion of reality. Emancipation is gained when relationships which appeared to be natural are 'bracketed' and our judgements about them suspended, our unguarded assumptions subjected to critical analysis. What previously seemed to be written in nature becomes visible under analysis as a product of relations of power whose strength derived from their not having been seen through (see Connerton 1980: 25).

Habermas (1970) proposes a theory of communicative competence as the rational foundation for the systematic elimination of distortion. He notes that the background consensus in any smoothly functioning dialogical context presupposes, at least, the tacit mutual recognition of four types of validity claim: the utterance is intelligible; its propositional content is true; the speaker is sincere in uttering it; it is appropriate for the speaker to be performing that particular speech act (Connerton 1980: 103). But this dialogical consensus may be challenged: by relativists who claim that one consensus is no better (or worse) than any other; or by positivists defending one universal consensus around the 'truth' of their austere view of rationality and science. Consequently Habermas develops the notion of communication into one of *dialogue*, which carries with it two additional entailments: 'The putting out of play of all motives except that of a willingness to come to an understanding; and . . . a willingness to suspend any judgment as to the existence of certain states of affairs and as to the rightness of certain values' (Connerton 1980: 103). Discourse, in this sense, involves participants in the presupposition that they are engaging 'under conditions which guarantee that the consensus which is arrived at will be the result of the force of the better argument and not of constraints on discussion' (Connerton 1980: 103).

In such an ideal speech situation the conditions which underpin truth-telling *are identical with* the conditions for democratic discussion in an ideal form of social life where all participants have an equal chance to initiate and participate in the discourse. A necessary presupposition of the ideal speech situation is that discussion is free from all constraints which are not themselves essential to the practice of rational dialogue; free, that is, from constraints of distortion, domination, power and ideology (see Connerton 1980: 104; Carr and Kemmis 1986: 142). Thus, the conditions of the ideal speech situation include elements which are the linguistic analogue of traditional ideals of freedom and justice.

Travelling a different route, but sharing Habermas's enlightenment credentials, R.S. Peters arrived at the same point via his philosophical analysis of the concept of education. For Peters, to engage with reason is logically to commit oneself to valuing the democratic form of life and its foundational principles. The rational person is one who, minimally, conducts her life in accordance with the principles of freedom (Peters 1966: 180–2), equality – not making distinctions without differences (p. 121) – and justice – the principle of making 'general rules for distinctive forms of action where there are relevant differences', the principle that condemns arbitrariness (p. 125). She recognizes the need for the giving of reasons, for justification, and rejects the warrant of decisions made by individual fiat or arbitrary choice (p. 122). These principles underpin the democratic framework within which reason can function. They extend one's commitment into the consideration of the interests of others (p. 172) and the fraternity of 'kinship with other rational beings as persons' (p. 225). This notion of *respect for persons* (pp. 208–13), a principle which has a long pedigree, including Kant's categorical imperative and the somewhat earlier example of Christ's Golden Rule,

> summarizes the attitude which we must adopt towards others with whom we are prepared seriously to discuss what ought to be done. Their point of view must be taken into account as sources of claims and interests; they must be regarded as having a prima facie claim for non-interference in doing what is in their interest.
>
> (Peters 1966: 215)

An important consequence of adopting the metaphysics of the ideal speech situation is that semantic concepts such as *truth* can no longer be analysed independently of (traditionally) ethical concepts such as *freedom* and *justice*, since the conditions for the arrival at and recognition of truth require the autonomy of linguistic practices; their freedom from distortion and the just-ice embodied in democratic rules of participation (see Carr and Kemmis 1986: 143). Reflective teaching's ethical and political commitment to a form of life in which autonomy and responsibility are possible is thus embodied in the possibility and in the structure of language itself (Connerton 1980: 104).

Critical strategy in the ideal speech situation

The critical theory of Habermas owes its strategic heritage to the *reconstructive critique* of Kant and the *criticism* of Hegel: Kant bequeaths the analysis of the absolute, subjective conditions which make knowledge possible while placing limits on its accessibility; Hegel supplies the blueprint for a critical analysis of the constraints on knowledge which are the human products of coercion and distortion (Connerton 1980: 22–4). Together these outlooks form the two dimensions of the critical stance, which is both a condition for and the out-come of the ideal speech situation; they are the critique of *condition and process* in reason and reflection.

Kantian philosophers have attempted to lay bare the essential conditions for knowledge (Hirst 1965; Peters 1966; Hamlyn 1978). This has involved the analysis of the universal rules governing rational discourse or activity; con-sideration of the objective phenomena of sentences, actions and the conscious operations of the human actor; and the excavation and mapping of the know-ledge presupposed in our ability to operate rules correctly. Hegelians, by con-trast, attend to the particular, to the conditions which shape the identity of an individual or group; calling into question assumed objectivities, suspecting distortions masquerading as realities and seeking to eliminate distortion and make possible the liberation of the truth which was distorted. Hegelians aim at emancipation by removing or changing the conditions which result in false or distorted consciousness (see Connerton 1980: 26).

Condition and process: while the Kantian imperative is to establish the framework conditions which must obtain if rational discourse is to be possible, it falls to the Hegelian tradition to police the contingent processes of actual attempts at reasoning, reflecting and engaging in discourse. Reconstruction describes the necessary conditions of the ideal speech situation; criticism creates and defends these conditions in particular social contexts.

The normative power of the ideal speech situation

The *ideal* speech situation operates as a *normative icon* in the critical theory of Habermas and in the reflective teaching approach to education of Carr and Kemmis, Winter, Peters, Siegel and others of the liberal, reflective and critical thinking traditions. Although one might question the possibility of such an ideal ever being fully realized, this does not prevent it from operating as an *idealization* of rational practice (Habermas 1970: 372); an articulation of the rational standards to which the practices should aspire which has normative implications for any procedure to be employed in ridding a given practice of distortion (e.g. Habermas 1976: xvii–xviii; Carr and Kemmis 1986: 192; White 1988: 56; Young 1989: 77, 1992: 50). Indeed, Habermas is explicit that 'the ideal speech situation is neither an empirical phenomenon nor simply a construct, but a reciprocal supposition unavoidable in discourse . . . it is a critical standard against which every actually realized consensus can be called into question and tested' (Habermas 1976: xvii–xviii). Consequently there is no reason to suppose, McCarthy argues, that the *ideal* speech situation cannot be 'more or less adequately approximated' in *actual* speech situations nor that it cannot 'serve as a guide for the institutionalization of discourse or for the critique of systematically distorted communication' (in Habermas 1976: xvii).

The transcendental argument

The necessary presupposition

Important questions arise with regard to the legitimacy of the rationality claims made within particular contexts. But what about rationality in general? What is the status of the framework of concepts and rules that enable us to say that one choice is better than another, that some reasons are more compelling, arguments stronger, evidence more relevant, justification more secure? The ideal speech situation is the prototype of the rational context in which these decisions are made and justified; but how is its foundational status to be defended against relativists – who argue that one *rationality* is as good as any other – or sceptics who doubt the very possibility of rationality? Alternatively, how is its democratic account of rational discourse and reflection to be defended against the oppressive, limiting, unitary vision of reason embraced by positivism? What is required is a general argument which will give absolute justification to the ideals of rationality constitutive of the ideal speech situation. The argument form which promises to fit the bill is the *transcendental argument*.

The ideal speech situation is claimed to be an *essential* presupposition of *any* context of discourse, such that the 'concept' of a language which did not assume the ideal speech situation is unintelligible. It carries the requirement that subjects engaged in communication are – by virtue of that act – *necessarily* committed to the standards and criteria which serve to define the ideal of undistorted, unconstrained communication. Thus, any linguistic act entails a commitment on the part of the actors to impersonal, universal standards of rationality and truth, together with concomitant assumptions of sincerity and a serious interest in achieving real understanding. The ideal which governs our rational and moral behaviour in any given context is thus *context-transcendent*:

No matter how the intersubjectivity of mutual understanding may be deformed, the *design* of an ideal speech situation is necessarily implied in the structure of potential speech, since all speech, even intentional deception, is oriented towards the idea of truth . . . Insofar as we master the means for the construction of an ideal speech situation, we can conceive the ideas of truth, freedom and justice.

(Habermas 1970: 372)

Our participation in discourse unavoidably commits us to the presupposition of 'an ideal speech situation that, on the strength of its formal properties, allows consensus only through generalizable interests' (Habermas 1975: 110). This 'strong universalization principle' entails that anyone engaging in argument must presuppose and value the validity of the rules of discourse and that the participants must, 'on pain of performative contradiction', admit that universalization is the only rule under which norms will be legitimized (White 1988: 57). For Habermas, Peters *et al.* any situation of dialogue, communication, speech or questioning involves universal validity claims and thus presupposes a commitment to shared criteria of truth, sincerity and reason which are objective and universal. They constitute the universal conditions of the possibility of intersubjective understanding and genuine agreement. Indeed, 'If we did not suppose that a justified consensus were possible and could in some way be distinguished from a false consensus, then the very meaning of discourse, indeed of speech, would be called into question' (Carr and Kemmis 1986: 143).

This is the transcendental argument. The principle of unconstrained, undistorted dialogue which is central to the notion of a critically reflective practice is justified through a demonstration of its necessary *presence* as a condition of the very possibility of intersubjective communication and understanding. The image and the normative authority of the ideal speech situation is thus presupposed by the very possibility of a language. In speaking a language, *even if only to call into question the ideal speech situation or raise doubts about the value of rationality*, we inevitably commit ourselves to the existence of the very ideals we sought to doubt and, on pain of unintelligibility, submit our speech and reasoning to the normative authority of the rational framework we set out to reject.

What the transcendental arguments of Habermas and Peters also affirm is that the form of life in which the transcendental values inherent in the ideal speech situation are realized is one in which the liberal democratic values of equality, freedom, justice, personal autonomy and respect for persons are central. The arguments are, therefore, transcendental refutations of technical-rationalism and its tyrannical bureaucracy of reason.

The transcendental tradition

Transcendental arguments have a long tradition in liberal and enlightenment philosophy. Employed most famously by Kant (1787), a transcendental argument – as its name suggests – transcends the context of a particular experience to address the issue of the very possibility of experience, knowledge or understanding *in general*. It concerns itself not with the question of what must be the case for a person to have this or that experience, to be capable of this or that piece of reasoning, of using this or that class of sentences, but addresses directly the question of what must be, or necessarily assumed to be, the case if any person at all is to be able to reason, use a language, have experience. This transcendental manoeuvre provides a tidy way of answering the sceptic, since if the sceptic raises doubts about, say, the value of autonomy, but autonomy can be shown by a transcendental argument to be a necessary requirement of the very possibility of intelligible thought, then the sceptic is confronted with an 'awkward dilemma'; for either his doubt must be groundless, and autonomy *must* be valued, 'or else there is no such thing as intelligible thought and his own doubt cannot be formulated intelligibly' (Walker 1978: 14). The sceptic is disarmed by being made to recognize that he is calling into question the very conceptual scheme within which alone his doubts make sense (Walker 1978: 14).

If successful, then, a transcendental argument will be a supremely powerful argument, as it will show what must be assumed in any thinking about experience, reason or language, and will precipitate conclusions which are unassailable by reference to the peculiarities of context or situation. The conclusions will be absolutely and universally true. It will also have the virtue of economy, since it avoids the need to consider particular cases in order to arrive at generally valid conclusions. All non-transcendental methods – which attempt to achieve generalization through a process of induction or analogy from the particular case – are vulnerable at precisely the point where they make the leap from premise to conclusion; questions can be raised about the justification of any such extensions from the particular to the universal. Given reflective teaching's criticism of positivism on precisely this point, it is clear that the transcendental argument will be the only method by which those committed to the principles underpinning reflective teaching will be able consistently to articulate and justify universal, context-independent or neutral *truths*.

Unsurprisingly, therefore, transcendental arguments have proved attractive to realist philosophers who wish to move beyond the authorization furnished by the justificatory charlatan that is common sense. In the 1960s and 1970s the worldwide influence of the liberal school in British philosophy of education was largely due to the persuasiveness of its transcendental arguments. R.S. Peters's work is saturated with transcendental arguments by means of which he attempts to show that it would be impossible for one to take part *seriously* in dialogical situations who lacked commitment to the principles of equality, justice and respect for persons referred to earlier. Meanwhile, others, like Hirst, Dearden and White, occupied themselves in transcendentally exhibiting the necessity of commitment to reason, to particular forms of knowledge and to personal autonomy. These arguments have, interestingly, been revived recently by the American philosopher Harvey Siegel, who has argued that rationality 'is *self-justifying*' , which is to say that

in order seriously to question the worth of rationality, one must already be committed to it. For to ask 'Why be rational?' is to ask for *reasons* for and against being rational; to entertain the question seriously is to acknowledge the force of reasons in ascertaining the answer. The very raising of the question, in other words, commits one to a recognition of the force of reasons. To recognize that force is straightaway to recognize the answer to the question: we should be rational because (for the reason that) reasons have force.

(Siegel 1988: 132)

This transcendental argument is extended by Siegel to include the justification of *critical thinking* as a fundamental educational ideal: in any case of conflict, resolution is only possible through resort to reason, which is to honour critical thinking itself (Siegel 1988: 137).

Transcendental arguments and conditions for their success

The transcendental argument promises once and for all to smash through the assembled enemies of reflective teaching – positivism, relativism, scepticism and ignorance – by justifying the form of life in which reflective teaching can take place as the only form of life that is rationally defensible.

If it is to stand any chance of successfully demonstrating that its categorial schema is necessarily employed in differentiating experience (Korner 1967: 318), the transcendental argument must be completely general; dealing with the conditions of anything's making sense, the conditions of all intelligible thought, and not just with the meaningfulness of this or that class of propositions (Stroud 1968: 251; Walker 1978: 14–17). Absolute generality is, of course, a necessity for the argument which claims to give a value-free justification of a particular value-system; of the value-system that all systems must assume. If the argument were limited to the particular, not only would it be open to opponents to deny its application beyond the context in question – thus threatening to precipitate an explosion of further arguments needed to cover a potential infinity of other contexts – it would also be possible to deny that any particular case of experience or reasoning or language use was precisely of that class to which the argument applied. The gambit of the transcendental argument is to raise the stakes to an *all or nothing* level; if successful its conclusions are true universally; if it fails it fails absolutely and cannot be salvaged for application to any particular context.

Realism

Some may think the account I have given of reflective teaching and its philosophical chassis too inclusive in the range of writers it draws upon for support in its construction. They may argue that important distinctions between the views of these writers have been overlooked and their similarities exaggerated.

Although there is some truth in this I hope that the introductory section of the previous chapter shows why I think I am justified in taking the inclusive approach. There I identified an overlapping threadwork of philosophical and theoretical traditions that are largely shared by the various writers I have placed within the reflective teaching movement. The traditions themselves are not identical with one another but, crucial to my story, there is a large region of agreement about issues, problems and approaches.

The agreement is where it matters; in providing potential support for the reflective teacher. In telling this story of eclectic support I have attempted to be faithful to the spirit of reflective teaching and its philosophy and practice. I have noted already how reflective teachers view theory as a voice in the emancipatory conversation, a voice to be valued in terms of its contribution to that conversation. A theory will not be valued for the things it says which do not make a contribution. This is a pragmatic approach to theory which, magpie like, takes arguments, visions, philosophies and theories out of their original context to embed what is thought useful in the new metaphysics staked out by the concepts of autonomy, emancipation, democracy and rationality and through the image of the ideal speech situation.

Alongside the genealogical and eclectic-pragmatic justifications for my style of exposition there is another reason why I am not too fussy about the differences in the subpoenaed positions: *they are overwhelmingly and irrevocably identical in their commitment to realism.* Given this, the differences become trivial border skirmishes; attempts to tidy the margins of the common agenda. Therefore I want to close the present chapter by reviewing one major thread in the weave of the previous one, that of realism.

Reflective practice upholds and extends the positivist commitment, drawn from enlightenment origins, of realism about the rules of reasoning. These rules assume a world in which they are universally applicable; a world which, in relation to reason's function, is entirely uniform. This view of reason supplements positivism by allowing for distinctive modes of rationality internal to different contexts of experience. This is not a relativist point about the incommensurability of the various modes of reasoning. It is, rather, a picture in which a universal, absolute framework of rationality guarantees the compatibility of all genuinely rational contexts.

Commitment to bivalence provides the logical, semantic warrant for this system by ensuring that no contradictions in reason are countenanced. Without such a commitment the unique contexts distinctive of reflective practice would still be possible but there would be no effective, overriding rational criterion to prevent them from degenerating into relativistically construed pockets of incommensurable rationalities. However, the commitment to contextual uniqueness presupposes a realism about the context of practice or discourse. Its boundaries and its range of membership must be realistically construed such that their description involves sentences for which bivalence holds. If realism at this point were rejected, the case for uniqueness would collapse, for the account of distinctive islands of reason presupposes the determinate reality of their setting.

Reflective teaching goes beyond the limits of positivism's realistic commitments to express an ethical realism in which general principles such as justice, equality and respect for persons – principles which underpin democratic practices – are given a transcendental justification. Because of the reification of ethical values embodied in the metaphysics of ends, persons and democratic community, an epistemology of discovery can be replaced by an ethics of improvement. Indeed, reflective practice entails that for a large class of statements – those which chart the action research enterprise, for example – these will amount to the same thing. Realism here carries with it a picture in which ethical reality exists independently of particular human practices, its denizens being ethical principles about which we must try to make discoveries. These principles may sustain different moralities in different social contexts but, as in the case of rationalities, the overarching, transcendentally grounded ethical framework will ensure that true moralities may be distinctive but must be compatible.

The objects in whom the ethical rights and responsibilities inhere are the autonomous persons whose nature is also realistically construed. Regardless of contingent difficulties in the process of discovering the facts of the matter, a person's essential nature and her authentic biography are truths which determinately obtain; truths which underwrite the primacy of autobiography over other-descriptions.

The commitment to bivalence is the semantic analogue of a metaphysics in which objectivity is possible. This enables us to recognize that in rejecting positivism's realism, reflective teaching does not jettison objectivity. What is rejected is positivism's empirical inductivist methodology for achieving objectivity; making way for methods involving essential reference to the particularity of the context of investigation. The commitment to objectivity testifies once more to the anti-relativist stance of reflective teaching. The danger of differentiating between unique contexts of practice is that this will precipitate a relativism 'in which all "rational" disputes boil down to un-analysable differences in world view' (Siegel 1988: 14). Relativism is avoided, however, objectivity preserved, through the adoption of rational criteria which are neutral across contexts, ideologies or world-views (Siegel 1988: 15).

The foundational role of realism in the metaphysics of reflective teaching is clear and its importance in the narrative of this book can now be expressed. Baldly put, from the point of view of postmodernism, the philosophies of reflective teaching and positivism are variations on the theme of realism. They are the historically located offspring of the enlightenment's metaphysics and epistemology; each is a distinctive working out of the common genetic inheritance of realism. To anticipate the journey into postmodernity of the rest of the book, if realism fails it takes with it positivism *and any other position which requires realism as its foundation*. Thus the mutilation of realism would reach further than the destruction of positivism to cripple also the rational framework essential to reflective teaching. Indeed, with its non-reductive complex structures of rationality across and within unique contexts, the metaphysics of reflective teaching is even more vulnerable to fallout from a collapse of realism than is positivism. It is such a collapse I wish to contrive. The scalpel I shall use to dismember realism and its reflective child is *deconstruction*, the strategies of which I sharpen and display in the next chapter.

Notes

1 Relativism is the spectre haunting both positivism and reflective teaching's pluralism for reasons I discuss in the conclusion to this chapter. Being such a universally reviled enemy, relativism tends to suffer critical and figurative attack in equal part (see Winter 1989: 188; Young 1989: 90; Siegel 1988: 108; McLaren 1995: 188, 252).

2 Reflective teaching and the critical theory of Habermas are linked by a particular view of the role which reflection has in emancipating those who engage with its process from views of the world – and of themselves – which are distorted by oppressive ideological forces. This interpretation of reflective practice, though influential, is by no means uncontroversial, and has been criticized by John Elliott (1991: 116) as being 'dangerous' because of its apparent denial that 'teachers' self-understandings of their practices can alone constitute a source of critical self-reflection and emancipatory action.' The difficulty with approaches such as Elliott's, however, and the merit of the theory of Carr and Kemmis, is that the former is not a relativist position but it gives no indication of the rational foundation which prevents it from *descending* into relativism. Reflective teaching – if it is to be capable of distinguishing itself from technical-rationalism while avoiding relativism – must invoke the ideal speech situation central to the critical theory of Habermas or something at least very much like it.

PART II

INCISIONS OF DECONSTRUCTION

6

DECONSTRUCTION: MANOEUVRES OF POSTMODERNITY

Deconstruction and fuel

> In general, the rule holds – LET YOUR ATTITUDE BE THE ANTITHESIS OF YOUR OPPONENT'S; and let your manner of emphasizing this different attitude put him in the wrong.
>
> NOTE. *Do not attempt to irritate partner by spending too long looking for your lost ball.* This is unsporting. But good gamesmanship which is also very good sportsmanship can be practised if the gamesman makes a great and irritatingly prolonged parade of spending extra time looking for his *opponent's* ball.
>
> (Potter 1947)

It would seem odd, outrageous, for a declared environmentalist to be the driver of a seven-litre gas-guzzler. The conspicuous contradiction between environmentalist principles and this style of transport would certainly draw attention to itself. After all, isn't such a vehicle the very incarnation of all that environmentalism opposes: the needless and excessive consumption of resources, the unnecessary pollution of the planet? Isn't the dude straightforwardly a hypocrite in the use he makes of the very devices which are the hallmark of his opponent's system of beliefs and values?

Well, he may be a hypocrite. There are a lot of them around. But too swift a dismissal of his behaviour might overlook a more subtle artifice at work, for the irony of his style may be deliberately contrived. He may have chosen to drive the gas-guzzler as a way of drawing attention to the weaknesses in his opponent's position. The nature of his gesture – of taking to extremes in his practice the *principles* of car ownership – may be intended to undermine the opposition by playing its permissive, free-market attitude towards the automobile to its absolute consequences; driving a car which both symbolizes the values of the pro-car lobby and parodies them at the same time.

Stephen Potter's 'gamesman' employs the laws of golf and sportsmanship in a similarly ironic way. He doesn't flout the laws of golf but on the contrary is absolutely scrupulous in his adherence to them. Nor does he offend course etiquette, he practises it *to extremes*. The gamesman's art is to take the laws and customs of his chosen game and then turn these rules upon themselves so that they are *forced* into subverting their own authority – the authority to guarantee fair play – and instead to work to the gamesman's advantage. The laws of the game become transmogrified in the hands of the gamesman into a special kind of manual on how to cheat.

These vignettes provide a not-too-misleading preliminary picture of what deconstruction is all about; for like parody and satire, dadaism in art or Potter's gamesmanship, deconstruction uses the ready-made devices already present in a position, theory, practice or text to undermine the position's (or theory's etc.) claim of authority and to show something of how it achieves its effects upon its audience. Indeed, from a deconstructive perspective all of these 'products' should be viewed as texts since their role as *position* or *theory* is simply one more example of an authority claim or *textual effect* which may itself be deconstructed (or parodied or satirized).

From this we can draw a few provisional observations:

1 Deconstruction acts upon texts and regards everything – whether it be the laws of golf, a stance taken on the environment, a conversation, an argument or whatever – as a text. It is texts that get deconstructed.
2 Deconstruction is a *strategy* for examining texts which works within the text's own system of beliefs and values. The text itself provides the fuel for the process of deconstruction; in deconstructing we borrow devices from *within* the text to use them *upon* or *against* the text.
3 Just as in the examples, deconstruction is *always* concerned to show up or exploit weaknesses, often working to turn supposed strengths into weaknesses. Like satire it is always *reactive* or *negative*, and never a positive or position-*constructing* strategy.
4 Because deconstruction is not a position but a strategy, it serves no particular mistress; like satire or Semtex it is for anyone to use. In the above stories there is no guarantee that our environmental satirist and gamesman will not in turn find themselves deconstructed.

Deconstruction and reading

Deconstruction is, at present, a little understood but much overused term. This situation has provided a fertile breeding ground for several myths which we should dispel from the outset.

First, deconstruction is often thought to be impossibly difficult. Well, just like anything else it is hard to be good at it, to do it with flair; but just like anything else it is possible to begin to build an understanding of the process. The real difficulty with starting is the paradigm-shift of perspective it requires – both emotional and intellectual – which will become apparent as we proceed.

Another barrier to understanding that is often cited is the impenetrable or tortured jargon which deconstructive writing employs. There is some justification to this charge; but when meeting any unfamiliar linguistic devices it is helpful in gaining an understanding first to share some sympathy for the motives which give rise to the language. Some of the challenges offered by deconstructive writing arise out of the peculiar strategies it employs:

- employing the already difficult language of the text under deconstruction;
- parodying the style of the text – academic or 'learned' styles, for example – by deliberately imitating and distorting its language;
- inventing new terms to express concepts, issues, relations etc. that are otherwise suppressed within the text;
- encouraging the reader to see as metaphorical a term which the text assumes to be literal.

The use of these manoeuvres will be amplified later. The general point about the challenge which deconstruction's linguistic complexities present to understanding is that deconstruction encourages a freer, more actively inventive use of language than traditionally respectable, authoritative genres such as academic or theoretical texts; a profligacy which can be quite shocking given the expectations and habits inculcated in many of us by our own academic upbringing.

Another myth is that deconstruction is synonymous with 'close reading' or 'analysis' and consequently nothing more mysterious than or additional to those notions: we take apart the text, therefore we are deconstructing! This is a mistake. Deconstruction does involve close reading and textual analysis; but it is *a particular strategy* of close reading and analysis. This strategy may be compared with gamesmanship. It does not just read the rules of the text closely but applies them beyond the normal limits which an etiquette of reading would require.

Some of the stylistic qualities which mark out a reading as *deconstructive* are summarized here:

- Unlike traditional close reading, deconstruction does not attempt to *comprehend* the text by exhibiting its *main* themes, *central* ideas, *unifying* patterns, the *meaning* of its content. While it may engage with these elements, this is merely as a preliminary to its strategic purpose to show how the text *eludes comprehension*, how its unity *disintegrates* and how its declared central concerns serve to *conceal* more crucial manoeuvres involving the *suppression* of unwanted rhetorical 'skeletons in the cupboard'. Deconstruction exposes what the text attempts to hide: *the method by which it achieves its effect upon the reader.*
- Deconstruction is concerned not to describe the devices which support the coherence of the text but, rather, works to demonstrate how the text is grounded in *aporia*: incoherence, paradox and contradiction.
- Deconstruction is over-intimate with the text, forcing the process of close reading to a location beyond the closeness hitherto considered appropriate or legitimate. Straining the concept almost out of recognition, it shows that beyond the level at which a reading can preserve and account for coherence

lies a reading in which the conditions required for the coherence of the reading break apart.
- Deconstruction attends to what, under traditional techniques of close reading, would be discarded as merely marginal to the text's manifest concerns. It attempts to show how the central concerns of the text cannot be decisively separated from the marginal; how, for example, the linguistic vehicles which the text employs to express its content cannot be divorced from each other to leave the content to stand independent of its mode of expression. The content of the text owes its existence to the particular language within which it is expressed.
- Because deconstruction is reactive, because it is the kind of close reading which attends to the *particular* devices employed within a *particular* text to achieve its *particular* effects, deconstruction will tend to use direct quotation more frequently than other styles of academic criticism.
- Deconstruction replaces the security of a rationally justified reading and replaces it with readings reliant upon the insecurities of talent alone: the manoeuvres are not algorithmic; their effectiveness depends, among other things, on their surroundings. In this it is more like satire than philosophy. A manoeuvre may only work because the context enables it to and not because it is inherently rational or funny. The audience becomes part of the context of the text and of the deconstructive con/text. This requires creativity, flair and style in a manner unacknowledged within but presupposed by traditional philosophical and academic writing.
- Deconstruction does not suppress its intention of causing trouble for and within texts and their positions or theories. It is never positive in the traditional sense of supplying arguments in defence of a position. From the perspective of reason, therefore, deconstruction constitutes a criminal act. It attempts to find a hole in the logic of the text; and when it does it doesn't attempt to patch it up but instead plunders and violates.

Deconstruction is often thought of as a very recent French invention. This is only part of the story. The French philosopher Jacques Derrida did name many of the devices of deconstruction and invented much of the vocabulary discussed in this chapter. This is a massive and original achievement. But the strategy of deconstruction is neither unique nor original to Derrida: the rhetorical strategies of the pre-Socratic Sophist philosophers of ancient Greece – particularly their arts of antilogic and eristic – presage much of the style of deconstruction. As will become evident, many of the deconstructive manoeuvres of the present book owe more to Wittgenstein than to Derrida. Derrida himself derives much in his approach from Nietzsche, Heidegger and Peirce (Rorty 1982, 1991b). And within Anglo-American analytical philosophy, Dummett's (1978) anti-realist undermining of bivalence, Quine's (1951, 1960) attack on analyticity and the determinacy of meaning and Davidson's (1974) assault on the idea of a conceptual scheme can be read as deconstructions of the conceptual system assumed by realism, deconstructions which, from a deconstructive perspective, are all the sweeter for their occupying a place at the centre of analytic philosophy.

The text

From a deconstructive point of view everything is *text*. Now any text – that is, any example of writing, any fragment of language, conversation, film, advertising poster – expresses itself, carries out its purpose, either through the overt employment of reasoning or at least on the assumption that its activities are supported by some underlying rational framework. Its arguments, descriptions, uses of evidence and explanation are all particular manifestations of an underlying logic, a rational system whose veracity, *whether or not it is made explicit*, is presupposed by the text in its writing, in the very possibility of its production.

I have said that the text assumes its system of rationality, but what does this mean? A text on education, say, or dinosaurs, Martian invaders or gas guzzlers, assumes, *whether these things exist or not,* the meaningfulness of the term 'education', 'dinosaur' etc. Insofar as they are meaningful, these terms must occupy a place within a system comprising other meaningful and related terms – those of *cause and effect* or *the physical world,* for example – together with general distinctions between *truth* and *falsehood* or *fact* and *fiction* that are embodied in the laws of logic which form the universally binding framework for realist thought.[1] The text will also assume, at certain key moments, the sincerity of its own voice and of its author. Texts which are particularly interesting from a deconstructive point of view are those which are reflexive or self-referential: texts which are rational only on the assumption of the very concepts they purport to discuss. Examples of this kind of text include discussions of the law of excluded middle, honesty, reality, rationality, autonomy, authenticity.[2]

Deconstruction, then, is a strategy of reading a text in order to turn the rationality expressed by or implicit within the text back upon itself to take apart its rational structure and reveal the devices of concealment and blindness where the text fails to meet the standards it sets for itself. In deconstructing a text one would first expose and describe the rational system; then assault it. The raw materials for the deconstruction are already present in the text as the assumed logical pillars of its arguments. No matter how strong the logic, how tight the reasoning, deconstruction operates like a virus on the text's immune system, turning its logic against itself.

For example, if a text expresses a doctrine of freedom, a deconstructive reading may endeavour to show how, in its mode of expression, the text attempts to limit the options of the reader, closing off possible lines of questioning. Deconstruction shows that the text actually contradicts or subverts its professed intentions to *describe* freedom by its employment of oppressive devices in its material expression. As a general point, by showing that there is an inherent contradiction concealed at the rational heart of the text – of any text – deconstruction situates rationality itself as simply a form of *rhetoric*, the art of selling the text's truth-claims to its audience.

The 'freedom' example serves to demonstrate the manoeuvre of object-language/metalanguage collapse.[3] The text employs a metalanguage in its attempt to elucidate the nature of freedom in the object-language; but in so doing it enables freedom to become 'freedom', a term in the text's own metalanguage, the *meta-metalanguage*; freedom becomes the signifier which is necessary for the description of the action of the text and which enables the text, therefore, to be judged according to the concepts which – as its ends or outcomes – it explicitly professes to analyse and describe, yet which are implicitly assumed in the performance of its analyses and descriptions.

Deconstruction is not interested in the fine tuning of the system on which it operates, to argue the toss over the truth of its particular claims or the rationality of its individual presentation. Instead it is concerned, in a sense to be made apparent, with the overthrow of the system itself.

Conceptual hierarchies

In our example the text explicitly favours *freedom* over other concepts, such as *oppression*, in a *conceptual hierarchy*. The hierarchical ordering is a symptom of the way in which a text *assumes the normality* of one pole of the opposition and sees the other as simply a negative, a distortion, a perversion or a parasite of the original concept. Texts, consequently, cannot be viewed as possessing a structure which is natural, value-neutral, uniform. Instead, the textual structure is an economy in which the currency of a concept is determined by its place among other concepts within a system of value exchange and difference.

This economy of the text is a function of a network of conceptual hierarchies. Other hierarchical oppositions common in the realist literature of Western philosophy, theory and reasoning include:

God/man
truth/falsehood
sincerity/deception
rationality/irrationality
autonomy/heteronomy
conscious/unconscious
transcendental/empirical
enlightenment/ignorance
foundation/superstructure
real/unreal
cause/effect
ideal/actual
male/female
soul/flesh
white/black
mind/body
good/evil
right/wrong
fact/fiction

stability/flux
inside/outside
origin/history
form/content
speech/writing
seriousness/play
literal/metaphorical
natural/synthetic
nature/culture
essence/accident
simple/complex
presence/absence
centre/periphery
depth/surface
theory/practice
positive/negative
higher/lower
sanity/insanity
real/imaginary
knowledge/belief
education/training
sex/masturbation
normal/perverted
lightness/darkness
necessary/contingent
permanence/change
profound/superficial
teaching/indoctrination
democracy/aristocracy

In each case of such binary oppositions, the former term is favoured – rationally, ethically, scientifically, semantically, metaphysically – over the second, subordinated or parasitic term. Taken together, they constitute in large part the economy of the normal form of Western intellectual and academic dialogue. If we follow Dummett in taking bivalence, the true/false opposition, as the essential feature of realism, then the rest become the children of bivalence, expressing the particular manifestations of realism as it devolves its authority across the economy of theoretical, intellectual, academic, pedagogic and everyday dialogue and writing. This economy has been variously described as racist, ethnocentric, sexist, logocentric and phallocentric depending on the particular hierarchies people have felt most oppressed by.

Reverse and displace

Derrida describes the movement of deconstruction following the identification of a conceptual hierarchy thus:

> In a traditional philosophical opposition we have not a peaceful coexistence of facing terms but a violent hierarchy. One of the terms dominates the other (axiologically, logically, etc.), occupies the commanding position. To deconstruct the opposition is above all, at a particular moment, to reverse the hierarchy.
>
> (Derrida 1981: 41)

Under deconstruction the hierarchical oppositions which mark the rational preferences of the text are unfastened and *reversed*. As illustrated above, the rationality of realist philosophy and theory is staked out by a binary logic which places in opposition a term and its negation: 'true' and 'not-true', 'rational' and 'not-rational', for example. The reversal which deconstruction engineers is not a reversal in the sense of defining 'true' in terms of 'not-false', but is, rather, a collapse, an obliteration of that binary distinction which opposes 'true' to 'false', showing truth to be *a special kind of falsehood*.

The reversal, then, is *strategic*, not *metaphysical*. Deconstruction does not arrive at a conclusion or a new end-point, a *position* in which black is white and true is false, for its strategic aim is not to institute a new metaphysics which is the *precise opposite* of the original. Deconstruction is not even concerned to demonstrate that the claims made within a text, its findings, conclusions or discoveries, are *wrong*. Such a dispute over the truth-claims of a text – weighing the evidence, providing counter-evidence etc. – is effectively to play the game of the text, to give tacit approval to the rules of debate which the text assumes. It is only at this point – the location at which the text's system of assumed rules of engagement is made visible – where deconstruction makes its incision and begins the post-mortem of the text's rational structure. Deconstruction is, partly, a refusal to read the text as the text would wish to be read. It is a refusal to engage with the text at the level of content and assertion.

The strategy of reversal has clear ancestral affinities with the Sophists' *antilogic*, which 'consists in opposing one logos to another logos, or in discovering or drawing attention to the presence of such an opposition in an argument or in a thing or state of affairs' (Kerferd 1989: 63). Indeed, in its deliberate, contrived determination to impose reversal upon texts, deconstruction may be seen to fuse antilogic with that other device of Sophistic rhetoric abhorred by the arch realist Plato, the *eristic* art whose concern is to secure victory in argument; a concern which subordinates truth to the imperatives of persuading or overcoming an opponent.

What gets deconstructed is the rational structure of the text – the conceptual hierarchies, values, rules etc. – which the text has to assume in the process of making its point. Unless the text is a book on logic or philosophy these rules will not normally be made explicit in the text, but they would include such items as the laws of logic, informal injunctions about avoiding fallacies, the hierarchical ordering of concepts noted earlier and those kind of context-specifying assumptions which, for example, make 'Henry VIII was greater than Napoleon' an inappropriate intrusion into a discussion of '>' or which rule out as criticisms of Einstein's general theory 'It doesn't rhyme' or

'It doesn't use God as an explanatory concept.' Normal engagement with the text will share these assumptions in order to describe, understand, debate the text's content. Deconstruction ignores the explicit content and addresses the structures which enable the content to be expressed. Under deconstruction the rational system, of which the binary oppositions form the structural elements, is *displaced* – not *re-placed* by a rational alternative, but shown to have *no secure foundation in reason or reality*. Reversal, then, is not an end in itself but a halfway house on the way to displacement; and deconstruction is a strategy, not a position, for positions are first texts which express a content. Reversal is a move to show the necessary and permanent insecurity of *all* positions. It is a *non-position*. And all rational systems can be deconstructed through a close reading of their rational/rhetorical structure.

Consider once again the example of 'freedom'. Under deconstruction 'freedom' is neither eliminated altogether nor rendered meaningless. The *possibility* of the strategy of deconstruction *relies on* the concept it deconstructs; applying the concept *to itself* to exhibit its meaning as arising out of a set of exclusions and oppressions, *as dependent upon the very concepts which it denies*. Thus, deconstruction is not a process that is legitimized or underwritten by some logical or rational principle which is *more fundamental* than the text itself. The incision of deconstruction is legitimized *by the text itself*, which, we might say, *self-deconstructs*. What is displaced through this operation is the economy which gives the term/concept its value. The currency of the term is not effaced. What is shifted in the displacement of the system is the exchange rate, *the value which the term commands among other terms in other linguistic contexts*. What is shifted is what we can and cannot employ the term to do.

This operation leaves the structure supporting the hierarchies of the text exposed. What holds them in place is made visible and shown not to be any necessity of logic or reason, nor any empirical imperative, but, rather, the dominating *rhetorical* force of entirely textual devices such as metaphor and metonymy, which 'encourage' us to be predisposed to see reality in a particular way.

Writing and presence

Since bivalence – the true/false opposition – is the central conceptual hierarchy in realism and in Western thought and reason, one might expect that the strongest anti-realist attack would be directed against bivalence itself. That would certainly be the case in analytic philosophy and, indeed, is the approach adopted by Michael Dummett (1978). Deconstruction, however, raises the stakes of the argument; for what it places in jeopardy is the very idea of the analytic enterprise itself. This means that a deconstruction of realist metaphysics will also be a deconstruction of its philosophical techniques and of the logical structures which enable them to operate. Thus, not only the central pillar of bivalence, but also the analytical, philosophical dialogue within which bivalence may be attacked or defended, is subverted by Derrida's displacement of the entire issue into a dispute over the primacy of speech versus writing.

The deconstructive manoeuvre is thus a double strategy in which the domination of the hierarchy true/false within the dialogue of reason, and the domination of truth over falsehood within the hierarchy, are reversed to favour the marginal by means of the engineering of a reversal of an opposition which is itself marginal to the philosophical tradition; the opposition of speech and writing.

It is easy to see the symptoms of the dominance of speech in our general approach to language. We tend, for example, to *talk* about what a book *says*, what a sign *tells* us, in what *voice* a book is written, what *audience* a book is addressing. These conventions, and the habit by which we often *hear* in our minds the words which we silently read, convey something of the primacy which speech appears to have over writing (see Sturrock 1986: 145–6). Writing is conceptualized and described in the vocabulary of speech. Indeed, is not the very foundation of rationality itself embodied, for Habermas, in the ideal *speech* situation?

In Derrida's hands, speech and writing become, respectively, metaphors for the analytic-realist and the deconstructive-anti-realist philosophical styles. Traditionally speech is favoured as the concept which best represents the semantic relationship of language to thought in virtue of its own essential and immediate causal proximity both to the thoughts which give it its meaning and to the thinker having those thoughts, expressing these meanings (see Derrida 1976: 11). Speech issues directly from its author, its progenitor. In this it embodies *authenticity,* of which other guarantees of authentication – the signature, for example – are mere simulacra whose status is parasitic upon the possibility of the spoken word. In *giving one's word*, the authentication is direct, self-defining, requiring no mediation through some device, medium or material which is independent of or remote from the speaker. Speech 'signifies "mental experiences" which themselves reflect or mirror things by natural resemblance' (Derrida 1976: 11). For the realist, 'Between being and mind, things and feelings, there would be a relationship of translation or natural signification' (Derrida 1976: 11); reality (or nature) *speaks to us in its own voice*, which we translate through our understanding, through our grasp of its essential message, its *logos*.

Here is the realist theory of meaning in a picture: we understand the world insofar as we can faithfully translate its logos; our statements are true insofar as they correspond accurately to nature's own statements; and the guarantee that our words stand in just this relation to nature's is underwritten by our own subjective authority, which comes of being the owner, author, direct and unmediated progenitor of our own speech. In every case, I know what I really mean or what I intended to say and I can have direct and immediate access to this fact through the simple, straightforward act of introspection.

This picture contrasts with the traditional view of writing, which is seen as lacking the transparent integrity of representation that speech commands owing to its temporal and spatial remoteness from the act of its creation and from the presence of the semantic and interpretive guarantee of its author.

In speech, meaning is alive, present, here, now; in writing, it is dead and requires resurrection. In the absence of a speaker who can resolve questions of interpretation by explaining what they *really* meant, writing suffers an indeterminacy which makes it an inadequate substitute for speech. Compared with the transparent communicative efficacy of speech, writing is an artificial surrogate; a necessary stop-gap, but no substitute. Human intersubjective understanding across the world would be better if writing could be replaced with speech in every instance and context of communication.

When its rhetoric is described in this way, realism is situated as having a phonocentric bias which is symptomatic of a deeper commitment: logocentrism or the metaphysics of *presence*. Presence manifests itself in various guises throughout Western thought but always it plays the role of grounding some region of understanding or experience in an underlying reality. Presence emerges as the ultimate, foundational reality which exists independent of ourselves and our thoughts and beliefs to ground our truths, our theories of truth and truth itself. It is the Logos of Christianity which constitutes the reality that is the world, its history and its destiny in the Word of God; the logos which informs and directs nature into a coherent design while doing the same for logic and mathematics. Presence appears as the things we see; as the immediacy of the ideas and representations we have; as substance, essence and existence; as the temporal present, the now of the moment; as the self-presence of consciousness, of subjectivity, as one's own inner experiences and ideas etc. (Derrida 1976: 12; see Culler 1983: 92–4). Presence constitutes the essential truth of reality; hidden from our sight possibly, but present in its entirety to some divine mind.[4] In consequence, presence becomes the object of discovery as it is revealed through processes of experimentation in the empirical sciences, excavation in palaeontology, analysis in philosophy, calculation in mathematics and revelation in religion. As the ultimate fact-of-the-matter with regard to meaning – the meaning that is immediately present to the speaker's consciousness – presence is also the essence of the ideal speech situation; the *ideal is* an unmediated, undistorted semantic presence at the centre of the speech context.

The metaphysics of presence is the desire for essence, for a centre, for an explanation, a truth. It is a desire which lies at the foundation of science and religion, philosophy and psychology, ethics and education. This longing for a centre – notes Spivak – spawns the hierarchical oppositions in which the 'superior term belongs to presence and the logos' (Derrida 1976: lxix). It nourishes the deific mythology of the voice of nature, which, in speaking to us, tells us how things really are; a divine voice which we must struggle to understand if we are ever to gain true knowledge (cf. Derrida 1976: 12–18).

In deconstructing the edifice of metaphysics that is realism – and its rhetorical consequences, the rational structure of the dialogue of the West from Plato, through the enlightenment, to the present – we shall be concerned to engineer a reversal of the hierarchy of the metaphors speech/writing to render speech as a special case of a more fundamental writing. The aim is not to situate writing as the more basic or general metaphysical concept; it is rather to displace altogether the system which holds the dualism fixed.

Under deconstruction, writing – as distance from the absent authority of the author's voice and the vulnerability, therefore, to interpretation which is unconstrained, un-*authorized* – displaces speech as *the* metaphor of language, thought, reason and metaphysics (see Wittgenstein, PI sections 242ff, 258, 265, 270 etc., 580, p. 207). All of these become species of a generalized form of writing, or *arche-writing*, since every employment of language, is, just like writing, remote from the jurisdiction of any absolute legislative authority.

We might say that *arche-writing* manifests itself in two forms: graphic writing and vocal writing (Culler 1983: 101). That is, the idea(l) of speech is a metaphysical myth: the mythology of presence. The metaphor of speech symbolized the ideal of an undistorted, self-authenticating truth which would constitute both the underpinning authority for human communication, reasoning, knowledge, and its natural object or goal. *Arche-writing*, Derrida notes, is not to be made the object of a science. It does not even occur as part of any linguistic system. It is, rather, the 'movement of *différance*', the differential condition of the possibility of language (see Derrida 1976: 60). It is a (non-) concept that can only be employed *sous rature* (see below). In opposing and overturning the closure of the possibilities of interpretation and distortion embodied in the metaphor of speech, writing re-constitutes language and thought within a setting of openings; openings, that is, to endless interpretation and re-interpretation. In its indefinite deferral of presence, writing turns language into a scriptease of distortion, mis-reading and artifice.

Through the metaphor of *arche-writing* we come to see language as a system not of self-present identities but of differences. Just as the vulnerability of the written text to unauthorized or 'erroneous' interpretation is owing to its materiality and the possibility, therefore, of its physical absence from its author, so language itself – together with the knowledge, reason, truth and reality that must express themselves through language – is textual, material, a physical sequence of marks or sounds, absent from any author(ity). All texts become, in this sense, already *written* – having no authoritative commentary. Even the author has no privileged access to her meaning but is in the position traditionally given over to the reader: that of having to interpret and understand the signs before her. All speech now becomes a special case of writing. On the model of writing, all language is mediated, has to be interpreted and is open to multiple and indeterminate readings.

Différance

daemon (de′-mon) *n.* an inspiring influence; a divinity; genius.
Demon (de′-mon) *n.* a spirit (espec. evil); a devil.

The fantasy of realism, and traditional theorizing in general, is that language and reason would be purer if in the conceptual oppositions of rational thought the negative concept could be eliminated altogether, if it could be forgotten or if it never had existed. But this can only ever be a dream; for the negative must, of necessity, exist since it is part of the meaning of the preferred, 'normal' concept. The preferred concept only has a meaning insofar as it is capable of enabling distinctions to be drawn between those cases to which it applies and those to which it does not. In other words, its meaningfulness presupposes that it is capable of being negated. This 'undesired' necessity provides an opening in the text upon which deconstructive manoeuvres can operate; a necessary imbalance in any text's logic which is part of the meaning of *différance*.

Différance – spelt with an 'a' – is the non-concept or strategic moment of deconstruction. *Différance* is Derrida's term, and indicates the possibility of the forming of concepts and inevitably brings with it the necessary openings or fault-lines which enable deconstruction to take place. *Différance* could be called a generalized absence. Derrida argues that the history of Western philosophy has been founded on a metaphysics of *presence* which is symbolized in its prioritizing of *speech* over *writing* as the more authentic representative of a person's true thoughts and meanings. In speech the author is present-to-her-words, can guarantee her meanings, her authorization of interpretations, in a manner which is precluded by the distance from the author in both space and time of the written medium. Her writing is vulnerable to misinterpretation in a way that her speech, because of her *presence*, is not. Taking a strategic tack which I shall develop later, Derrida plays with the homophony (in French) of *différance* and difference to begin to question the unambiguous authority of speech over writing, while exploiting the collapse into *différance* of the twin notions of *differing* and *deferral* to initiate a subversion of the metaphysics of presence along both spatial and temporal dimensions.

> The play of differences supposes . . . syntheses and referrals which forbid at any moment . . . that a simple element be *present* in and of itself, referring only to itself . . . No element can function as a sign without referring to another element which itself is not simply present . . . This interweaving, this textile, is the *text* produced only in the transformation of another text. Nothing, neither among the elements nor within the system, is anywhere ever simply present or absent. There are only, everywhere, differences and traces of traces.
>
> (Derrida 1981a: 26)

Deconstruction exploits the notion that every text is an economy, a system of differences and imbalances. The text's currency, its terms or concepts, has its role or value defined by its place in differing from other terms or concepts. The concept of 'education', for example, is not simply a single, unique, self-defining concept but is, rather, situated within a galaxy of other concepts – indoctrination, training, instruction, pedagogy etc. – by differing from which it establishes an inventory of legitimate applications.

Différance, moreover, signals the tension between structure and event: an event's uniqueness, its differing from other events, yet its requiring the structure within which it may become a 'kind of . . .' and share a meaning with other events. But the structure itself – as simply a network of differences – does not supply the necessary framework. It is assumed within each event, yet contact with it is endlessly deferred.

We find a permanent possibility of deconstruction. It seems that any resting place, any position, must immediately collapse, must differ from itself because of the way in which it fails to meet the standards it sets by which to judge its own coherence and integrity. The elements which would validate its ultimate coherence, identity (presence), are deferred. Their presence is pointed at by the text's assertions but denied, absented, by the structure which enables it to say anything at all. Ironically, because it is possible for the text to mean, that meaning must be subject to endless deferral, must be constantly different from the promise of a determinate act of reference. If the rationality of a text is nothing fixed or solid, but is held in place only by the internal coherence of the text itself, then the idea of the text actually corresponding to, referring to or depicting something external to the text is just another example of the text's rhetoric. This leads deconstructive writers to embrace Derrida's slogan: 'There is nothing outside the text' (see Derrida 1976: 50, 91, 101, 158–9; Wittgenstein PI: sections 504, 384).

The trace

> Her government, under the administration of the
> dogmatists, was at first despotic. But inasmuch as
> the legislation still bore traces of the ancient
> barbarism, her empire gradually through intestine
> wars gave way to complete anarchy; and the
> sceptics, a species of nomads, despising all settled
> modes of life, broke up from time to time all civil
> society.
>
> (Kant 1781/1787: A.ix)
>
> The (pure) trace is *différance*.
>
> (Derrida 1976: 62)
>
> The trace is in fact the absolute origin of sense in
> general. Which amounts to saying once again that
> there is no absolute origin of sense in general.
>
> (Derrida 1976: 65)

By emphasizing the metaphor of writing over that of speech, deconstruction does not simply usurp the latter to replace it with the former in a reconstituted realist metaphysics. The re-styling of philosophy as *writing* does not result in a position at all but instead issues in the displacement of all systems through its dissolution of the authority of presence. Presence is never pure; it is always inhabited, infected, by the *trace*. Writing, as Spivak says, 'is the name of the structure always already inhabited by the trace' (in Derrida 1976: xxxix).

Texts cannot be self-contained with regard to their meanings and the significance of, for example, their movements of characterization and emplotment. They are neither self-contained nor self-coherent but bear the *trace* of various readings – prior readings and possible readings – and other texts which might influence their interpretation. A text is therefore always already a *palimpsest* of multi-layered writings and interpretations.

The trace symbolizes the impurity of presence; the fact that wherever presence is required in metaphysics it is inevitably only available in a distorted form. It is the inevitable pollution of our concepts by intrusive elements which subvert our ability to give a term a determinate context for its correct application or understanding (Quine, 1960). The mark of realism is that in every region of thought and experience where it occurs – be it common-sense experience, scientific theory, academic debate, ethics, philosophy, critical reflection or whatever – it manifests itself through a hankering after a presence: the world, God, reality, nature, space, time, the self, the mind, reason, causality, the ideal speech situation etc. In each case some origin, or originary force or principle, is posited as the foundation for the discipline, which, in turn, investigates its consequences. The point of theory, for example, becomes, on this model, one of enabling us to break through the surface impressions and beliefs available to common sense to achieve a clear view of the underlying reality that determines the surface features.

Deconstruction is a strategic dismantling of this mythology, whose pure, natural god of presence is usurped by the distorting, artificial devil of the trace:

> The trace is not only the disappearance of origin – within the discourse that we sustain and according to the path that we follow it means that the origin did not even disappear, that it was never constituted except reciprocally by nonorigin, the trace, which thus becomes the origin of the origin.

> (Derrida 1976: 61)

The trace, we might say, is the image of the absence of a presence; it signals that while a constituting or foundational presence is required by a text it is unavailable except as a product of the text; the text constructs its own foundations. Thus, although Christianity requires God as its constituting presence, the lesson of the trace is that God Himself is the textual product of the dialogue of Christianity, which has created the presence, the origin – now visible as corrupted and contrived – that the very possibility of that dialogue necessarily presupposes. The origin – that is, the trace itself – does not exist (see Derrida 1976: 167).

In the move from common-sense assumption to full-blown philosophy, realism relies upon the projection of a picture or metaphor. It takes the characteristics of immediacy, solidity, familiarity, externality and objectivity of the physical world around us, the everyday world in which we lead our lives, have breakfast, go to school, make discoveries, and develops the picture into a model of *reality* itself, such that, for example, this table has much in common with the ultimate nature of the universe: its objectivity, its extension in space and time, its being subject to causal laws and so on. Realism reifies the consistency and coherence of description and explanation uniformly across the universe. The stories of the table, of Jupiter, and beyond, are consistent because they share the same fundamental narrative of description and explanation.

But even within this picture (from which realism sources its stories of absolutism, essentialism, objectivity and truth), the trace inhabits the manifestations of presence which are the foundations for the picture. In tracking the influence of the trace, deconstruction reveals the picture of universal coherence to be self-contradictory; a picture constituted by incompatible locations of presence each of which is inhabited by the trace of the other, a trace which has to be suppressed and concealed if the story is to retain any semblance of coherence, authority and its mythology of presence.

Applying this story of *presence which is eternally already inhabited by the trace* is a key manoeuvre of deconstruction. The manoeuvre has important precursors in the history of philosophy, however, and in exemplifying its strategic application it will be instructive to draw upon these.[5] Immanuel Kant provides an excellent summary of the predicament of realism when the story of the trace is written into its metaphysics of presence in his treatment of the antinomies of pure reason.[6] In the antinomies Kant argues that for every 'essential metaphysical foundation' (presence) that is presupposed by realism there is another essential foundation *with which it is incompatible*. The presence bears the trace of the other. Each antinomy is set out as a thesis and its antithesis:

Thesis	*Antithesis*
1 The world has a beginning in time, and is also limited as regards space.	The world has no beginning, and no limits in space; it is infinite as regards both time and space.
2 Every composite substance in the world is made up of simple parts.	There nowhere exists in the world anything simple.
3 There is both the causality of the laws of nature and causality owing to human free-will.	There is no freedom; everything in the world takes place solely in accordance with laws of nature.
4 There belongs to the world, either as its part or as its cause, a being that is absolutely necessary.	An absolutely necessary being nowhere exists in the world, nor does it exist outside the world as its cause. (See A426/B454–A460/B488)

The issue of presence, then, arises with regard to the oppositions of finite/infinite, simple/complex, determinism/free will, necessary/contingent. In the first antinomy the world is posited as requiring an origin in time, yet the possibility of such an origin is denied by the antithesis in which the world is seen as requiring a different, contradictory presence: the self-presence of being its own originating principle; that is, having no origin (beginning) in time. Kant offers a similar argument to establish another dual requirement of contradictory presence in the case of space. These antinomies of presences which reason compels us to assume jointly leave the reality of the world suspended between two sets of incompatible requirements of presence, so that the world must be thought of as having an origin in time (be of finite duration) yet cannot have, and must have a limit in space (be of finite size) yet cannot have. The world bears the trace of both an origin and of an infinity, that is, the trace of founding narratives that are unreconcilable–*différance.*[7]

The dilemma of the second antinomy arises in a variety of situations where surface complexities are supposed to be clarified and explained following a process of analysis which reveals their simple components. This general picture covers such cases as the movement from complex physical phenomena to simple atoms in the explanations of physics; from complex concepts such as education to simple, constituting criteria in philosophical analysis; from human and social events to God's *Logos* in religion.

However, as Wittgenstein has shown, what constitutes *the simple* is a matter of some relativity; it is dependent upon the role something has in a particular story we wish to tell or explanation we wish to give. In what sense, asks Wittgenstein, is 'broomstick and brush' an analysis of 'broom'? Does

> someone who says that the broom is in the corner really mean: the broomstick is there, and so is the brush, and the broomstick is fixed in the brush? . . . Suppose that, instead of saying 'Bring me the broom', you said 'Bring me the broomstick and the brush which is fitted on to it.'!
> – Isn't the answer: 'Do you want the broom? Why do you put it so oddly?'
> (PI section 60; see PI sections 46–8)

Not only is *what is* simple or complex *whatever counts as* simple or complex relative to some text (story, set of interests or purposes etc.), this effacement of the absolute necessity of the distinction entails that the simple itself is always already inhabited by the trace, that is, *constituted by a system of complexities*; it is already a text, an *anthology* of possible stories. What is simple or complex is, then, written backwards as product rather than cause of the text.

> The trace is not a presence but is rather the simulacrum of a presence that dislocates, displaces, and refers beyond itself. The trace has, properly speaking, no place, for effacement belongs to the very structure of the trace.
> (Derrida 1968: 156)

Our stories about time suffer similar displacement when the metaphysics of presence is replaced by the disruption of the trace. The pure instant of the present moment can only be thought, identified, named insofar as it is constituted as a member of a series of moments. The simple instant is already a complex of relations of pasts, futures, presents- and pasts-to-be:

> The presence of motion is conceivable, it turns out, only insofar as every instant is already marked with the traces of the past and future. Motion can be present, that is to say, only if the present instant is not something given but a product of the relations between past and future. Something can be happening at a given instant only if the instant is already divided within itself, inhabited by the nonpresent.
> (Culler 1983: 94)

Zeno's paradox does not demonstrate the unreality of motion. It suggests, rather, that its possibility cannot be conceived through a metaphysics of presence, since the stories of presence-as-instant and presence-as-space cannot be reconciled in a narrative of change. The temporal present can thus be seen to be an effect of *différance*, of differing and deferral.

The impact of the antinomies on the question of the trace is this: in some of our stories about reality we must assume the world to be finite, composed of simples and so on, while in others it must be infinite or non-simple. The narrative of the trace leaves us with the necessity of unreconcilable stories. The problem for realism is that it needs, on pain of incoherence, a reconciliation of the stories or, within each opposition, the domination of one over the other. At this point we begin again the identification of the conceptual hierarchies to articulate within their story the adventures of the trace.

Metaphor

Metaphor is a manifestation of the subversive actions of reversal and the operations of the trace in the infusion of one word-image-set by another. The literal/metaphorical distinction is particularly important in realist philosophy; it is employed, for example, in drawing a distinction between serious and non-serious writing, academic and colloquial language, research and poetry where, in each case, the former, truer, more referential medium is legitimized partly by the extent to which it manages to exorcise metaphor from its modes of expression.

The importance of this distinction for those practices in which rationality, truth, clarity and wisdom have traditionally been valued makes metaphor, *as the subordinate, suppressed term in the traditional hierarchy*, a powerful weapon when wielded with deconstructive intent.

Metaphor is itself a metaphor for the meaning-displacing characteristics of deconstruction:

- In its interpretation metaphor clearly bears the trace of other beliefs, memories of other texts.
- The interpretation of metaphor is indeterminate.
- Its interpretation requires the reader to supplement the literal term with something marginal to a serious, reference-respecting reading.
- Its role is con/text-relative.
- Metaphor has no metaphysical pretensions. It does not attempt to refer beyond the textual relationships it can enjoy. Indeed, it does not attempt to refer at all.
- Metaphor is, we might say, inhabited by *différance*: *its object* – that which gives it a role, opens the possibility of interpretation – is never present but always distant, other-than, deferred and different from its context of application, *the object* which it purports to describe.
- Metaphor is the embodiment of a reversal in which image supplants truth as the determinant of the term's currency within textual exchange.
- Metaphor opens potentialities of understanding rather than fixing understanding determinately and uniquely. A metaphor is permanently an opening for re-reading, re-interpretation; every metaphor is at once a palimpsest.

Thus, *différance* could be construed as the generalization of metaphor across all texts. Contrary to traditional metaphysics, no term object or text is straightforwardly identical with itself, as it is nothing more than an interpretation which is always vulnerable to dissolution through re-interpretation. Texts are, we might say, inevitably metaphorical in nature, without any determinate literal base.

No term, therefore, can have ultimate metaphysical or referential stability. *That* would require a *presence* at the end of the process of reference or signification, whereas all we have is endless metaphoricity of the play of *différance*. No term has a self-present meaning. Meaning is, rather, subject to indefinite and ultimate deferral and differing (the twin aspects of *différance*).

The strategy of deconstruction is to expose the assumptions on which the logic or integrity of a text is based and without which it would either collapse into falsehood, self-denial, nonsense, or metamorphose into a different literary genre, from educational textbook, say, to fiction, subjective biography or poetry. A text, realistically construed, forgets its metaphorical setting of the terms it deifies as 'literal'. Indeed, the use to which a term is put within a text is a manifestation of the forces at work within the text which establish and maintain its economy; that is, the actual use is an expression of the text's (assumption of a) deeper logic, its rules or *logos*. But deconstructive attention to the metaphorical nature of language enables us to read the dominant terms of the hierarchies listed earlier as metaphors for the text in which they appear. The dominant terms of the text, therefore, stand in a metonymical relationship to the text itself; they contain the blueprint for reading the text, they contain its DNA.

None of this should be taken as implying that deconstruction is a critical method which differs from traditional theorizing only in that it employs, or requires, a *systematic theory of metaphor*. Any attempt to construct such a theory would miss the point of the deconstructive impact of metaphor's displacement of the literal; for systematizing metaphor would require the reduction and regulation of the possibilities of interpretation. It would necessitate, in other words, the conversion of metaphor into literal expressions. However, what is un-found in this process is metaphoricity itself; eluding systematization as the literal referent of the (putative) theory, metaphor re-appears as the text-DNA to disclose the theory as itself *non-literal*.

The point we have reached – the metaphorization of all attempts to be literal – places us in a position to appreciate some of the more shocking manoeuvres of deconstruction. Deconstructive writing employs a style which subverts the stylistic conventions of realism; conventions which attempt to conceal their conventional status, style which pretends not to be a style but masquerades as the pure, neutral, transparent, representational form required of literal writing which refers to facts, truths and reality.

In deconstructing we will employ whatever textual tricks we can to force the reader to attend to the stylistic aspects of presentation, to shock the reader into seeing the text in a different way: once again the family resemblance of deconstruction to dadaism and satire can hardly be missed. These devices might include puns, jokes, mis-readings, invented terminologies and typographical innovations.

- *Puns*: 'con/text'; the separation '/' makes play with the idea of the text setting a context (passive) and the (active) process of selling, persuading by a confidence trick. The con trick here is the method by which we are swindled into committing ourselves to the claims to literalness of the text through our (misplaced because displaced) confidence in its authority to underwrite such claims. Similarly, 'textile' and 'text-style' sets up the potential for a novel reading; 'term' (word) and 'term' (period) oscillate to signal the historicity of a meaning. Puns 'connect events of the narrative with events of reading and writing' (Culler 1983: 240). They are symptomatic of deconstruction's fashioning of the language of the text into its own metalanguage, the process by which the text is coerced into supplying the tools for its own self-deconstruction. Deconstructive readers will be on the look out for punning clues in the writings of fellow deconstructors.
- *False etymologies*: 'criticism' and 'crime' may be linked through a false etymology to construct a new metaphor for the critic, who now becomes the criminal who violates and plunders the text in its author's absence (see Norris 1982: 100 for a variation). Similarly, the psychological violation of therapy is committed by the*rapists*. It is a commonplace assumption of realism and liberal theory that the etymological origins of a term are irrelevant to its *present* meaning. Philosophical analysis is not etymology. Deconstruction is not etymology; nor is it concerned at all with the origins of words, whether these be etymological, conceptual, metaphysical or otherwise text-independent. Hence the ironic joke of false etymologies: to ridicule the very concept or authority of origin and to trivialize the analytical search for deep, meaningful origins while setting up an imbalance in the interpretive potential of the text.
- *Jokes*: Wittgenstein thought that all philosophy could be expressed as a series of jokes (PI section 111). Jokes *are* jokes only on the assumption of some prior context of seriousness and propriety. Mirroring the strategy of jokes, deconstruction offends the formalities and conventions which preserve such institutions. By playing their game to distort their priorities deconstruction is gamesmanship to reason's fair play.

Like any joke, these gain maximum impact within the proper context. In itself this point serves as a reminder of the importance which deconstruction attaches to the notion of context and the con/text-relativity of readings and interpretations.

Strong mis-reading

One of the biggest jokes in the deconstructor's armoury is that of strong *mis-reading*. The term is borrowed by Richard Rorty from Harold Bloom to represent the determined and chancy activity of creating one's own meanings and imposing them on a text without reference to, or respect for, the intentions, self-interpretations or rights of the writer whose traditional role as the prime *author-ity* on matters of interpretation is thus written off. It is a *mis*-reading, therefore, only on the assumption (*present* at the outset of any debate) that the interpretations of third parties are to be judged for veracity solely in terms of their goodness of fit to the author's own account. The expression '*mis*' recognizes the rhetorical advantage of authorial privilege while advertising the fragility of that privilege in its dependence on a transient public fashion that, for the moment at least, continues to find it useful to regard the author of a text as having the (initial) last word on its meaning.

Mis-reading signals the deconstructor's strategy of regarding any understanding of the text as a particular kind of mis-understanding; one whose misses are not felt to matter.[8] *Mis*-reading also enables play to be made with the perpetually missing *presence* and with femininity's '*miss*'; the spurning of phallocentism through the seductiveness of a reading *and* her refusal to be wedded to any master-text. This passive source of semantic instability oscillates with the simultaneous, active mis-readings pursued through the stupration of *différance*.

A special operation of mis-reading is the havoc which deconstruction makes with the notion of intertextuality and the opening up of the strategy of *reading-as*.[9] In its innocent, passive state, intertextuality simply refers to the kind of literary understanding which can be gained from seeing one text as a member of a corpus, as deriving some of its meanings, references, modes of characterization and emplotment from other texts; even to the extent of relying on other texts to support or supplement the reader's understanding. However, texts, now visible not as self-complete, self-identical narratives but as palimpsests, are simply *opportunities* for interpretation or re-inscription. Deconstructive play with intertextuality distorts the intertextual relationship and its assumed hierarchies of interpretation to impose one text upon another, bullying the victim-text into taking on the values of its tormentor. It will read one text *through* another text to render it an unwilling slave to an alien literary genre – politics as theory as novel as philosophy as magazine . . . *Dr No* as educational theory, *Ethics and Education* as pornography – imposing a logic on the text rather than passively accepting a prior logic to displace once again its rational system.

The supplement

Philosophical analysis in particular, and critical reflection and interpretation in general, traditionally seeks to establish a clear separation of what is central and peripheral, essential and contingent, in the meaning of a term or concept or in the understanding of a text. Supplementarity is the strategy of seizing upon the peripheral in the text to show its absolute necessity to the text's purpose. Supplementarity approaches the subversion of the text's hierarchies from the opposite direction to the strategy of strong mis-reading, where overtly external intertextual strategies are employed to erode the inside/ outside impermeability of the text. Supplementarity involves attending to the marginal to find an outside within the text, an externality produced by the text, an element of the text which is both supplementary to its declared intentions yet, by virtue of its very supplementarity, a necessary element in the situating, the stage-setting of the text's story. The logic of supplementarity is that the text weaves for itself the ghost of a context, a virtual space within which it tells its story. Supplementarity is the highlighting of something otherwise suppressed or forgotten by the text – its contextual margins.

For example, in his deconstruction of Rousseau's naturalism, Derrida focuses upon the distinction which Rousseau draws between natural or normal sex and masturbation. Rousseau tells us that this *dangerous supplement* which

> shame and timidity find so convenient, possesses, besides a great attraction for lively imaginations – that of being able to dispose of the whole sex as they desire, and to make the beauty which tempts them minister to their pleasures, without being obliged to obtain its consent.
>
> (Rousseau, *Confessions*; cited in Derrida 1976: 151)

But because of this range, because this supplement 'has not only the power of *procuring* an absent presence through its image; procuring it for us through the proxy (procuration) of the sign, it holds it at a distance and masters it' (Derrida 1976: 155). Now any sexuality can be read as a special case of its supplement; that is, of a generalized masturbation.

The forces of the trace, *différance* and supplementarity subvert the self-integrity of the context. The necessary inside/outside distinction is collapsed, reversed and displaced. The text becomes visible as the model of a Klein bottle; for what supplementarity does is displace the very distinction, *inside/outside,* which I used in differentiating between it and intertextual strategies of mis-reading. There is no longer any determinate inside/outside at all.

Sous rature

> The results of philosophy are the uncovering of one or another piece of plain nonsense and of bumps that the understanding has got by running its head up against the limits of language. These bumps make us see the value of the discovery.
>
> (Wittgenstein, PI section 119)

> When philosophers use a word – 'knowledge', 'being', 'object', 'I', 'proposition', 'name' – and try to grasp the *essence* of the thing, one must ask oneself: is the word ever used in this way in the language-game which is its original home?- What *we* do is to bring words back from their metaphysical to their everyday use.
>
> (PI section 116)

Terms with metaphysical pretensions, which traditionally command ultimate status yet which, under deconstruction, are vulnerable to re-inscription in the ways described, are placed *sous rature* – *under erasure* – signifying their necessary role within a text but the provisionality of their status within the legitimizing framework of a particular reading. '*Sous rature*' is Derrida's expression[10] to signify this necessity for the use of a term in a particular dialogue, narrative, text or language-game[11] and the contingency of the language-game itself. The term's *truth* or *authority* does not ground the language-game but, in a striking example of deconstructive reversal, depends upon the language-game for its role. But, since the language-game is itself ungrounded, is a web of contingencies, the term has no absolute necessity. The term's semantic integrity or stability is nothing metaphysical, absolute or permanent; it is, rather, that *within* this or that language-game, *now*, the usefulness of the term is, *for us*, that it brings with it, *as part of the role it can play*, a story (*trace*) of permanence and stability.

Thus – to anticipate a case to be examined later which is close to the heart of the philosophy of reflective teaching – 'rationality' has a role within a language-game in which we differentiate between the giving of good reasons in support of a conclusion, decision, action or whatever and the failure to do so; between valid and invalid arguments. When, however, we attempt to 'go metaphysical' to step outside of the language-game and talk about rationality in some context-independent absolute sense, then, we might say, we attempt to preserve the role of the term though we have removed it from the theatre within which its role was legitimate and useful.

Philosophers are particularly vulnerable to the temptation to go metaphysical with terms like rationality, to make statements not about this or that example of reasoning but about rationality in general. Consequently, it is important for those anti-realist philosophers who want to talk about terms like rationality but who don't want to take the metaphysical leap out of the con/text provided by a language-game/text to have a means of reminding their readers that in saying something about the use of the term in the particular case they are not attempting to issue a universal rule. Indeed, they are much more likely to be engaging (reactively, negatively, deconstructively) in dispute about some absolute or universalizing conception of a term *only* to reject the possibility of that conception.

This act of making use of a term while rejecting its metaphysical implications is sometimes signalled by simultaneously writing and crossing out the term (e.g. ~~rationality~~) to place it *sous rature*; asserting the term while recognizing the metaphysical groundlessness of its role; showing its necessity in assertion but its strategic, non-referential status by its (self-) denial and effacement; its implication of '"both this *and* that" as well as "neither this nor that" undoing the opposition and the hierarchy between the legible and the erased' (Spivak, in Derrida 1976: 320). Under deconstruction, the meaning and stability of a ~~term~~ or ~~concept~~ must acknowledge, through the device of *sous rature*, its provisionality, its system-relativity and the everyday, non-metaphysical sourcing of its authority to participate – as a currency with no fixed, permanent value – in textual economies.

~~Position~~

This ~~position~~ is sometimes referred to as *post-structuralism*. Post-structuralism is postmodernism in philosophy; though *pretermodern* would be better than postmodern since it carries 'beyond' but contains the trace of past and present in its pun. It is not really a position at all, however. It is a refusal to have a position. It is reactive upon positions. It is better to name it as a style – *textualism* will do. The style is *textualism*, the strategy is *deconstruction* and the attitude is *ironic*. This will become apparent as we proceed.

Notes

1 The basis of realist logic – a logic which assumes its own transcendental status – lies in Aristotle's 'laws of thought', so called because they are taken as defining the necessary conditions for intelligible thought. They are:

- The law of identity: everything is identical with itself or '$a = a$'.
- The law of contradiction: 'no statement is both true and not true' or 'not a and not-a'.
- The law of excluded middle: 'every statement is either true or false' or 'a or not-a'.

2 But explicit self-referentiality is not necessary to deconstruction. Under deconstruction, every text is made to become self-referential.
3 The object-language is the referring language we use to speak to each other. The metalanguage is the language we use to talk about that object-language, its meanings, its conventions for referring, for questioning and so on. This realist theory of language thus assumes there to be a determinate hierarchical structure to the linguistic levels. Deconstruction confuses the levels to make trouble.
4 This is not to say that all realists are religious. It is, rather, that the story of an omniscient presence is a useful metaphor for realists in describing the fact of events which happen in remote regions of space and time that may forever be beyond *our* finite, human capacities to verify them *and* the belief in the unity, uniformity and universality of the laws of nature, nature's *logos*.
5 Not only does this serve the purpose of situating deconstruction within a tradition, it also enables something of the trace of the trace within the dialogue of Western philosophy to be accentuated. In properly deconstructive terms this ~~tradition~~ should be placed *sous rature* as it can only now be conceived as a tradition. Only now that we have the vocabulary of deconstruction can we re-write (*strongly mis-read*) the history of philosophy to make it point towards the deconstructive opening of the text.
6 An antinomy is a 'kind of pseudo-rational inference . . . directed to the transcendental concept of the absolute totality of the series of conditions for any given appearance. From the fact that my concept of the unconditioned synthetic unity of the series, as thought in a certain way, is always self-contradictory, I conclude that there is really a unity of the opposite kind, although of it also I have no concept. The position of reason in these dialectical inferences I shall entitle the *antinomy* of pure reason' (A340/B398). This use of Kant as an ally of deconstruction is deliberately arch. His concern with architectonics – philosophical system-building – makes him in many ways the very antithesis of postmodernism. Nevertheless, he steadfastly attended to and described the limits of pure reason and it is in this that his writing provides deconstructive leverage.

7 Kant's summary of the crisis in reason heralded by the antinomies could almost be read as an account of the operation of the trace: 'Human reason is by nature architectonic. That is to say, it regards all our knowledge as belonging to a possible system, and therefore allows only such principles as do not at any rate make it impossible for any knowledge that we may attain to combine into a system with other knowledge. But the propositions of the antithesis are of such a kind that they render the completion of the edifice of knowledge quite impossible. They maintain that there is always to be found beyond every state of the world a more ancient state, in every part yet other parts similarly divisible, prior to every event still another event which itself again is likewise generated, and that in existence in general everything is conditioned, an unconditioned and first existence being nowhere discernible' (A474/B502).

8 Culler (1983: 176). Wittgenstein's deconstruction of the realist conception of following-a-rule is an elaboration of this slogan (see Chapter 7).

9 Wittgenstein on *seeing-as* provides many of the strategies for initiating this process of (mis-)reading (see PI sections 193–208. Kuhn's (1970) notion of the paradigm is another relativistic application of this idea.

10 The expression is derived from Heidegger and (apparently independently) mirrors much in Wittgenstein's anti-foundational philosophy (e.g. see PI sections 115–33).

11 Wittgenstein's name for what I have otherwise referred to as 'the text'.

7

DECONSTRUCTING REASON: THE SHIFT TO POSTMODERNITY

reflect (re-flekt') *v.t.* to throw back, esp. rays of light, heat, or sound, from surfaces: to give back an image of; to mirror; *v.i.* to throw back light, heat, etc.; to meditate; to attend earnestly to what passes within the mind; to consider attentively. – **to reflect on**, to cast discredit or dishonour on; to disparage.

practice (prak'-tis) *n.* customary actions; custom or habit. – **sharp practice**, dealings that border on the dishonest.

The autonomy of language

If I were to say that a presupposition of reflective practice is the *autonomy of language* this would probably appear to be an unduly figurative way of representing things: people can be said to be autonomous, but what does it mean to anthropomorphize language – words, sentences, texts etc. – to say that these too must be free of coercion, manipulation, deception or distortion?

Reflective theorists – because of the requirement of the perspicuity of the reflective process – cannot countenance any view of language in which the literal/metaphorical distinction is collapsed. Their concern with *reasoning* as a criterion of personal autonomy has implications for the view they must take towards the language within which that reasoning is carried out and judgements about its cogency are expressed. If the structures of the language, its words, its rules of combination and transformation, become distorted, then the reasoning process itself becomes contaminated and the autonomy of the individual is lost.

We can begin to see how distortion of this kind might thwart our desire for clarity and precision in the processes of reasoning by looking at the way in which vagueness operates within everyday language. If we take the word *'good'*, for example, it is easy to see how inadequate it is to the task of building an ethical theory of sufficient precision to command, if not universal agreement about its truth, *universal agreement about its interpretation.* In its everyday, shop-worn use, *'good'* has an imprecision which enables it to serve an enormous range of (possibly conflicting) purposes: a tool might be a good tool, but a good hammer isn't a good saw; nor is it good like Mother Teresa. A man might need a good woman; but not, in every instance, a Mother Teresa. Indeed, words like *'good'* find a use – *are useful* – precisely because their vagueness and malleability enables speakers to avoid commitment to levels of clarity and precision which would otherwise inhibit and stultify the flow of conversation; notice, for example, how poor some clarity-obsessed academics are at everyday conversation and interaction.

Of course, the dialogue of reflection sees itself as an engagement which takes place at a much deeper semantic and epistemological level than *mere* conversation. The rational standards embodied in reflective teaching *do* require clarity, precision and freedom from distortion of the language in which they are expressed. This requirement predisposes supporters of reflective teaching to value conceptual analysis as a means of purifying language of vagueness and distortion so that language – and the concepts to which it refers – can be brought into precise alignment. So the term 'good' would be made fit for ethical theory by being purged of colloquial uses, misuses, secondary meanings, metaphorical and connotative baggage, and elevated to the level of a technical term within a technical ethical language of precision and clarity. This is the situation with mathematics, for example, whose language of 1, 2, 3, . . . , +, – etc. outstrips in precision and economy what can be achieved by use of language such as 'one point three seven four times six point nine equals nine point four eight zero six'. The ultimate goal of analysis, then, is to eliminate distortion by establishing a technical language whose structure and vocabulary stands autonomous of particular human interests, idiosyncrasies and failings by being precisely aligned with the structure and inventory of reality.

Linguistic autonomy and the *ideal speech situation*

Realism's desire for precision is inherited by reflective teaching. Its criterion of adequacy for an educational theory is that the theory should provide a method by which interpretations of the practice situation – together with one's own self-reflections and self-understandings – can be rendered immune to the distorting effects of ideology, custom, habit, tradition, coercion, authority and institutionally imposed and maintained definitions and expectations; the very forces which nurture conservatism.

The elimination of distortion is identical with the realization of the ideal speech situation posited by Habermas and his followers as the necessary foundation of the kind of critical, rational processes required for reflective teaching. Clearly much of importance hangs on the cogency of the ideal speech situation; and it is the purpose of the transcendental argument outlined in Chapter 5 to demonstrate the normative inescapability of this picture. Now, whatever the merits or problems of transcendental arguments in general,[1] one obvious, minimal condition of their success is that the conditions, the necessary presupposition of which the transcendental argument is invoked to demonstrate, *must be able to be conceptualized, described, expressed, understood*. In the present case this simply means that the view of language embodied in the ideal speech situation *must be realizable*, or, more weakly, must at least be *thinkable* – able to be represented in some way, to ourselves and to others, as an *ideal*, a set of norms or standards to which reason, if it is genuine, is answerable. In other words, this presupposes that the picture of the distortion-free, ideal speech situation is one which is capable of being sustained by language; *that our language is such that it enables the picture to be expressed meaningfully*.

Essential to the notion of the ideal speech situation – with its conceptual scaffolding of *'rational* consensus', *'justified* consensus', 'orientation towards the idea of truth', 'freedom and justice' and *'genuine* agreement' – is a commitment to the *autonomy of language*; to the idea that that the speech-act neutrality of language – the independence of meaning from any particular form of words or their use on any particular occasion – enables it, at least in some idealization, to exist free of any distorting effects of particular practices, readings, interpretations, iterations, paraphrasing, connotation, innuendo etc. In this idealization our linguistic representations, our mental pictures, have some kind of self-ratifying power of intrinsic reference; free of distortion they cannot but *refer uniquely*. Language, on this view, somehow corresponds to the state of affairs to which it refers. This idealization, it is suggested, is presupposed in our capacity to put limits on vagueness in reference and variation in interpretation. It is presupposed in the possibility of eliminating *distortion*.

Reflection requires that there be some rigid correspondence relation which language and thought can stand in with regard to reality which guarantees referential success; to empower the dialectical process, for example. This presupposes, minimally, that any categories employed or referred to retain an identifiable, determinately prescribed role throughout the dialectical process. The elimination of distortion is, therefore, not merely the goal of reflection; the absence of distortion is *a necessary precondition of its procedures*. Any distortion inherent in language at its origin would be fatal to the reflective process, since the integrity of that process depends upon assumptions of purity, consistency and determinateness in the function of language and its various components.

This autonomy, then, is visible as a deep-level precondition of the reflective process. Only on the assumption of such autonomy can language become a tool fit for the purpose of expressing views and engaging in processes of reasoning which are themselves free of distortion. Only through its autonomy can language be a medium capable of faithfully transporting premises to conclusions via a rational process and underwriting the validity of that process. Language must be an ultimately pure, transparent medium through which the world can be properly seen, described and represented unmediated by the distorting effects of interpretation. It must be capable of shedding the non-literal baggage of metaphor, implication and connotation. In other words, the language employed in the reflective process has to be autonomous in having a clarity, a consistency and an integrity which is independent of how individuals might use it and interpret it or play with it and distort it. Its *real*, literal meaning, we might say, must transcend its physical realization in practice, where matters of style and suggestion can interfere with the process of divining pure, unmediated literal meaning from the sounds in the air or the marks on the paper in which that meaning is carried. Correspondence of meanings to our attempts to express them is, on this view, a tenuous affair which frequently fails; the job of ensuring semantic success falls to the critical, rational and democratic processes which constitute the ideal speech situation.

It is this realist picture of language that I wish to deconstruct.

Realism, rationality and reflection: following a rule

The realist's philosophy of language conceives command of a language as an ability to follow its deep rules faithfully. The semantic rules of a language, realistically construed, issue in a family of pictures or metaphors: the structure is a pattern which guides our decisions and to which our moves must conform if they are correct; in order to fulfil these demands the pattern must obtain determinately and independently of our attempts to grasp and keep faith with it; its rules are pictured as rails which stretch beyond our local concerns and usage to an infinite end, guaranteeing ultimate correctness of use in all future cases or applications if the lines are followed; the structure is a machine grinding out its functions with a certainty and consistency which is guaranteed *because inherent in its structure.*

Dependent upon this picture is the realist's view of rationality; the view of rationality which lies behind the commitment to reflection as the metaphor of a pathway to knowledge and truth, the view of rationality which is one of a cluster of metaphors embodied in the picture of the ideal speech situation, where particular examples of reasoning are judged according to standards which are independent of any particular person's subjective opinions about their correctness. Thus, the question 'What is it to think rationally?' is a question about rule-following on at least two levels. Clearly an answer would have to make reference to *the rules of reasoning*, or some such standard; but the cogency of this response can only be judged according to the criteria acquired through a more general and inclusive question: 'What is it to have grasp of a language?'[2] If the picture of language is faulty, the view of rationality becomes untenable.

A deconstruction of this picture of language, and of what conformity to its rules consists in, should take, as its points of textual incision, three locations in its metaphorical setting:

1 The idea that conformity to the rules of a language involves conformity to objective standards that are independent of *language users*. The idea that *linguistic rules* are appropriately conceived as regulating an infinite series of potential applications (*the objectivity requirement*).

2 The requirement of consistency in conformity to the user-independent standards; that is, the relationship of language users to the linguistic rules through public practices of interpretation and application (*the consistency requirement*).
3 The requirement that, corresponding to the consistencies of 2, there are regularities in inner or mental structures; structures which support self-consistency and self-understanding. This is the subjective (or idiolectic) case in which a language user understands, is consistent with, her personal practice of using and interpreting her own linguistic constructions (*the idiolectic-regularity requirement*).

In what follows I shall dismantle each of these elements of the picture. The deconstructive strategy I employ will drawn upon Wittgenstein's play with rule-following.

The objectivity requirement

Realism promises to supply, though more commonly assumes, an account of how, *in general*, the meaning of a term (or expression, or fragment of language) is determined. As a corollary it holds that a term's meaning determines the set of conditions which must be true of each and every context in which the term's use is objectively legitimate.

Accordingly, the realist owes us an account of the rules which regulate a term's use in a variety of situations and which link the contexts of correct application. These rules, realism asserts, obtain as a property of our conceptual world independently of our knowledge *of*, or adherence *to*, them. At a deep level – the level at which the ideal speech situation is conceived and justified – the rules constitute the essential precondition of the possibility of anything's being intelligible. A term, or a concept, is viewed as having a determinate pattern of application which obtains independently of anyone's actual knowledge of that pattern and even independently of our contingent, human capacities for acquiring such knowledge.

The backdrop to these convictions is provided by the realist's picture of reality as extending beyond our known or experienced universe; beyond the relatively local realms in which our statements can now, or ever, be verified as true, or false, to its own self-determined infinity. This picture feeds the belief that there is no in-principle problem in thinking of statements which are intended to apply to unknown, or non-surveyable, regions of reality as being both meaningful and determinately either true or false, even though *which value they in fact possess* is unknown, or unknowable, to our Earth-bound minds.

This picture is viewed as the transcendentally justified necessary condition of intelligibility: if our language is to be at all intelligible, that to which it applies must be an independent, determinate and stable world and our concepts must themselves possess a corresponding structure and rigidity. This picture is presupposed in the idea that in engaging in empirical investigations we effect discoveries about the nature of things – anything: electricity, God, dinosaurs, Caesar, children's learning, effective reading schemes etc. – whose reference has remained stable throughout the history of our fluctuating beliefs about them. All of which is simply the working out of the commitment to bivalence; the principle that our statements are determinately either true or false independently of our knowledge or beliefs.

Reversing the picture: anti-realism

The system which gives rise to this picture can be displaced by first confronting it with a reversal, an anti-realist alternative. In this picture there is no practice-independent pattern determining in advance what is to count as a correct move or application, for the pattern itself, insofar as it exists at all, is *created* out of the actual moves, the actual applications, which happen to be made (Wright 1980: 21). Following Wittgenstein we shall reject the thought that achieving a true understanding of our own language and the world to which it refers will involve us in digging beneath the surface of our linguistic practices to discover the pattern or essence which lies hidden from our unreflective gaze (PI sections 92, 77). Rather, *the surface is everything*. Nothing is concealed; all is open to view (PI sections 126, 435). The realist has given himself a false picture. The pattern of application does not extend beyond the results of our investigations or our linguistic practices. The concept – conceived as pattern or rule – cannot function as the determinate standard against which our *actual* practice, of employing the concept in the particular case, is right or wrong according to whether or not it *really* conforms to that pattern.

π

Wittgenstein deconstructs the picture of the practice-independent, determinately obtaining blueprint for correct applications of a concept by attacking one particular manifestation of the pattern metaphor: the realist's conception of the reality of mathematical progressions. Here the realist (and commonsense) belief is that we can give a determinate sense to the assertion that a mathematical series continues, independently of any actual results of our investigations, to infinity, such that any statement we make about some element in that series will be determinately true or false whether or not we can ever discover which. So, given the realist's commitment to bivalence, although, in the case of the decimal expansion of π, for example, we may never know whether the group '7777' occurs in the series, we do know, *with certainty*, that the assertion 'Either the group "7777" occurs, or it does not' *is true* (PI section 352). If this realist picture is to prevail it presupposes that the region of reality which constitutes the concept 'the decimal expansion of π' must be fully determinate prior to our investigations.

But, Wittgenstein observes, as long as we lack an effective power for giving our expressions a purpose, we cannot claim to have fixed their meaning unambiguously (PI section 426); to be able to empower our words with meaning we must master the technique of verifying the statements in which they occur (PI section 353). But in the case of π we do not even know how to begin to try to verify the assertion 'Either the group "7777" occurs, or it does not.' Here the natural temptation is to discharge responsibility for providing an account of our understanding of the meaning of a statement to the picture in which the statement refers to a reality which transcends our investigative capacities; a reality which, in the picture, God can see but we cannot. But this is no help in clarifying how meaning, in such cases, is possible, because our understanding of what it would be to possess the necessary super-human faculties is no less problematic than our alleged understanding of verification-transcendent patterns.

The worship of bivalence presents us with a picture in which either reality accords with the statement or it does not. 'And this picture *seems* to determine what we have to do, what to look for, and how – but it does not do so, just because we do not know how it is to be applied' (PI section 352). In other words, the very meaning of the principle of bivalence is just as 'shaky' as the question, in any particular case, of whether a statement or its negation is true (RFM V-12). In answer to the realistic assumption that the rules governing the legitimate expansion of π must determine the series completely and, consequently, must 'determine *all* questions about the structure of the series', Wittgenstein responds: 'Here you are thinking of finite series' (RFM V-11). As for non-finite or unsurveyed series, what it is to apply notions of truth and falsity, what it is for our expressions to *correspond to the facts,* is precisely what is in question (OC section 199); and prior to our determining a method for turning up a result we have nothing which fixes a meaning for such applications.

What we *do* have is a family of pictures which find application in familiar situations within our mathematical practice. We have, for example, a perfectly serviceable idea of what it is for the series '7777' to appear as a result of the calculation '2711.08 ÷ 4 = 677.77', and we can verify statements which assert its occurrence in an indefinite number of cases. We can also attach a clear meaning to statements asserting that the series '414' occurs in the expansion of π. The question is, however: how do such examples entitle us to project our understanding of meaning from decidable cases into cases in which truth is undecidable and thereby attach a meaning to statements whose verification is beyond our capacities? The unverifiable assertions about the remote regions of the expansion of π may *appear* to have a determinate meaning *because they are formally grammatical,* and because we know, for example, what it is for '415' to occur in the series. But 'our understanding of that question reaches just so far, one may say, as such explanations reach' (PI section 516; see RFM IV-8). We are yet left with the question: what entitles us, out of an indefinite range of possibilities, to make *just these* projections into verification-transcendent reality?

The flickering of reality

The realist metaphor presupposes that we can step outside of the normal, everyday situations in which no doubts about the correctness of our assertions arise to grasp the meaning of concepts as they apply in regions where such doubts do arise. The ground for this is that we can know our way about in hitherto unexplored regions of experience if we have a sufficiently sound understanding of the requisite conceptual patterns. But how do we recognize correctness of understanding here?

Imagine, for example, that we are in possession of two algorithms for determining some nth place character in π's expansion; algorithms whose veracity has found universal agreement among mathematicians. Imagine also that the choice between which algorithm to use has been either purely aesthetic or relative to the particular skills of the individual mathematician. For us, the correctness and reliability of each method is beyond question.

Realism about mathematics holds that all mathematical expressions must conform to the principle of bivalence: without exception they are true, or they are false. But suppose now that our trusted algorithms throw up conflicting results regarding the existence of the '7777' sequence within the expansion. Realism asserts, necessarily, that something must have gone wrong. But what? Initially we might check the results by repeating the tests; but if we get the same discrepancy on each occasion, what then? The matter becomes even worse if we suppose ourselves to get *different* results on each occasion.

Various narratives can be attached to this episode, each of which can claim to give the *true* picture. Perhaps we make systematic errors in our calculations. Perhaps our errors are not systematic but appear so by chance. Perhaps our computer has a faulty program or there is some quirk in its physical structure. Perhaps a wilful demon deceives us. Perhaps mathematical reality *undulates* – a mathematical statement at one time true becoming at another time false. Or perhaps there really is a plurality of correct and incompatible expansions of π. The conceptual determinateness required by realism is becoming unstable:

> If you say that the infinite expansion must contain the pattern ... or not contain it, you are so to speak shewing us the picture of an unsurveyable series reaching into the distance. But what if the picture began to flicker in the far distance?
>
> (RFM V-10)

To regain control of his picture the realist must show what sort of criteria are relevant to deciding between the alternative pictures and solving the problem. Not only must he show which, out of an indefinite number of incompatible narratives, is the one which actually corresponds to reality; he must also show that the reasons he gives for justifying this decision are the ones which are *bound to give the right result*.

But now the whole argument can be repeated: the realist is evidently in a regress in which he is unable to say how he can recognize the truth, grasp of which his picture presupposes. In the absence of verification-independent compelling reasons for making a choice between the rival accounts, there appears to be no possible motive, licensed by realism, for supposing that such a choice is required.

That we can make a decision to act in a particular way here is true. And the justification for so acting might be framed in terms of the *success of a*

method, which for the anti-realist is not separable from the success *it appears
to us* to have (see PI sections 320, 324). But realism requires something more;
it requires that the correctness of that decision be underwritten by its *conformity to the way reality actually is*. We have seen, however, that reality is
impotent in 'picking out' one narrative as *the* uniquely correct description of
how things are. An answer to the question of how we might begin to rein-
state bivalence in radical cases is unavailable to the realist, for he is unable
to read off from the world how the world's answer should go. In the π
example our results have collapsed the normal distinction between *proof* and
experiment: now we are not even sure which statements should remain fixed
and which tested.

The deep need for decision

The point we have reached is that there is no antecedently correct answer
to the question of which move we should make and which picture we
should preserve. A *decision* is required for which there are no constraints
independent of our own interests and practices. The ground for this decision
does not exist *out there*; it has to be *invented* (RFM I-166–8, V-9). The statements which we are used to verifying within familiar contexts do not, after
all, empower our claims that reality *must* go one way or another in its unfamiliar regions. *We* have to decide, *in this new practice we are creating*, which
results are *symptoms* of error or *criteria* of correctness (PI section 354), which
moves are *experiments* and which *calculations* (RFM I-161–2, III-68–74, VIII-
17–18, 61–2), when we should predict that *x will* occur and when we should
say that *x must* occur in accordance with the application of our rules (RFM
VI-15). Our narratives, we might say, have become texts which have no interest
in *corresponding with reality*. Instead, they are expressions of our decision to
regard reality in a certain way.

We can, under this reversal, legitimately form a conception of things being
thus and so just as far as we can explain our conception to ourselves and
others. Without this capacity we are incapable of manifesting our understanding of a statement, even to ourselves; which is precisely the predicament
in which the realist finds himself. Thus, at this point bivalence fails and realism becomes unintelligible. Although we might appeal to the authority of a
further test which supports the results of one of our competing algorithms
there is nothing which can serve to determine that such confirmation is actually *confirmation of its correctness*. If reality were surveyed by God,[3] He might
find that the unconfirmed method is the uniquely correct one and that no
further confirmation exists. In this case, if we are persuaded by further evidence we will actually, but unknown to us, part company with the truth.

What this suggests is that such a decision-independent picture of truth can
have no work to do in explaining our understanding of our own language
and its concepts. In going beyond the criteria which govern the correct employment of a concept within our local practices we do not *discover* independently existing regions of the conceptual pattern. Rather, we *create* these
regions; *we* determine how the pattern is to go through our interests and

decisions. Prior to our deciding, no answer exists; just as there is no answer to the question of whether the hero in a poem has a sister or not before the poet has thought about it (RFM V-9). In calculating we derive new rules which the series obeys (RFM V-11), we expand mathematics (RFM V-9). Thus, what correctness of application *is* grows outward, as it were, from our existing practice, from our actual acts of application, and not 'inward' from some fully determinate, independent reality as the rigid template to which correct practice must conform.

These arguments reflect the realist picture back on itself. If we can give no grounds – independent of the agreement of our community – for deciding between rival descriptions for which communal assent has not hitherto been sought, then all reason is removed for supposing that such standards actually do exist. If we cannot decide between rival descriptions what possible grounds can we have for believing that our communal practice might actually be founded on a mistaken grasp of patterns? It becomes impossible to say, prior to securing agreement in judgements, that a particular practice is wrong (cf. Wright 1980: 215–22).

Realism: the inexpressible picturing the unintelligible

These considerations enjoin us to 'revise what counts as the domain of the imaginable' (PI section 517). The realist, overlooking the fact that often we need to perform a calculation to settle the question of whether a statement makes sense (PI section 513), supposed that we could represent something which it turned out we could not. His commitment to bivalence involved him in holding that we could form a determinate idea of what it would be for '7777' to exist somewhere in the expansion of π and that we could similarly form a clear and determinate idea of what it would be for '7777' to be absent. It cannot but be an embarrassment to the realist to find that he has committed himself to the unintelligible 'belief' that *we can have a clear and determinate idea of what it looks like to falsify a necessary truth*; as if we were able to form a picture of a world in which '$1 + 1 = 2$' were false (see RFM V-18; Kielkopf 1970: 135).

What we have to jettison is the picture in which we are imagined capable of surveying the whole future pattern of use to which sincere employment of a concept commits us. We can have no privileged access to the character of our own understanding beyond those situations in which we are *normally* required to manifest that understanding (Wright 1980: 32). There can be no fact of the matter regarding questions of the correctness of applying particular concepts in particular situations *prior to our decision to apply them* (OC sections 49, 146, 362, 368; RFM III-27, V-20, 33, VI-24; PI section 186). The realist's mistake was in thinking that our decisions needed a justification which rested on something more basic, more fundamental, than agreement between speakers of a language. If established linguistic practice does not furnish a context in which correct understanding of a pattern can be fully manifested then it is senseless to suppose that there is any such context and any such pattern.

What goes for the expansion of π goes also for the extension of any concept. When we extend its rules beyond the context of our immediate practices we involve ourselves in the enterprise of *creating* new rules and not in an investigation which *discovers* rules which were already there. The philosopher, like the mathematician, is an *inventor*, not a discoverer (RFM I-168, II-38, V-11). Getting this the wrong way round is the mistake on which the history of philosophy, positivism and reflective teaching has been founded.

The consistency requirement

Realism, in holding that rational reflection makes genuine discoveries about the world, including our reasoning about the world, is wedded to a picture in which there are facts about our linguistic and rational practices which are not transparent to our unreflective self-descriptions, and our understanding of which, therefore, is not completely manifested at the surface of our linguistic practices in the use we actually make of language. For the realist, there is a *deeper* conceptual reality which underpins and regulates all of this. Meaning, within this metaphor, is use-transcendent; and any analysis of the conceptual structure which is portrayed as underpinning our linguistic and rational practices is, *if true*, required perfectly to describe, represent, correspond to, standards which are inherent in the nature of a determinate reality which is fully independent of our attempts to describe it. The question of what constitutes our *correct* application of a concept or fragment of language, now, or at any future time, is settled in terms of fidelity to the underlying mental picture or model and the set of rules of application which it embodies. Here, the appropriate metaphor for *understanding* is, we have seen, the grasping of a mathematical formula which automatically, and necessarily, determines whether or not any given number in an infinite series has a particular property; that is, fits or does not fit the formula.

The machine as symbolizing its action

This, of course, is the picture we are deconstructing. Although we can, in cases where the application of the concept normally has a point, say whether the concept has been correctly understood – we look at its application within our familiar practices – beyond established practice we can form no uniquely valid conception of what 'applying the concept correctly' can mean. There are just too many ways in which it can be interpreted that are consistent with all our previous applications, and no further, practice-independent signposts to motivate a decision on which application is correct.

As an explanation of the underlying deep structures which enable us to understand a language or engage in rational processes, realism gives us a metaphor of the concept as *containing* all its future applications; a picture as containing all its legitimate interpretations. But this explains nothing. Wittgenstein extends and distorts the metaphor into a picture of a 'machine as symbolizing its action': the rule regulating application of the concept is conceived as an adamantine machine inexorably grinding out all its correct applications (Baker 1981: 52), so that 'If we know the machine, everything else, that is its movement, seems to be completely determined' (PI section 193). But we forget here that the machine may break, its parts melt, its gears wear out. The same goes for the concept, or rule, or formula; for *how are we to establish which of its properties are not subject to flexing?*

Continuing the series

The realist needs an argument to separate *correctness* of application from *seeming to be correct*. This translates into the need for a demonstration that some concepts, at least, are self-interpreting; that correct understanding of a concept (rule or formula) compels us to use it in just *this* way. Again we can distort the picture:

> 'But am I not compelled, then, to go the way I do in a chain of inferences?' Compelled? After all I can presumably go as I choose! 'But if you want to remain in accord with the rules you *must* go this way.' Not at all, I call *this* 'accord'. 'Then you have changed the meaning of the word "accord", or the meaning of the rule.' No; – who says what 'change' and 'remaining the same' mean here? However many rules you give me – I give a rule which justifies *my* employment of your rules.
>
> (RFM I-113)

Whatever set of rules are given in an attempt to specify what is to count as *the correct application* of a concept, we will be able to point to examples of behaviour which conform to those rules under certain interpretations but which offend under others.

Wittgenstein's illustration of this employs the metaphor of the pupil who is taught to continue a number series (PI sections 143, 184ff). On being given the rules for constructing the number series up to 1000 by using '+n', the pupil is asked to continue the series '+2' beyond 1000, at which point he writes '1000, 1004, 1008, . . .' Here it is not doubted that the pupil has gone wrong. *Of course* he should have written '1002, 1004' and so on. The point is that the distinction between going right and wrong is not licensed by anything in the realist metaphor; whatever reasons we give him to show that he is mistaken there will be an interpretation of our rules which makes his action come out correct.

We might, for example, tell him that we wanted him to carry on after 1000 *in the same way* as when he constructed the series up to 1000. This achieves nothing, however, since what is *correctly* meant here by 'same' and 'different' is precisely what is at issue. Suppose, then that we write down the first figures of the series for him; what now compels him to copy these as '1000, 1002, 1004' rather than as '1000, 1004, 1008'? We might *translate* his idea of 'same' through such expressions as: 'When we add two above 1000 he adds four', or 'For him what is involved in the operation "+2" below 1000 is the same as what is involved in the operation "$n + 4$" where $n > 1000$'.

Such interpretations look bizarre; but that is a fact about how things seem to us and not about what is right or wrong absolutely. We postmodernists can rest content with just this conclusion; the judgement concerning the perversity of the alternative courses *is* relative to our own practices. Realists, however, have a problem. They must show that the rejected interpretations are not simply bizarre but *bizarre because they are incorrect absolutely*. They are, by their own standards of rationality, required to show why it is that an application of the concept cannot be thus bizarre yet, in fact, be correct. And if they want to maintain that the bizarre options are *sometimes correct* (as indeed they must if they want to be able to distinguish between their own deep, reflective theory and superficial, common-sense intuition), then they owe us a general account of how we are to conceive ourselves capable of effectively recognizing – in fidelity to some antecedent criterion – those cases in which being bizarre does in fact come apart from being incorrect.

In our story, *we do say* that the pupil is wrong and we do try to give him examples that will persuade him to behave in ways which *we* take to be appropriate. This is not enough for realism, however, for its disciples want to say that the reason why the pupil is wrong is not simply because his behaviour is out of step with that of his peers. There must, the realist wants to assert, be a determinate fact which constitutes the correct understanding of the pattern, some fact which corresponds to *sameness* in the continuation and reapplication of the pattern:

> 'But you surely can't suddenly make a different application of the law now!' If my reply is: 'Oh yes of course, *that* is how I was applying it!' or: 'Oh! *That's* how I ought to have applied it!'; then I am playing your game. But if I simply reply: 'Different? – But this surely *isn't* different!' – what will you do? That is: somebody may reply like a rational person and yet not be playing our game.
>
> (RFM I-115)

There simply is no fact which will enable us to distinguish between the uniquely correct application and erroneous ones; no fact which fidelity to the set of rules consists in. At this point the metaphor of rules and their application deconstructs. Its metaphors have come apart and have nothing to offer by way of guidance to our understanding.

The idiolectic-regularity requirement

In order to resist the implications of these deconstructive manoeuvres the realist may look to the subjective realm of the individual's understanding of her own thoughts, ideas, images and meanings to provide the appropriate picture which will salvage the intelligibility of his metaphors of understanding a language. He might argue: whenever I think of something I understand what I am thinking, the meaning of my mental image is immediately *present* to my consciousness; I can, without error, intend my image to attach to words or correspond to objects in the world. Even if I am mistaken about how others use the word to refer to objects, *I can't be mistaken about what I myself mean by it.* I *know* what I mean by following my own 'inner' rules. I know how to interpret and apply my own images. I know what the *correct* interpretation of my image is; and we all know this in our own subjective cases.

The conclusion which will be drawn from this is that the private, subjective realm of the idiolect, with its certainties of self-interpreting mental pictures, provides the foundation for our understanding of public, intersubjective situations of communication. The idiolectic picture demonstrates the model for correctness in interpretations and applications of a concept in the public realm *and* provides the blueprint for the ideal speech situation presupposed in critical reflection.

Ducks, ants and Winston Churchill

This picture of private certainty rests on a mistake, an illusion fostered by a misleading metaphor. The mistake is to forget the overriding semantic importance of *context*. The picture of purity at the centre of the ideal speech situation trades on a context-free image of language. I shall deconstruct the metaphor by showing how *différance* is traced within even the single thought and the very possibility of representation. The realist account depends upon the metaphor of an image's or a picture's determination of a particular (correct) interpretation. The crucial question, therefore, centres on the conception of what it is for a picture to project a determinate interpretation which will legislate for what counts as right and wrong applications in future cases.

But the metaphor self-distorts into a picture that cannot be cashed in realist currency: from any image we can make any number of mutually incompatible projections each of which is 'correct' according to its own criteria. A single picture may represent the head of a duck or of a rabbit; but it can do neither independently of our convention to so regard it (see PI 194ff). For how could one object stand in the requisite relation to another independently of our placing it so? And to ask which one it *really* represents is a silly question if asked outside of a context in which our interests give it a point: we may use the picture to represent ducks when we are keeping a tally of ducks and hens on the farm; we may use it as a road sign depicting rabbits when we want motorists to drive carefully past Watership Down. Nevertheless, the fact that such agreement can be secured does not entail that it *must*; and even less does it imply that there is a particular projection which all rational beings must agree on independently of their practices. Every aspect of a picture, every point in a pattern, is open to a variety of incompatible interpretations that are consistent with the picture, the pattern and the rules of projection. Conversely, every move we make can be made out, via a suitable interpretation, to be in accordance with the picture (PI section 201).

That we do rule out some interpretations and favour others is of course correct. Realists, however, require that this practice is underwritten by something deeper, more secure, than the approval or disapproval of one's peers. Their 'correct' cannot, without abandoning realism altogether, be allowed to collapse into 'seems correct to us'. Collapsing the *is/seems* distinction at this point would entail that understanding has nothing to do with interpretation, thus displacing the realist's metaphor.

In alluding to the subjective case, realists hope for a demonstration that we can sometimes have privileged access to absolutely correct interpretations. This hope is fuelled by the illusion that our own ideas, images or representations have some self-validating power of intrinsic reference. But a line traced in the sand by a foraging ant might look to us like an image of Winston Churchill (as might a cloud or a heap of horse dung), but the 'picture' does not depict, does not *refer to*, Winston Churchill (see Putnam 1981: 1–5). It might be argued that what is missing here is an *intention* that the picture should *depict*. But the thought that the picture's capacity to represent is empowered by intention presupposes a capacity to know, to be able to recognize, whatever it is to which one wishes to refer; and *being able to do this* presupposes that some representations simply correspond to reality in some unique and self-correcting manner. We are back where we started.

Language-as-tool

When seen as a tool, the role of the sign is determined not by some intrinsic, essential, context-independent nomological feature of language or concepts, but is a function of the *use* we make of it when we employ it within a particular context:

> Isn't the question 'Have these words a meaning?' similar to 'Is that a tool?' asked as one produces, say, a hammer? I say 'Yes it's a hammer'. But what if the thing that any of us would take for a hammer were somewhere else a missile, for example, or a conductor's baton?
>
> (OC section 351)

Contrary to what is required by the ideal speech situation, words do not simply *mean*; a move is not simply *a move in chess* (PI section 53). What is required is a context (OC section 350), a *framework* within which there is some point to the move:

> A coronation is the picture of pomp and dignity. Cut one minute of this proceeding out of its surroundings: the crown is being placed on the head of the king in his coronation robes. – But in different surroundings gold is the cheapest of metals, its gleam is thought vulgar. There the fabric of the robe is cheap to produce. A crown is a parody of a respectable hat.
>
> (PI section 584)

Wittgenstein mobilizes various illustrations of the metaphor to show that what goes for language, tools and crowns goes also for thoughts; ideas do not *intrinsically* represent and concepts do not *intrinsically* determine a pattern of correct application. An ostensive act of pointing to an object to name it – intuitively, *the* paradigm case of an undistorted referential performance – can be variously interpreted (PI section 28), *even when made to oneself*. Wittgenstein presents us with a picture: is it an old man walking up a path?

How? Might it not have looked just the same if he had been sliding down-hill in that position? Perhaps a Martian would describe the picture so.

(PI section 54)

The representation contains no intrinsic rules which can be 'read off' from it and which tell how it is to be applied (PI section 292). If there were such rules, how would we interpret them? Would, for instance, the picture be one of *portrait* or *genre* (PI section 522)? Does it depict a unique individual, event or state of affairs, *or a general class*?

How rules should be taken, understood, interpreted or applied cannot be unambiguously given (PI section 454). What makes my image an image of someone is not its *looking* like him (PI section 177, see section 434–5, 683). Otherwise the figure 'I' could not have the role of representing *me*.

Here the problem begins anew, for our representations and concepts have no more intrinsic referential or semantic links with the world *or with each other* than do marks in the sand. It appears as if *nothing less than a perfect copy* could possibly stand in a relation of representation rigid and pure enough to meet the demands of realist theory; for otherwise a *convention* – the socially constructed dirt in the pristine mechanism of meaning – would be required, would, out of necessity, insinuate itself between word and object, image and reality, language and the world, to bridge the chasm of difference inherent in the individuality and separateness of copy and original to license *just that* representational connection. But now, given a *perfect* copy – a copy which is indistinguishable from its original by means of any test we can imagine – one erases the distinction between representation and object. Now it cannot be established what role each is to play.

Subjective understandings as public expressions

If you say 'How am I to know what he means, when I see nothing but the signs he gives?' then I will say: 'How is *he* to know what he means, when he has nothing but the signs either?'

(PI section 504)

The gambit of appealing to the picture of the private, subjective realm was supposed to provide the model for a defence of realism. Instead we have found that the private realm is itself defined by the very metaphors which fall apart under deconstruction:

What is essential is to see that the same thing can come before our minds when we hear the word and the application may still be different.

(PI section 140)

There is nothing to be achieved in protesting that we might hold the *application* to come before our minds for the intelligibility of such a move is precisely what is in question: how is the *picture of the application* to be projected? Just as an external model or picture requires interpretation if it is to be able to *represent* something for us, so it is with an internal picture in the mind, even in the purely idiolectic case of one's representing something to oneself.

But if the relation of picture and interpretation is to be understood in turn by means of the application of some further picture, the whole question is raised anew. How does *this* picture represent? How do *I* know what *I* mean by *my* picture? How do I know that the idiolectic, private pattern of interpretation and application to which I am now faithful is *the same pattern* to which my previous judgements were faithful?

This is not a sceptical point about memory; for the deconstruction of the metaphors of realism shows that even given perfect memory there could be nothing in my past applications which determined how those applications should be interpreted in licensing future applications. Once again, commitment to realist mythology and common-sense intuition inclines us to impose on the case a picture in which my own understanding of my own meanings reaches beyond all the examples and explanations I can give to myself or anyone else:

> but then, whence the feeling that I have got more? Is it like the case where I interpret what is not limited as a length that reaches beyond any length?

(PI section 209)

That our applications are not limited does not mean that there is a determinate pattern of correct use which continues to exist beyond the borders of our actual practice. Rather, I do not know any more about what commitment to my idiolectic patterns is a commitment to than the explanations I can give to myself; and if I can give them to myself I can give them to anyone (PI sections 209–13); indeed, part of the role they play for me *as explanations* is that I see that others find them acceptable. Once such explanations have been given in satisfying a particular purpose in a particular practice the idea that there is anything more to understanding the truth of the matter is senseless. There simply is nothing more to it to be understood (or misunderstood).

The idiolectic case of my subjective self-understandings cannot provide a model for our grasp of public language and objective standards of rationality. The deconstructive reversal of this picture presents us with a story in which the veracity of those self-understandings is itself dependent upon standards of public understanding, upon, in other words, the very set of metaphors of interpretation and application which have been shown to be incoherent by their own lights. The reversal of the picture suggests that private self-understanding is not something additional to, deeper and more certain than, our understanding of others; for our private understandings, insofar as they are intelligible, have to be framed in terms of a language.

The superficiality of depth

The realist's mistake is that understanding and rationality are deep matters about which discoveries can be made through the use of the privileged reflective method. The mistake lies in the deification of a metaphor in which context-based understanding is judged somehow incomplete and inferior to the greater understanding to be had by an omniscient, omni*present* God.

I have argued, however, that understanding is not relative to an absolute context-of-all-contexts but *is* relative to a particular, provisional and redescribable context of use; a context in which the use of a concept is given a point by its role in a practice. Incompleteness and misunderstanding are therefore relative only to what counts as full understanding within the local practice-context. There is nothing *deep* behind our understanding in such circumstances. It is the circumstances themselves which are crucial to our decisions as to whether someone has a complete understanding. There is no deeper truth than that which is produced when our moves in a language-game are justified in the eyes of our fellows. No deeper rules are needed; our signposts are in order if, under normal circumstances, they fulfil their purpose (PI section 87); and what *normal* is here, is for *us* to decide.

Recognition of this removes the yearning for a more secure understanding of conceptual reality through the reflective exercise of digging below the distortions of practice to expose its authentic conceptual foundations. 'Foundations' dangle from actual practice as epiphenomena of our justificatory interests at a particular time. Our practices exist unjustified; our reasons dissolve into rationalizations which are no more foundational than our assertion: *this is how we act!* (PI sections 1, 211, 217, 228). It turns out that all along our practices – of speaking a language, of reasoning and thinking, of reflecting – have lacked foundations.

This displacement of the metaphor of underlying essences and mechanisms for our language simultaneously dissolves the possibility of any systematic theory offering a clarification and explanation of our linguistic practices. Because meaning exists at the surface of practices, any attempt to describe semantic structures at some 'deeper' level immediately precludes itself from being an *explanation* of meaning (see Wright 1980: 258–9, Chapter XV). This is not to say that no links can be drawn between the candidate deep explanation and the structure of surface practice. It is rather that any number of incompatible 'deep' stories of 'explanation' can be told about practice. And none of these could take the role of *explanation* since they simply constitute another story, another surface with which to confront the surface of practice. Not deep, that is, just different.

Textuality

Deconstruction of the picture of an ideal speech situation precipitates an alternative metaphor in which the act of *clarification* itself becomes a form of distortion, a process which destroys, which smooths over, the very features that were necessary for communication to take place:

> The more narrowly we examine actual language, the sharper becomes the conflict between it and our requirement. (For the crystalline purity of logic was, of course, not a result of investigation: it was a requirement.) The conflict becomes intolerable; the requirement is now in danger of becoming empty. – We have got onto slippery ice where there is no

friction and so in a certain sense the conditions are ideal, but also, just because of that, we are unable to walk. We want to walk: so we need friction. Back to the rough ground!

(PI section 107)

Wittgenstein's point is that any idealization of language which is motivated by the view that clarity – the elimination of distortion – is inherently virtuous overlooks the fact that the closer we examine our idealization the more we find it to be dependent upon those strategies of interpretation and unjustified leaps from premise to conclusion that are characteristic of the elements of distortion which we imagined ourselves to be abolishing. We find, moreover, that language, when shorn of the features of distortion, becomes a tool unfit to the purpose of communication.

We are naturally tempted by the thought that the purity of clear, undistorted language will be enlightening and emancipatory.[4] Instead, what we find is that the price of *lustration* – of the purification of language to make it a medium fit to support the ideal speech situation – is the sacrifice of the very ingredients which are necessary for meaning. If we want meaningful dialogue then we have to face up to, and embrace, its inherent impurity, its promiscuity of readings and interpretations, its inevitable involvement in distortion.

In short we have to recognize the *textuality* of language, thought and reason: the signified is, we might say, *always already a signifier*, open to the *play* of textuality, to re-reading, re-inscription, re-interpretation (see Derrida 1976: 7, 15). That is to say that anything to which we are able to refer – objects, events, people, words, thoughts etc. – has a meaning for us only within a framework of other words, phrases, linguistic constructions, which enable it to have a role within our expressions. The object – no matter how 'solid' – *cannot* serve to fix meaning but instead has meaning bestowed upon it by the role which expressions within which it appears can play within other regions of language. This table, for example, has the significance it has for us, not because of its possessing some intrinsic power to induce us to react to it in a particular, determinate way – like a relation of cause and effect – but, rather, it gains its significance because, for us, it can have a use, a role, in a range of language games such as making and eating a meal, writing a letter, entertaining, playing cards or table football; and it does not have a role for us as a hat stand, a car or a knife. The object does not determine the role it will play in our language games, in our social interactions, in our conversations. The object does not serve to ground – to determine – the meanings it will have. Since meaning now becomes visible as ungrounded, unfixed, undetermined by its object, it also becomes visibly mobile under human intervention and linguistic creativity. This foundation – or, rather, non-foundation – of language in free-play or *différance*, unrestrained by any *necessary* rules, operates *even within the act of representation* which proves to have no self-present identity but carries the trace of a perennial alterity; the self-present identity required at this point for the purposes of critical reflection being subject to perpetual detour through the interplay of forces of textual dis-placement.

The signified concept is never present in itself, in an adequate presence that would refer only to itself. Every concept is necessarily and essentially inscribed in a chain or a system, within which it refers to another and to other concepts, by the systematic play of differences. Such a play, then – *différance* – is no longer simply a concept, but the possibility of conceptuality, of the conceptual system and process in general.

(Derrida 1968: 140)

Reflective practice requires that the causal mechanisms underlying 'distorted self-understandings ... be clarified, explained and eliminated' (Carr and Kemmis 1986: 137), that they should be made transparent to those whom they affect. We might have imagined that the purely idiolectic case of one's own personal deployment and interpretation of the language one speaks would provide a *prima facie* sympathetic environment for the ideal speech situation; and, indeed, the self-integrity of the idiolect *is essential* if reflection is to realize its emancipatory purpose and enable individuals to distinguish between distorted and pure self-understandings. Instead, however, we find that the referential context of the idiolect can secure no guaranteed privileged access to one's own meaning, no present-to-consciousness of a self-identical element of sense. All we find are the very referrals and alterity of *différance* that are constitutive of the operation of the sign. Representation is never pure, unmediated, undistorted, but is inscribed by the *trace* of *différance*; the perpetual possibility of re-inscription; that disappearance of an origin that 'was never constituted except reciprocally by a non-origin, the trace, which thus becomes the origin of the origin' (Derrida 1976: 61).

There is no *absolute* clarity which we could give our concepts; the above arguments show that we cannot even make the notion intelligible. In our attempts to be clear, to gain absolute precision, all we succeed in doing is ripping our language, our signs, out of the contexts in which they have their impure but manageable employment; viewing them in a context in which we do not know what we should say about them because in idealizing our signs *we have distorted them* out of all recognition.

The term *rational*, for example, carries with it in the reflective dialogue the promise of pure, undistorted standards governing the manner in which legitimate thinking can be undertaken. It intimates the suggestion of clear and measured progression from the premises in arguments to their conclusion in a fashion which permits no room for interpretation, no room for doubting the sincerity and truthfulness of the process, and no room for different individuals or groups arriving at different, incompatible and equally legitimate conclusions. In situations of disagreement this idealized standard of rationality guarantees that at least one of the disputed claims will be wrong, and, moreover, that keeping faith to the standard will enable us to judge which one!

But what kind of algorithm is this standard supposed to give us? In preserving the purity of reason we remove the criteria for its application to particular cases. Does reason alone enable us to move from the statement 'Jones murdered Smith' to the conclusion that we should forgive Jones?[5] In order to reach and exhibit the sign in pure isolation we are obliged to disembowel language; revealing the sign not as a pure, self-functioning organ of meaning but, rather, leaving both the sign and its corporeal surroundings as lifeless surrogates of the embodied whole which formerly intrigued and confused but impressed us. Alternatively, the metaphor of the ideal speech situation and our attempts to secure it may be replaced by a metaphor in which we attempt to judge the result of a horse race by examining photographs of the finish magnified to reveal the atomic structure of the relevant region of the world. Thus, where at first we see horses' noses and a finish post, now, we might suppose, not only do we suffer quantum indeterminacy, we also have no way of knowing which particles belong to the horse and which do not. We no longer know where the horse begins and ends. Suppose that the magnification to this degree reveals the differences between objects to be blurred. Now we have to retreat to the more familiar ground which is less pure, less *clear*; but at least its lines are definite (cf. PI sections 71, 88).

The absence of presence

In violation of what has just been said, critical analysis and reflective teaching presuppose that the reality constituted by and of the sign is ultimately stable and, in its unmediated presence-to-consciousness, *self-interpreting* – leaving no distance between the sign and its interpretation this immediacy is assumed to provide the pure, undistorted framework on which reason can be securely mounted. Only by being given such an ultimately solid structure within its linguistic carriage can the critical or reflective process be conceived of as strong enough to bear the burdens of its self-delegated responsibility to improve rationality and objectivity by making interpretation and judgement more coherent and free from unreflective dogma.

It is this belief in the consistency of language which underpins the view, for instance, that reason and reality are essentially convergent such that the dialectical process is able to bring about the ultimate resolution of contradictions (Carr and Kemmis 1986: 33–4). For the reflective teacher, reality abhors incommensurability and paradox.

The supposition, however, that the sign can provide a pure, unmediated environment within which reason can free itself of distortion to achieve absolute self-integrity is a myth. Any *show of integrity* advertised by reason is not a necessary product of its fidelity to its essential destiny mapped in the genetics of its semantic inheritance, but is, rather, an effect *actively created* out of the obliteration, suppression and concealment of the permanent possibility of alterity; that is, the self-integrity of rationality to its own standards is a special case of deceit. Reason, Wittgenstein shows us, is, like the interpretation of the sign, a permanent opening of literary possibility whose closure is secured only by an act of enforcement, a decision to go *this* way.

The conviction which underpins the theoretical foundations of reflective teaching maintains that although we cannot in general – because of the distorting effects of ideology, tradition and so on – guarantee that our linguistic practices faithfully reflect the true structure of the world and our predicament within it, sometimes, when conditions are favourable, we can attain clear and unmediated grasp of truth or, minimally, make progress towards such grasp, providing that in our efforts we are sufficiently thorough in our application of the correct analytical method of discovery. It is through its application of analytic method that critical theory claims to distinguish itself from mere social anthropology to become emancipatory, as opposed to simply descriptively hermeneutic, and to facilitate the realization of a rational, democratic and just society and bring about improvement of the concrete situations of educational practices and institutions (Carr and Kemmis 1986: 157, 160–1).

The problem with the attempt to free our reason of distortion is, however, not contingent upon the effectiveness or purity of our analyses; the above discussion shows that the corrupting play of *différance* is always already a necessary element in the very conception of the sign. We postmodernists will say that the language in which analysis is conducted is itself the *arche syncope*[6] bearing the innate necessity of ~~distortion~~, meaning that language, in its origin, its constitution, is both distorted and distorting; always inviting, rather than resisting, varieties of interpretation and reading; constantly eager to slide from one sense to another to elide any obligation to determinateness of expression or integrity to a standard of correctness.

Metaphors of reflection

The critical reflective enterprise requires that the language which constitutes its sharpest analytic scalpels is referentially crystalline; purged of the distortions of metaphor and the need for interpretation. A deconstructive reading, however, reveals the play of *différance* at the heart of the text's rationality; the text itself being implicated in a conspiracy of distortion and deception. This reveals itself in the text's reliance on metaphor to power its analytic mechanism.

Critical theorists, reflective teachers, realist philosophers, are the authors of that same metaphor-infested *literature* which their philosophy abhors; unwitting accomplices to the crime of distortion. The central concept – analysis – is itself a metaphor which strains to hold the rhetorical framework of the enterprise in place by means of its capture of an image of investigative, experimental methodology; claiming for itself the authority which in certain contexts we reserve for the scientist to present the picture of a process through which are precipitated the elemental ideas and principles which determine the essential properties of a concept and, in consequence, the role it can play in a language purged of distortion. This picture of the scientist trades upon a cluster of related images: the *men* in white coats who discover truths about the world, who eliminate ignorance, who improve our lives through technological advances, who enable us to have control over our environment, our dirty washing, our kitchen utensils.[7]

This rhetoric is aided by the ocular metaphor, which contrasts the clarity achievable through the application of analysis with the fuzziness of unreflective vision. The insight achieved by the scientist-philosopher reveals a structure of our conceptual or semantic reality which is in some sense already present and potentially visible to those with the eyewash of analytic method. On this view, our linguistic practices do not manifest the full story of our meanings at their surface; for if they did there would be no need for the process and expertise of analysis. Analysis – and critical reflection – would be superfluous because practice itself would be the last court of appeal.

The ubiquitousness of another cluster of metaphors – *clarification, purification* the elimination of *distortion* – has the rhetorical purpose of establishing the literalness of the analytic enterprise by sustaining a picture in which the material which is the object of analysis – its goal – is in some sense *already there* but obscure to those lacking the method. Were this not the self-portrait which reflective theory was concerned to promote, the excessive employment of the rhetoric of clarification at the expense of alternatives such as *make-up, fabricate, create, invent, concoct, romance* would be difficult to explain other than as mere fetish. Clarification works to impose on the dialogue of reflection an image of discovery and enlightenment; of seeing accurately what was there all along but concealed from uncritical, non-reflective reason. It borrows its structural authority within the critical dialogue from activities such as purifying a substance through distillation, turning on a torch at night to view our surroundings, wiping a fogged glass to see what lies beyond; analysis works like a car's demister, helping us to keep to the true road by enabling us to see properly where the road leads.

These metaphors are the textual devices of persuasion by which realism/objectivity is assumed; devices which strive to control the structure of further argument. Without their suggestion of a concealed, self-identical *presence*, the nature of which analysis can reveal, we may as well confess philosophy as another player in a game of ~~distortion~~; analysis as a form of literature which *creates*, rather than *discovers*, its characters of clarity, coherence and truth for persuasive narrative effect.

If, as I have argued, the reversal of the literal/metaphorical hierarchy is legitimate, indeed, is required in any account of our capacity for using and understanding a language, then the process of analysis – judged according to its own criteria – is a deception and the analytical scalpel of reason a piece of sharp practice. For there can be no overarching set of criteria – independent of the narrative concerns *internal* to a particular story – for taking the plot of analysis in one direction rather than another. What the most rigorous analysis reveals is nothing pure but unlimited levels of undecidability. Analysis presupposes a presence at the end of the process, a presence which gives justification to the enterprise; but by its own lights it cannot establish how its supposed presence – as pre-existing, awaiting discovery – can be distinguished from its being constituted as a narrative effect of the process under local, literary imperatives of characterization and emplotment. In short, the distinction between ground and effect is reversed and the rhetorical hierarchy of analysis is displaced. By turning analysis upon itself we reveal no ground but a system of rhetorical tropes. The distillate of analysis exhibits itself as nothing pure, nothing simple, but as already complex, suspended within a framework of traces which run through the history of its emplotment and the possibilities of its future applications. Its semantic status is a function of its role within a context of other terms or narratives; it inevitably carries with it the traces of its emplotment within its sustaining structure and thus, instead of being constituted by a single, self-identical presence, it is a literary artifact, a construction out of absences, of deferrals, of pragmatic exigency, of *différance*.

Postmodernist metaphysics: new metaphors

The metaphysics of postmodernism arises out of the reversal of the realist picture of language and the recognition that the deconstructive fracture is a necessary by-product of the possibility of meaning. Some of the most striking metaphysical outcomes of the displacement of realism are the reversals of its foundations of objectivity. The realistic picture of the nature of existence has the following features:

- the world exists independently of our perceptions and judgements;
- the world is one – a complete, coherent singular whole – and it is unique;
- the world is 'out there' waiting to be discovered.

These, we can now see as metaphors: the world is personified as an individual with his own unique identity and his own voice, an individual whom we are invited to meet, find out about and discover his thoughts and opinions.[8]

Here is an alternative, postmodern story of metaphysics.

The world is ours and speaks in our language

The deconstruction of the realist's picture of understanding a language shows us that in interpretation there is no unique, point-by-point correspondence of language to interpretation. When, therefore, we are confronted by an alien language, we meet it with ours *en bloc*, or rather, what our language meets are the particular, singular experiences which we take to be constitutive of another language. As Davidson has argued, we achieve an understanding of the alien language

> by holding belief constant as far as possible while solving for meaning. This is accomplished by assigning truth conditions to alien sentences that make native speakers right when plausibly possible, according, of course, to our own view of what is right ... If we cannot find a way to interpret the utterances and other behaviour of a creature as revealing a set of beliefs largely consistent and true by our own standards, we have no reason to count that creature as rational, as having beliefs, or as saying anything.
>
> (Davidson 1973: 137)

Davidson's point is that any intelligible translations of the alien language must hold its speakers to subscribe largely to our view of the world. But, after deconstruction, we can use Davidson's argument as a metaphor with which to combat the realist's metaphor of the world: any intelligible translation of the world must hold it to fit *our* view of the world. *The world must speak in our vocabulary.*

This is the is/seems collapse. Reality-*in-itself* must align itself with reality-*for-us*. To see the pointlessness of the realist's metaphor let's borrow for a moment his picture of the God's-eye view of the universe. Imagine that from this perspective we can view the panorama of different communities speaking their different languages. From this privileged observatory we may discover that the speakers of one language systematically misunderstand the behaviour of the speakers of another. Although the speakers of language Ω believe that they have fully understood the speakers of language ¥, grasped their thoughts and customs, and so on, from our heavenly panopticon we can see that they are in fact mistaken; the behaviour which Ω-speakers regard as manifesting particular thoughts, intentions and meanings is in fact no such thing. It is actually not a language at all but the meaningless by-product of the motion of beings whose bodies transcend spatial dimensions, whose temporal and causal processes are the reverse of those of the Ω-speakers and whose thoughts are thus completely inaccessible to the Ω-speakers, whose actual experience of the ¥-beings is that part of them which pokes through into their region of space-time; though even that is travelling in the opposite direction through time (I have tried to make the ¥-beings about as alien as you can get).

Interestingly enough, to a realist this constitutes a possibly correct, albeit fantastic, description of the situation between speakers of English and speakers of any alien language. To the postmodernist it is just a story; a story, moreover, which cannot picture what it is supposed to depict for the panopticon, the meta-perspective which it assumes makes no sense. Given such a perspective we deprive ourselves of any criteria we might have had for drawing a distinction between reality and illusion; for where are we to look for confirmation that the so-called meta-perspective is indeed just that and not some other perspective that is on a level with Ω and ¥? What if it is an illusion and it is we ourselves who are mistaken? Realism assumes that there is a definitive answer. Postmodernism rejects the whole scenario. Suppose, now, that we are in fact the Ω-speakers. It makes no sense to suppose that the 'meanings' expressed in the 'behaviour' of the ¥-beings are anything other than what *we* say they are; what is important is that their behaviour is intensional, meaningful, *under our description*. It is not something about which we can be mistaken in the manner required by realism because *the correct description*, in the only sense of 'correct' that has any work to do, simply is *that description which satisfies us*. The only criteria for legislating between the alternative descriptions are those criteria which make sense to us, those we employ. If the above pandimensional story makes sense and language Ω is English, then the story is false. It can only be intelligible if it is false. Our ¥-speaking friends speak to us in our language! And so must the world.

The world is multiple, contradictory

Given the picture in which truth is a product of the stories we tell, one consequence of this is that there will be as many truths as there are stories. If we accept this then it seems we are committed to a further picture; one in which the stories we tell may contradict one another at certain points in their narrative. But since we have already accepted that truth is story-relative, we are faced with the inescapable conclusion that some of the truths we hold may be mutually incompatible. And since the world is whatever a true statement is about, the conclusion we must draw is that the world itself contains facts which contradict one another. The world, in other words, is not a singular, self-consistent reality but a multiplicity of incommensurable realities.

Given the multiplicity of different practices in which we engage, there is no *a priori* reason why those practices should not throw up conflicting results. What we reject here is the realist's further step of insisting that at least one of the results in a conflict must be wrong. *That* move, we have seen, is not rational *except when licensed by the metaphysical picture which we have deconstructed.*

But even within what we take to be a single practice there can be multiple and incompatible realities. Within a practice, meaning gets settled in case law by the criteria we happen to adopt for what constitutes the legitimate use of a term. As Wittgenstein has suggested, the criteria themselves, like the cases of use, will be multiple. They will determine what we regard as *necessarily good evidence* for the legitimate use of the term. The list of criteria and of the conditions for overturning them will be indeterminate; and between the cases and the criteria there will not be a rigid rule of sameness but a much looser family resemblance.[9]

Consequently we may find that an assertion is both verified and falsified if the criteria are present which justify its assertion and the criteria are also present which justify the assertion of another statement which contradicts the original. The multiplicity of criteria, our tests for truth and falsity, our methods of verifying and falsifying may, through their legitimate application, turn up unexpected or startling results. In displacing realism we have abandoned any notion of correctness independent of our practices of verifying and falsifying. There is, therefore, no higher constraint on our practices which could rule out the possibility of our practices precipitating such contradictory results.

Take, for example, statements about *the past*. Realism and common sense hold the past to be singular and unique; there is just one true chain of history leading from the dawn of time to the present day. We may tell different versions of that history but our stories are true, or false, only insofar as they faithfully represent, or fail to represent, the facts. For postmodernists, however, there is no *a priori* reason why we should favour this story of how the past behaves; no reason why the pictures of the past derived from the application of different procedures of investigation and verification should be incapable of throwing up contradictory results. Within this new picture we have no right to say, for reasons of the results alone, that the past must align itself with one story or the other, or neither, because, as yet, *we have no further test for coherence for how past-tense statements ought to behave beyond the very practices that have given rise to the picture.* Consequently, Caesar can have both crossed and not crossed the Rubicon. And if we want to insist that this conclusion is unsatisfactory then we are simply hankering after the already-deconstructed realist view of the past which asserts that, whatever happens, the past cannot be different from the present *in just this respect!*

This picture of the past as a multiple and contradictory reality is important. It is the dissolution of a picture which has been very solid for us. Indeed, the certainty of the past, that it has happened and is self-complete, if inscrutable, has provided us with a metaphor for reality itself as a fully determinate, practice-independent story. Because of the persuasive power of this metaphor its deconstruction will make it much easier to find acceptable the multiple and contradictory realities of educational practice which inhabit the postmodern world and which I shall describe later.

The world is made, not found, by us

What should we do with our twin Caesars? The short answer is that it is for us, not the world, to decide. The world speaks our language, fits our criteria. Consequently we can decide to hold the past stable and legislate away at least one of our Caesars; or we can accept the multiplicity picture. The point is, there is nothing which the past or reality can tell us outside of the vocabulary we have prepared; and when it speaks in that voice it is for us, within our multiple practices, to decide how to regard its story. We limit our stories along some dimensions and leave them free to move along others. Reality thus behaves like an old Hollywood set, extending just as far as our purposes require.

The activity of persuasion and the achievement of local consensus is central in a postmodern picture in which truth coincides with our decisions. If we could be persuaded that Everest did not exist then it would not exist. If one denies this then I should say: 'You mean there is a possible situation in which we are all persuaded that Everest does not exist and yet it does? Then why not say that Everest may not exist though we are all persuaded *now* that it does?' It is not faith here that moves mountains. It is rather that the world coincides with how we take it to be and persuasion can only go one way or another by taking the world with it.

I have sometimes been told that the truth of realism will be demonstrated beyond all doubt if I climb a tall building and jump off![10] And what if I should fly? Would that demonstrate the correctness of postmodernism? Of course not. This is not an empirical *thesis*. It is, rather, a picture of the conditions of empirical discourse.

Notes

1 Criticisms include Korner's demand that the transcendental argument supply a uniqueness proof of the conceptual schema it is employed to justify (Korner 1967), and Stroud's and Rorty's view that transcendental arguments can only work if the verification principle is accepted, a move which, they argue, would make the transcendental argument redundant (Stroud 1968; Rorty 1971).

2 It is this latter question that is ignored or overlooked in realist theorizing on

the assumption that language can ultimately be rendered as a transparent medium and carries with it no metaphysical implications. This oversight is repeated in the reflective canon which, in common with all forms of realism, sees rationality as a holy grail which is achievable once the distortions of language are clarified.

3 God is another realist metaphor for a reality which transcends, in its infinity and self-completeness, our experience and practice; a reality which, nevertheless, exists and is in principle perceivable. The role of God in the metaphor is to underwrite the picture in which the truth would be clearly visible to one whose perceptions were not limited by her being physically confined to a location in a particular space at a particular time. The God of this picture knows how the universe came to be, why the dinosaurs became extinct, who killed Kennedy and what I am really thinking. The metaphor of God works to persuade us that in each of these cases, and any number of others, there is a fact of the matter, a truth which could be known and described, even though that knowledge may never actually be acquired by us with our limited sensory resources.

4 For example, 'The extent to which the ideal speech situation varies from the actual speech situation is the extent to which communication, and from it emancipatory knowledge, are smoothly shaped or distorted' (Groundwater-Smith 1988: 259).

5 The conclusions we could draw are infinite and, as is made clear by Wittgenstein's dialogue on rule-following, each of the possible conclusions is equally justifiable on rational grounds. In general this involves our intervention; our imposition of a picture on the situation which gives it a sense and which makes some conclusions more plausible than others. But it is crucial to recognize that it is the picture which determines the reasonableness of the conclusion and not the process which determines the reasonableness of the picture. Thus, in the mundane – though not for Smith – example of the murder, any number of conclusions can be legitimized by embedding the situation in a range of different pictures: 'Jones murdered Smith so . . .'; 'Jones must be punished'; 'Jones did us all a favour'; 'Smith probably deserved it . . . brought it on himself . . . was acting provocatively . . .' The choice between these conclusions and their pictures is not a matter of our moving through a clear, rational process.

6 As I indicated in Chapter 6, it is the intention of deconstruction to show language to be metaphorical at base; which is to say that it has no foundation at all. Deconstructive writing, therefore, will typically employ textual devices which play upon the multiple possibilities in the meanings of words to help remove the illusion of determinacy which attaches to the over-used, stale metaphors which pass as literal truths in our day-to-day exchanges. Deconstructive writing will, in other words, invent poetic constructions for employment in contexts where we might least expect to find them – in academic or theoretical writing, for instance – in order to keep our normal, blind, literal linguistic intuitions permanently off-balance. The metaphor of the *arche-syncope* plays with the notion of the origin of language – presumed to be secure in some foundational, ostensive gesture by traditional semantic theories in general and critical-reflection in particular – to include within the picture the images of elision – an original absence or *distortion* – and fainting – the loss of consciousness wherein language forgets, loses touch with, swoons over its own insincerity in its denial of elision. Of course, explaining this is a bit like explaining

a joke or a poem. The effect of the image is more important than its meaning; and its effect is not to be gained from paraphrasing its meaning. Again, deconstruction plays with this reversal whereby the effect and the meaning are separated and the meaning is subordinated. Not only is this a reversal of traditional semantic theories in which the *legitimate* effect is seen as a determinate causal outcome of meaning; it establishes the postmodern fashion of viewing language and meaning as a permanently open possibility of interpretation.

7 Interesting, then, how much of this image trades on representations which no longer command universal assent. The scientist–male identification now appears old fashioned and the optimism about the benefits of technological progress now seems much more like an advertising illusion sold to developing countries to prime them for exploitation.

8 In most forms of enquiry, when the world expresses itself to us it is in a masculine voice. Our world has, for a long time, been man-made!

9 See Hacker (1972: 301). Wittgenstein's *Philosophical Investigations* can with some justification be seen as a working out of his concept of the criterion and its implications for a range of philosophical issues. The picture of family-resemblance is also drawn from Wittgenstein (PI sections 66–7), who uses it to displace the idea that there must be something common to all the things which we use a term to refer to. His famous example is the case of 'games'.

10 A rather desperate manoeuvre and not at all in keeping with the usually polite injunctions of realists to stay within the boundaries of rational argumentation. It must have been something I said. The move is simply an updated version of Dr Johnson's 'refutation' of idealism. Johnson kicked a stone. It is not remembered as one of his more articulate moments.

8

DOUBT AND AUTONOMY: THE PLAY OF DECONSTRUCTION AT THE HEART OF REFLECTION

> Sometimes, in his wild way of talking, he would
> say that Gravity was an errant scoundrel, and he
> would add, – of the most dangerous kind too, –
> because a sly one ... the very essence of gravity
> was design, and consequently deceit; – 'twas a
> taught trick to gain credit of the world for more
> sense and knowledge than a man was worth.
>   (Lawrence Sterne, *Tristram Shandy*: 20–1)

Chapter 7 choreographs a deconstruction of the linguistic and rational foundations of realism; the theoretical framework which sustains reflective teaching and, indeed, its cousin and rival, positivism. For either of those positions to be defensible realism had to win the battles of Chapter 7. But it lost. Reflective teaching claimed a deep justification; a foundation that was, in the normal run of things, silently assumed, implicit in reflection's discourse, but always ready to step forward to support the rational coherence of its off-spring practices. These deep foundational assumptions have now been hunted down and exhibited as shallow, textual creations of myth and metaphor; not foundations at all. *My deconstructions had to operate at the assumed depth* to remove any possible sanctuary where further arguments, justifications and foundations might remain untouched by my incisions. What remains is to trace the implications of this deconstruction as it works within particular manifestations of the reflective stance to unravel their coherence. I have chosen two examples. Doubt, because the whole motivation and practice of reflection assumes its *presence*: without doubt, all reason for reflection is removed. And autonomy, because the autonomous person is *the character* of reflective teaching. She is emancipated reflectiveness made flesh.

Reflection, doubt and questioning

Reflective teaching's concept of open-mindedness is created out of the hier-archically opposed duality of the concepts *certainty* and *doubt*. The rhetoric of reflective teaching operates upon technicist, positivist research to engineer a shift in the location of these concepts. The old certainties of tradition, cus-tom, technical efficiency and nomological universality are rejected as rational grounds for practice and replaced with a process of dynamic interrogation. The process of rationality itself becomes *the new certainty* through the opening-to-doubt of established 'truths' or methods of truth-production which have formerly constituted the fixtures around which practice has revolved. The capacity to articulate doubt becomes the mark of the attitude of seriousness; of an ability to recognize the true depth and gravity of the situation. Within the open-minded dialectic, rationality *through* doubt becomes the principle means by which the distortions of ideology and other impediments to reflect-ive teaching are exposed and eliminated to leave the way open for the proper development of the autonomous person and the democratic community. This idea of open-mindedness – the exhortation *constantly* to question, criticize and change – issues in a culture of *radical doubt*.

Open-mindedness or the absence of closure?

There is something seductive to postmodernists in the irony of the perman-ently open or, rather, the absence of closure, as a remedy to realism. However, for postmodernism the failure of reflective teaching to provide an appropri-ate remedy to positivism is consequent on the fact that it shares with its opponent too much of the conceptual and rhetorical pedigree of realism for it to be effective as a cure. This common genetic inheritance can be seen in the eulogizing of rationality as well as in the strategy of doubt (the *sceptical* route to truth of traditional realism). Neither of these pillars of critical reflect-ive rhetoric can provide a foundation for an alternative *attitude* to realism. We postmoderns will *agree* with the claim that objectivity arises out of a con-text of intersubjective agreement rather than through correspondence with reality, but will *reject* the additional, metaphysical step of seeing objectivity as an outcome of open and impartial rational argument. Postmodernism views this as a contradiction brought about by a commitment to strategic doubt which fails to place the key concepts – ~~open~~, ~~impartial~~, ~~rational agreement~~, ~~participants~~ – *sous rature*.

Reflective rhetoric fails to recognize fully the implications of the point that questions about meaning and doubts about the truth of our statements bottom out *not in essence but in decision*; not in the discovery of some essen-tially compelling reason or fact but in our *creation* of ~~reasons~~ and ~~facts~~ by *our deciding* that to continue with our questioning would be nonsensical, boring or passé. At this point doubt becomes illegitimate *because* nonsensical. It no longer can play a part in our game. This involves not a direct rejection of tradition but, rather, in displacing the system of realism, a re-inscription of tradition's role. What is required is an appropriately postmodern account of

certainty which avoids realism altogether. Wittgenstein provides it in his book
On Certainty:

> I did not get my picture of the world by satisfying myself of its correctness;
> nor do I have it because I am satisfied of its correctness. No: it is the in-
> herited background against which I distinguish between true and false.
>
> (OC section 94)

> The questions that we raise and our doubts depend on the fact that some
> propositions are exempt from doubt, are as it were like hinges on which
> those turn ... If I want the door to turn, the hinges must stay put.
>
> (OC sections 341, 343)

These things, we might say, are exempt from doubt. Doubting here requires a
picture that we cannot formulate; requires that we step outside of our framework to provide ourselves with a perspective of which we have no conception.
Doubt here drags all into chaos (OC sections 69, 279, 456, 490, 613–17).
Driving an epistemological wedge between what *is true* and what *seems true*
at this point leaves the reflective teacher semantically and metaphysically
stranded; unable to give meaning to the constructions her thesis posits as
essential.

Certainty is not secured through rational reflection achieving conscious
grasp of *presence*; this is why it is not vulnerable to sceptical doubt in the
manner presupposed by realism and critical theory. Certainty is given in the
meaning a statement has for us, in the role we decide that it will play in our
language-game; it is a non-ratiocinative ceremonial icon. Thus, the truth of
many empirical propositions belongs to our frame of reference (OC sections
83, 114, *passim*). We do not understand someone who doubts *here* because
she offends our whole pattern of verification, she fails to play *our* game. If
someone appears to doubt here we cannot confidently claim to understand
her signs as signs of doubt (OC section 154). If I myself doubted these things
I must also doubt the meanings of my words (OC sections 369–70, 456).

We do not know what our radical doubter could possibly count as evidence
(OC section 231). Further, without the stability of Wittgenstein's 'hinges', we
are unable to see how she could even represent her evidence to herself. This
has consequences for our conception of epistemology, for the distinction
between knowledge-grounds and semantics is collapsed: If I am wrong here
I have no guarantee that anything I say is true (OC section 69). *This* doubt
lacks a framework (OC sections 17, 24, 102 and others). But the only framework which could give it a meaning – *our framework* – outlaws such doubt
(OC section 56).

> The argument 'I may be dreaming' is senseless for this reason: if I am
> dreaming, this remark is being dreamed as well – and indeed it is also
> being dreamed that these words have any meaning.
>
> (OC section 383; cf. 676)

Arguments-from-illusion have been a popular device in the critical theory
strand of the reflective teaching movement, where, it is argued, ideology

prevents people from correctly seeing their situation, their real, authentic interests, by peddling an illusory account of reality (see Carr and Kemmis 1986: 138). Wittgenstein's parable applies directly to the arguments from general ideological, traditional, habitual and customary illusion to displace the rational basis of many arguments for critical theory and justifications of the need for reflective practice. Textualism finesses the problem of scepticism, placing it as a set of unintelligible bleats; childish questioning which has outlived its usefulness and become boring in its iteration. What constitutes a verification is given in our conventions; there being no sense to 'right' beyond our practice of *taking-as-right* (OC sections 17, 24, 32 and others). The *use* we make of a proof, for example, determines that it is to be *exempt* from doubt (OC section 39); further checks are not necessary (OC sections 77, 212). The sense of certainty is given in the *attitude we take* to these situations (PI section 217). This certainty is not simply reserved for mathematical proof – nor for the structures of *reflecting* – for the stage setting of the necessary reasoning requires that many empirical statements also have this status:

> If the proposition $12 \times 12 = 144$ is exempt from doubt, then so too must non-mathematical propositions be.
>
> (OC section 653)

> For the mathematical proposition has been obtained by a series of actions that are in no way different from the actions of the rest of our lives, and are in the same degree liable to forgetfulness, oversight and illusion.
>
> (OC section 651)

The contrast between the propositions of empirical description embedded in custom, habit and tradition and those propositions through which we conduct our activity of reflecting, analysing, becoming critical *according to standards of rationality* cannot be drawn. Dependency on the validity of this distinction was the mistake of reflective teaching, with its commitment to a picture of an undistorted rationality.

The call of nature or public convenience?

The postmodernist is not haunted by these sceptical doubts and does not require them in the fashioning of an alternative to realism, save for turning them back upon realism itself. Instead, certainty becomes the norm rather than the exception. As Wittgenstein has shown, we exist within a network of everyday facts (OC sections 17, 24, 247, 111, 250ff, 417). *This*, we might say, is how things are (OC sections 212, 254; PI section 325, p. 224). This settlement rests on decision rather than upon rational foundations. It is secured through *creative* rather than *catechetical* activity; it is made not found (OC sections 166, 196, 204; PI sections 480–6). We create foundations which go just as deep as our practices warrant (RFM III-74, VII-40). In order to make sense of doubting, we must know what it would look like for our doubt to be false (OC section 625). Doubt is not imposed on the system from without, but rather the very possibility of doubt dangles as an epiphenomenon of our practices, of our language-games (OC section 247). Our certainty often goes unjustified but at this point doubt requires not *argument* but *therapy*.

There is, therefore, no sense in asking if the criteria we employ, in general, are correct. Such questions can only be raised *within* a system (Rorty 1980: 298, 341). No meaning can be attached to the construction that global error (PI sections 345, 391, 420), and error in certain local cases about, for example, the existence of the shop at the end of the street, is possible. These possibilities exhibit themselves as legitimate only by franchise of realism in a theory of meaning.

On this postmodern view the criteria which govern the decision to revise our picture of the world – to reject our ideology – are not *discoverable* in the world; they become reasons following our decision to adopt them as the rhetorical signposts in our rationalization of practice. There is no fact which constitutes an antecedent constraint on the decision, for example, to change our view (OC sections 497, 516, 632, 634, 667; PI section 224). If our normal criteria for applying the epithets 'true' and 'false' run out then these slogans can have no application; we are free to create one. At this point we also run out of reality to talk about. Conversely, if our criteria *are* fulfilled then doubt is senseless (OC sections 68ff, 77, 114–17, 154, 247–9, 459, 613–17, 632). A change here is a change in meaning (or reality) (OC sections 63–5, 492, 558–9, 617; PI section 142, p. 224). If we accept that the meaning of a statement is given – completely – in the use it has for us, then part of the use which certain statements have is that they should stand fast for us in certain situations. A change of meaning here would be a change of the world.

Correctness, then, is textual and negotiable. We create realities within our narratives; the plurality here signalling the openness of the ways in which we can refuse to negotiate further. Richard Rorty has described the pragmatics of the kind of postmodern culture which embraces this attitude:

> In such a culture, criteria would be seen . . . as temporary resting places constructed for specific ends . . . A criterion *is* a criterion because some particular social practice needs to block the road of enquiry, halt the regress of interpretations, in order to get something done. So rigorous argumentation – the practice which is made possible by agreement on criteria, on stopping-places – is no more *generally* desirable than blocking the road of inquiry is generally desirable.
>
> (Rorty 1982: xli)

In such a culture rational argument is seen as a particular kind of manoeuvre which is parasitic upon decisions which are *irrational*. It operates *only on the authority of a* decision to obliterate openness at a particular point. Any general limitation on the possibility of alternative narratives – alternative stopping-places, gestures of *closure* – would require a realist conception of truth; natural stopping places rather than *public conveniences*. But practice is groundless. There *are* no *deep* explanations of our picture of the world, for what lies there is written in stories constructed by ourselves:

> There is nothing deep down inside us except what we have put there ourselves, no criterion that we have not created in the course of creating

a practice, no standard of rationality that is not an appeal to such a criterion, no rigorous argumentation that is not obedience to our own conventions.

(Rorty 1982: xlii)

This, we shall see, has devastating consequences for the conception of autonomy which is foundational in the philosophy of reflective teaching.

The mythology of autonomy

In Chapter 4 I outlined the way in which the vocabulary essential to the story of reflective teaching includes the term *autonomy* and its satellites *freedom* and *emancipation*. Within the theatre of reflective teaching the concept of *autonomy* has an important and complex role operating at many theoretical and practical levels. Within socio-political contexts personal and collective autonomy stand as the ultimate emancipatory goals of reflective teaching.

To view autonomy as simply *the* goal of reflection, however, would be seriously to undervalue its rhetorical importance; for as well as gaining a large part of its significance from its *orientation towards* autonomy as a desirable end-state, the reflective process itself *presupposes* at some minimal level the autonomy of the reflective individual or group to engage in the activity of reflection within a democratic framework, where processes of reasoning, debate, discussion, argument and assertion are free from coercion, manipulation and non-rational or distorting interference. The process of reflection itself – *if it is to be consistent with its own standards of rationality and truth* – must be carried out in a situation – both public and subjective – which is free from external interference. The only standards to which it is answerable are the standards of rational inquiry; and these are not the product of this or that interest group or in the sole service of this or that political perspective.

Within the theory of reflective teaching autonomy operates on at least these two levels: it stands as the richly conceived, democratic goal of the reflective process and as the minimalist freedom from certain kinds of distorting interference that is a necessary condition of the very possibility of that process.

Self-fidelity: a metaphysics of presence

Central to the reflective view of autonomy is the idea that one cannot act autonomously in ignorance. One lacking personal knowledge of his situation within a system of knowledge and of how his motives, interests etc. stand in relation to public knowledge lacks autonomy, for he is inescapably involved in self-deception. Autonomy, as Dearden (1968: 88) has said, 'gains in value with every increase in understanding and appreciation of the basic constitutive elements in rational choice.' This is, of course, a matter of degree – autonomy is not absolute – but this does not diminish the force of the point that autonomy is inextricably bound up with knowledge. If this were not so, the concept would collapse into one in which the mere *seeming to oneself* to be acting freely would be sufficient for autonomy; and the brainwashed, the indoctrinated and the insane would all count as autonomous.

Self-knowledge, then, is essential for autonomy:

> The better we know our motives, wishes, purposes, typical reactions to others and so on, then the greater is the possibility of bringing our thought under conscious control. But if the explanation of our thought and action lies in what are at present unconscious motives, then only *true* beliefs about them will create such a possibility of conscious control. False beliefs will leave them unconsciously operative as before.
>
> (Dearden 1975: 66)

Reflective teaching – through the exercise of *ideology-critique* – aims to reveal how the distorting, deceiving forces of ideology 'generate erroneous self-understandings' (Carr and Kemmis 1986: 193). In the achievement of a perspective from which to describe and eliminate the effects of ideology, however, the critical process itself requires a certain essential autonomy of features of communication through which the participants' self-understandings may be analysed and validated against criteria determined by the necessary conditions of free and open dialogue (Carr and Kemmis 1986: 31–2).

The concept of autonomy thus operates within and upon the *critical* dialogue to establish the independence of the mechanisms of thought from the play of textuality, as manifested in the assumption, at strategic points, of an immediate *presence*, or self-consciousness, which is immune to the distorting effects of *différance* and metaphor. Autonomy is thus *the* concept/metaphor which is characterized as both the *emancipatory end* of analysis and the *essential presupposition* in the linguistic embodiment of the practice. Its necessity within the dialogue of theory and practice is evident from its centrality within a galaxy of concepts such as freedom, independence, integrity, sincerity, authenticity, truth, rational choice, real interests and so on. Its moral authority has been called upon to provide a foundation for arguments about the nature of education (Peters 1966) and the curriculum (White 1973) and arguments opposing sexist (White 1983: 145) and religious indoctrination (White 1983: 146ff; Dearden 1968: 57).

The role played by autonomy as the foundational concept in the process of critical reflection – a concept which is at once a synecdoche of the process itself – can readily be seen in Dearden's (1968: 47) grounds for why autonomy must be positively sought after:

1 'Through it we can achieve integrity and thus not be involved in self-deception, or the deception of others.'
2 'It permits us to develop an intelligible and well-grounded knowledge of our true situation in the world.'
3 'It permits and encourages us . . . to pursue the good as we ourselves judge it, though correspondingly it makes us responsible for our choices.'
4 'Consistency with its . . . principles already requires that we be fair in our dealings with others.'

These 'grounds' expedite my deconstructive move towards a *'double reading'* – taking autonomy as at once concept and synecdoche – for they are the very slogans which serve to establish the *ante-lingual* conceptual hierarchies of truth/falsehood and sincerity/deception, which originate and regulate the rational/rhetorical structure and self-warrant of *legitimate* theoretical dialogue; falsehood and deception are subordinated as the unwanted but necessary polar opposites of truth and sincerity and serve, in their opposition, to determine the sense of the superior concepts. The critical-reflective dialogue is, therefore, one in which truth and sincerity are both the guaranteed outcomes of the process *and* the essential regulatory concepts of its normative structure.

Autonomy – as the absence of arbitrary action and the freedom from distortion in the originative psychological conditions for action – clearly involves thinking and acting *in fidelity to something*. Whatever this *something* is, its role is to establish a person's choices as *her own* rather than someone else's and, moreover, as *her own authentic, sincere and rationally conceived* choices rather than arbitrary whims. This presupposes, of course, that the rules of rationality are not themselves *arbitrarily written*; that they are, in other words, autonomous in their self-integrity. The standards to which the autonomous person is faithful, then, must somehow be necessarily contained in – be constituted by – his or her own peculiar *nature* but regulated, policed, authorized, by an independent legislative rationality.

The trace of instability

This commitment to autonomy, and its satellite concepts, as both ground and consequence of reflection adverts to a paradox in both liberal and critical theory which upsets the fine balance between the twin structural metaphors of *nature* and *rules* (see Ryan 1983: 156ff). David Cooper (1983: 59) has highlighted the dissonance in the liberal idea that acquiring knowledge involves initiation into established, rule-governed activities *and* into critical activity. At such points the hierarchies of freedom/submission, opening/closure – mirrored in the reflective teacher's dual concerns of open-mindedness and wholeheartedness – cannot be established within the liberal system of reason, which has, for instance, nothing to say on the question of when in fact a rule is being *obeyed* and when it is being *created*. The assumption that we do recognize such cases, as somehow written in reality *autonomous* of our reading, is precisely the realist mythology deconstructed in Chapter 7.

In the construction of story – the story of *history*, for example – nature and rules collapse into literary artifact:

> No given set of casually recorded historical events in themselves constitute a story; the most that they offer to a historian are story elements. The events are made into a story by the suppression or subordination of certain of them and the highlighting of others, by characterization, motific repetition, variation of tone and point of view, alternative descriptive strategies, and the like – in short, all of the techniques that we would normally expect to find in the emplotment of a novel or a play.
>
> (White 1978: 47)

The individual person is one event embedded among others within a narrative history; and these events are themselves constituted out of further stories which come together to form their history. The narrative construction of history is, consequently, the narrative creation of the person; a situation that issues in a rhetorical environment which is hostile to the conditions necessary to the flourishing of reflective teaching. We saw in Chapter 5 that essential preconditions to critical discourse are four *validity claims*, among which are that what is asserted is true and that the speaker is sincere in her utterance (Habermas 1970). But these preconditions *cannot be sustained*, cannot play the required role, since the claims of 'truth' and 'sincerity' are not to be satisfied by any naturally occurring elements whose mere existence guarantees them that status. If an autonomous act cannot be a singularity independent of a life in which it occurs, then we must concede that it gains its sense, its significance, only within the stage setting provided by the story of that life. But that story is a literary device; it is *textual*. Indeed, the textuality of the ceremony – the bestowal of title to autonomy – is not simply a necessary outcome of the literary act of weaving the menu of events into a narrative (devastating as that is for reflective teaching); for the events themselves, the story elements, the entries on the menu, are nothing more solid than the twists and turns of the plot of another story. Autonomy becomes a function of inter-textuality and mis-reading; authenticity a trace of the palimpsest of *arche-writing, différance, supplementarity, re-emplotment, distortion*.

As a consequence, the very idea of the *person* as a concept fit to support the notions of autonomy, self-integrity and so on becomes vitiatingly mutilated as the picture of the person dissolves into overlapping, self-interfering strong mis-readings of the events within and surrounding her life. Just as *who a person is* is largely a matter of decision as to what kind of story in which to emplot her life, so the very act of attributing autonomy is *story*-relative and negotiable. Such acts of giving title to autonomy are ceremonial performances: verbal fictions, contrived literary devices or poetic gestures rather than accounts which are discoverable and assessable for truth with reference to reality's inherent, story-independent criteria. The way in which a person comes to autonomy is, therefore, not a matter of her recognizing and keeping faith with her own self-present essence in some moment of rationally conceived, unmediated grasp of undistorted truth, but is, rather, a matter of the way in which a title is, by the authority of others, granted or withheld according to one's role in a narrative.

Autonomy as a war of literature

If the argument that autonomy is a function of the trace is persuasive then we are faced with the conclusion that one's own autonomy is dependent upon a war of literature, upon the battle to establish the charm of a text (Staten 1985: 134). What determines the status of an autonomous act on this view is not a general philosophical-critical account of the structure of language, thought, ideal speech situations or whatever, but the particular local style of narrative-setting. What is rational or natural no longer dominates the conceptual system underpinning an individual's achievement of self-description, but is itself parasitic upon the contrived, irrational forces woven through the text-style within which the metaphors of autonomy, integrity, rationality and nature are placed.

While it is true that critical reflective theorists are committed to a view in which reality is *at least partly* constituted by activities of social construction, it is also true that they must strongly resist the extension and elaboration of that insight woven in the present text if the notions of autonomy and self-hood essential to the thesis are to be salvaged. Blocking the move into textuality is a matter of life and death to the critical enterprise. Nevertheless, the deconstructive leverage by which the rationality of critical reflective theory is dismantled comes ready-made in the very furniture of social construction. Critical theory/reflective practice supplies, in short, the materials for its own deconstruction.

Take, for example, the critical theorist's view of social reality, that

> Understanding 'what man is' is always a matter of grasping the underlying process imminent in man's present situation and in terms of which he strives to transform himself in order to realize his true 'potentialities' or 'essence'.
>
> (Carr and Kemmis 1986: 141)

In consequence the sense of any manifestation of social or individual behaviour is not to be grasped without reference to a specific, historical context within which the meaning that the manifestation possesses *within local commerce* can be made apparent:

> Coming to mean does not happen in a vacuum. It is a process which takes place in and through history, even if only the history of a small group or only over a short period of time. To understand any human activity ... requires seeing it in an historical, as well as a social, framework.
>
> (Carr and Kemmis 1986: 181)

This conviction is echoed – though within a quite different conceptual framework – by Alasdair MacIntyre (1985: 208), who argues that narrative history, in which we place the agent's intentions in causal and temporal order with reference to the dual contexts of their role in *his* history and their role in the history of *the setting or settings to which they belong*, is 'the basic and essential genre for the characterization of human actions.' The rationale behind this attention to historical and narrative setting is that 'behaviour is only characterized adequately when we know what the longer and longest-term intentions invoked are and how the shorter-term intentions are related to the longer' (MacIntyre 1985: 208).

It must be noted here that the structure of these contextual elements is inextricably tied up with the rhetoric of a particular reading. The context of longer/longest, moreover, like the context of group-size and time-period in the Carr and Kemmis version, always already contains, as *différance,* its own textual over-spill – its own *supplement* – in that its overt narrative always remains incomplete, partial, a victim of the literary imperatives of storytelling.

Thus *longest-term*, in MacIntyre's picture, is a rhetorical device of closure: bringing the curtain down on questioning, blocking further readings; deriving its authority not from its correspondence with reality but from the persuasive style of its story. By *strong mis-reading* of MacIntyre we will agree that understanding a piece of behaviour requires that we establish for it a historical, social and institutional setting which itself has a history

> within which the histories of individual agents not only are, but have to be, situated, just because without the setting and its changes through time the history of the individual agent and his changes through time will be unintelligible.
>
> (MacIntyre 1985: 206–7)

However, we postmodern textualists will place *historical setting* as one, albeit important, element in our rhetorical strategies of emplotment. It is one literary device *among others* which may serve our purposes in establishing a style of conversation. It does not set limits on story-form but is itself nothing outside of the telling of a story, and story is always an indeterminate collage of trace and supplement. Tradition does not control the narrative, for tradition is itself nothing more than a *currently fashionable* literary artifact. Thus, *contra* MacIntyre (1985: 221, 194), it is not so much that a person finds herself born with a past, inheriting a tradition, but rather that she is, along with history and tradition, already constituted out of intersecting conversations, literary styles and *différance*.

The narrative constitution of the self

An essential component of the reflective person's concept of autonomy is the fundamental semantic and veridical priority given to the individual's autobiographical story, her own view of herself. When personal knowledge

> arises out of one's own rational reflection upon one's own considered action, it may be regarded as authentic. This implies that the actor alone can be the final arbiter of the truth of an interpretation of a considered action and, hence, that the correctness of the interpretation of an action is not a matter to be decided by external reference to rules or principles or theories ... The criterion of authenticity thus acts as a defence against the politics of persuasion in educational research; the actor can only be expected to alter his or her own understanding of a situation to the extent that he or she understands others' interpretations as relevant.
>
> (Carr and Kemmis 1986: 190)

Contained within this rhetoric of privileged perspective is another manifestation of the metaphysics of *presence*. It appears as the story of the *private object*, the self-present-to-consciousness autonomous *simple* which legislates that there is such a thing as 'achieving a correct understanding of individuals' meanings' (Carr and Kemmis 1986: 104). This flies in the face of Wittgenstein's famous deconstruction of the possibility of a private language:

Suppose everyone had a box with something in it: we call it a 'beetle'. No one can look into anyone else's box, and everyone says he knows what a beetle is only by looking at *his* beetle. – Here it would be quite possible for everyone to have something different in his box. One might even imagine such a thing constantly changing. – But suppose the word 'beetle' had a use in these people's language? – If so it would not be used as the name of a thing. The thing in the box has no place in the language-game at all; not even as a *something*: for the box might even be empty. – No, one can 'divide through' by the thing in the box; it cancels out, whatever it is.

   That is to say: if we construe the grammar of the expression of sensation on the model of 'object and designation' the object drops out of consideration as irrelevant.

(PI section 293; see sections 294, 304, 580, 670)

The double-bind in which the theorist of reflective teaching finds himself is that while a *metaphysically posited private object* can have no semantic work to do, privacy – construed as a *textual product* – cannot have the privileged legislative function required by the theory. The concept of one's own personhood – and its inner functions – consists in seeing oneself as a certain sort of thing, as falling under a description; but the very possibility of description rests on the available tools of description, the criterial frameworks which we have acquired in learning a language. The public nature of meaning entails that 'private' meaning, far from being *uniquely secure*, is up for grabs through its location and re-location within a range of (possibly incommensurable) narratives. One result of this is that in making judgements about a person's meaning, the speaker's word cannot be regarded as *necessarily* the final court of appeal (Rorty 1980: 349). The speaker's meaning – like her identity, her self-integrity, her sincerity, her sanity – is a poetic device in the aesthetic of a narrative; an epiphenomenon of the literary imperatives of characterization and emplotment and, as such, the embodiment of *différance*, of the absence-to-privilege of a reading.

   Because truth is con/textually wayward, fractured and disseminated across texts whose provisional, local dominance is founded on blindness, suppression, deception and artifice, sincerity is only possible on condition of our becoming blind to alternative textual possibilities; on condition that we can locate its enactment within a drama in which the demarcation of true/false is produced through the suppression of contradictory styles of emplotment. Sincerity is therefore a species of deception – *a particular act of generalized insincerity* – while autonomy depends for its status upon the contrived, manipulative authority of the text. The autonomy/authority conceptual hierarchy essential to the architectural integrity of realist philosophy and reflective teaching is thus reversed through this analysis and its rational system – which underwrites the distinction – is displaced.

   Consequently, human action – private and public – may be regarded as *enacted narrative*. MacIntyre provides a clue to the textuality of the setting in his account of the dramatic nature of dialogue:

A conversation is a dramatic work, even if a very short one, in which the participants are not only the actors, but also the joint authors, working out in agreement or disagreement the mode of their production. For it is not just that conversations belong to genres in just the way that plays and novels do; but they have beginnings, middles and endings just as do literary works. They embody reversals and recognitions; they move towards and away from climaxes. There may with a longer conversation be digressions and subplots, indeed digressions within digressions and subplots within subplots.

(MacIntyre 1985: 211)

The fault lines exploited by deconstruction are evident in MacIntyre's text as the literary devices whose employment, in the reading of conversations, the text is ostensibly *about*, but which inevitably *reflexively* work to infect the textual form of their own application. The allocation to genres of conversational or literary moves, the location of the moments within the conversation as beginnings, middles, ends, the reversals, the placing of the climaxes, the location of digressions, digression/story relations, plot/subplot negotiability and the re-inscription of the levels; these are necessary devices to the understanding of human agency but inevitably they render the product *literary* rather than *literal*. For critical theory they are the necessary *and suicidal* elements of rational social theory; they are the essential constituents of the theory which deconstruction shows to be simultaneously fatal to its self-integrity.

Changes or distortions in any of these devices must reverberate through the whole text to re-constitute its rationality. The notion of longest-term, for example, is rendered permanently unstable by its susceptibility to re-inscription and dis-placement because its dramatic role within a narrative is as an ending of a story which follows on from and which partially determines – and is determined by – a particular beginning and a particular middle. A consequence of this is that the narrative role of the story elements is incommensurable with their role in providing an appropriate medium for objective or critical discourse. Louis Mink makes the point well:

A narrative must have a unity of its own; that is what is acknowledged in saying that it must have a beginning, middle, and an end. And the reason why two narratives cannot be merely additively combined – in the simplest case, by making them temporally continuous as the parallel chronicle is continuous – is that in the earlier narrative of such an aggregate the end is no longer an end, and therefore the beginning is no longer *that* beginning, nor the middle *that* middle . . . [Therefore], narrative histories should be aggregative, insofar as they are histories, but cannot be, insofar as they are narratives. Narrative history borrows from fictional narrative the convention by which a story generates its own imaginative space, within which it neither depends on nor can displace other stories; but it presupposes that past actuality is a single and determinate realm, a presupposition which, once it is made explicit, is at odds with the incomparability of imaginative stories.

(Mink 1978: 143)

What Mink describes is the displacing effect of supplementarity. The contextual requirements which MacIntyre places on narrative in the form of long-term intentions cannot be anything outside of their telling, for they cannot possess an identity which remains unmodified by their re-telling and their grafting on to other narratives. The con/text is a dramatic property of a text just as much as are those properties which MacIntyre acknowledges. Autonomy, as a property of a historically situated life, is therefore a gesture of the play of dramatic narrative which is necessarily and permanently vulnerable to re-inscription through the re-situating of its context. An acceptable reading is a particular kind of mis-reading; it is simply that process of *transformation, distortion, modification and closure* – characteristic of all understanding – which passes unnoticed or which is suppressed.

Because there is no fact-of-the-matter to autonomy with which to confront, with immediate and decisive presence, questions as to the autonomy of this person or that person, the rational leverage is removed by which a distinction between the coercive, distorting influences of custom, habit and ideology and the idea of theory as the consciously held product of reflection can be determinately drawn and maintained, intact, across contexts of textuality.

Reflective teaching requires, minimally, the transparent self-integrity of consciousness – the determinate meaning of what is *before*-consciousness. Displacement of the system of rationality which supports that view renders theory as a special case of ideology, a particular custom which has certain rituals of academia attached to it. The displacement, moreover, collapses the distinction drawn within some approaches to critical theory between implicitly and explicitly held theories. Carr and Kemmis, for example, find unacceptable the claim that teachers operate, possibly unconscious of the fact, according to implicit theories, where 'teachers can be understood as acting *as if* they were following a set of principles' (1986: 189).

But for we postmodernists the concepts presupposed to possess enduring, essential semantic and metaphysical stability in order to drive the desired wedge between the assumed polarities of implicit and explicit commitment – *consciousness, intention, authenticity, personal identity, custom, habit* etc. – are placed *sous rature*. The story-relative essence of autonomy entails that 'acting *as if*' is all there is to be discovered at the end of the most rigorous analysis of behaviour, consciousness or intention. Given the dispersal of the story of autonomy across a multiplicity of re-inscriptions – an infinity of incommensurable narratives – there can be no such thing as *the* story, the *correct* representation of the essence of the autonomous act. Instead each story documents its own *as-if;* like any fiction which *creates* a transient, persuasive world of characters and plot out of scattered fragments of language, each narrative situates events within a theatre whose devices of enchantment preserve its *as-if,* momentarily, from collapse under the *irony* of the simultaneous assertion and effacement of the story's authority. But the ironic stance is necessary; in the absence of a story possessing guaranteed facticity the realization of each *as-if* is not in some determinate, immediate, self-present alignment of conscious representation and external reality but, rather, is permanently un-realized – deferred across the endless chain of reference to further *as-ifs*.[1]

The irony is that at the end of enactment is further enactment, where all assertion is also its own denial and every commitment is a commitment *sous rature*.

Autonomy is necessary for the enterprise of reflective teaching but won't do the work required. It functions as a metaphysical slogan, a persuasive device, but depends only on its image to persuade. By its own standards of rationality it fails and therefore the whole story fails. Autonomy is just another ideology.

So should we give up on reflective teaching? No. But it needs another story which recognizes irony. We need to forget that our practices are only legitimate in the service of autonomy and recognize that autonomy is itself a product of other values. We create autonomy within our creation of a selection of values within which autonomy can have a role, and in which we can draw a distinction between behaviour which fits and behaviour which does not. What is required is the relativism of postmodernity.

Note

1 Devitt (1984) uses the as-if manoeuvre in order to defend realism, inferring that the best explanation of why a theory is successful is that the world is experientially as if the theory says it must be. The arguments given here show that the generation of possible as-ifs is far too promiscuous to enable the notion to meet the strict requirements of realism.

PART III

POSTMODERNITY

9

REFLECTIVE TEACHING IN THE POSTMODERN WORLD

Ironism ... results from awareness of the power of
redescription. But most people do not want to be
redescribed. They want to be taken on their own
terms – taken seriously just as they are and just as
they talk. The ironist tells them that the language
they speak is up for grabs by her and her kind.
There is something potentially very cruel about that
claim. For the best way to cause people long-lasting
pain is to humiliate them by making the things
that seemed most important to them look futile,
obsolete, and powerless ... The redescribing ironist,
by threatening one's final vocabulary, and thus
one's ability to make sense of oneself in one's own
terms rather than hers, suggests that one's self and
one's world are futile, obsolete, *powerless*.
Redescription often humiliates.

(Rorty 1989: 89–90)

It is difficult for us to give up our belief in god or fairy tales. The old stories
gave us a sense of security in their familiarity and in their theme of the permanence of a way of life. The metaphysical and spiritual security to be found
in the idea of a language whose semantic structure, like the structure of the
reality it represents, is essentially stable and transparent to inquiry, coupled
to the picture of the self as constituted by an essentially determinate, enduring, rational nature, has, in the flux of contingency and change, an obvious
psychological and emotional appeal. Its power, evident from its centrality in
Christianity, social and physical science, democracy and almost everything
that passes as serious academic dialogue, marks it as the logo-type of the
West's self-description.

The deconstructive manoeuvres of this book constitute what Rorty (1989)
has called a process of de-divination through the re-description of language,
reason and autonomy. From the strategic location we have reached, the claims
and commitments of reflective teaching become re-described as the symptoms of a maturing philosophy on the way to becoming properly postmodern.

Reflective teaching is a moment in the evolution of literary style. It is a style which has rejected a number of enlightenment commitments but which retains enough of the fashions of realism in its story of language and reason for it to appear awkward, old-fashioned, archaic, passé to postmodern taste. In postmodernity – in a world that is made not found, a world in which there is no truth that we have not put there, no reason except for the rules we live by, no deep significance that is not superficial – reflective teaching retains too many of the old mythologies for it to do a substantially different job from traditional realist or positivist writing. It is, in its apotheosis of reason and logos, simply too *Old Testament*.

Reflective teaching tried to break with universalism, positivism, technical-rationalism, but was like a plane shedding seats and a few passengers in the futile hope of escaping the influence of the spirit of gravity to achieve freedom. Postmodernism makes the escape by refusing to be bound by the rules of the game, by becoming *immaterial*. The price of holding on to reason is the inevitability of universalism and realism. But if realism is jettisoned reason becomes no longer important. It only seemed so while we were under its spell.

Difference and distortion

Symptomatic of reflective teaching's failure quite to break through into post-modern, anti-realist writing are its worries about its literary management of the vocabulary of *'bias'*, *'partiality'* and *'relativity'*; worries which arise out of the general difficulties which critical-reflective writing has in dealing with the stylistic implications of difference and *différance* within a literature which emplots difference parasitically upon the characterization of *similarity* and *identity*.

In tracing the boundary between bias and neutrality, however, the reflective teacher assumes once more the external vantage point which is presupposed in all her attempts to conceptualize the notions of distortion and error. Consequently, postmodern irony enacts a re-description of the critical-reflective claim that 'the very purpose of critical self-reflection is to expose and identify self-interests and ideological distortions' (Carr and Kemmis 1986: 192). A vocabulary of *bias* is legitimized only on the authority of the surrounding vocabulary of *reliability* and its mythology of the divine bivalence of language. The stylistic imperatives of the characterization of the *value-free, neutral medium* determine that bias will have a literary role whose importance is guaranteed in virtue of its being the parasitic mirror image of the narrative adventures of *the neutral*. This distinction, however, is itself parasitic upon the bias of a text. The ceremony of awarding the epithets *'self-interest'* or *'ideological distortion'* involves, as an ironic gesture, a particular device of emplotment by which these characterizations are *creatively* written on to some other fragment of narrative. Their placement – how they may be described and employed, what we categorize as falling within their compass – is up for grabs. The decision to regard a particular case as an example of ideological distortion is not to be judged against some neutral standard *discoverable* through critical reflection, for the decision to regard-as-neutral is itself ungrounded by anything other than its literary surroundings. Contrary to the rhetoric of reflective teaching, we do not *expose* self-interest and ideology in any sense other than by persuading our fellows to re-describe the events of the life of an individual, group, institution or nation using the vocabulary of self-interest and ideology instead of the vocabulary of neutrality and truth.

On this view, the idea that the teacher might set out 'deliberately to examine where his or her own practice is distorted by taken-for-granted assumptions or ideology' (Carr and Kemmis 1986: 192) is simply to acknowledge the competition between a multiplicity of available descriptions to seduce us and, within this scene, to note the individual's own precarious efforts at self-description, which are perpetually vulnerable to re-description and displacement. Distortion is not a property inhering in certain ideologically influenced perspectives but not others. Its *being* is text-relative; distortion is assigned as a particular move in emplotment which, under any number of re-descriptions, may be variously staged or absented altogether. The struggle to read distortion *on to* a narrative is the struggle to give warrant to re-description. It is the struggle to humiliate.

The questions of ideology versus theory, irrationality versus rationality, distortion versus clarity, illusion versus truth, which are centrally important in the dialogue of *reflection*, are finessed by postmodernism. It is not that they are rejected as nonsense, or as false dichotomies, or collapsed so that the distinctions cannot be drawn; they are not rejected as being wrong at all. It is, rather, that they no longer seem to be interesting or useful questions to ask *in general* outside of the consideration of one particular case or another. In a postmodern light they come to appear like questions such as 'What is beauty?', 'How many angels can dance on a pinhead?' or 'What is the nature of goodness?' Within some vocabulary, at some point in history, these questions may have been useful or interesting. All that postmodernism urges is that in the vocabulary of the educated West on the threshold of the twenty-first century these questions, and those of critical dialogue, are burnt out, passé. They are irrelevant because they are unhelpful in resolving locally important questions such as 'What are the forces of oppression operating in this university?', 'What are the coercive effects of central government's educational policies?' or 'How does the bureaucracy of this institution distort academic and pedagogic concerns?'

Reflection reinscribed

The transition to postmodernity does not involve a straightforward rejection of the dialogue of reflective teaching on grounds of its failing to represent social reality accurately; nor is the intention to replace that dialogue with something *closer to the truth*. Instead we are provoked by the postmodern impulse to give up the game of trying to produce better-because-truer theories and abandon the thought that there can be a general theory of how rationality, justice and theories themselves can be improved. That idea was one more example of our old commitment to the mythology of presence, to the meta-story that some stories can be shown to be better than others by virtue of their point to point correspondence to nature's own story. Nature, if she speaks at all, speaks *our* language, employing the devices of whatever literary form *we* have prepared.

Instead of *replacing* reflective teaching we are engaged in producing *re-descriptions* of its themes; taking its characterizations, its plots, its rhetorical manoeuvres and re-inscribing them in a vocabulary which is post-metaphysical in that its characters are un-anchored by *presence* and stabilized only by the inertia of their embeddedness in a story. So what are the implications of an ironic postmodernism for teaching and teacher education? If the question is, 'What does a postmodern curriculum look like?' or 'What is the structure of a postmodern course?' then the question is not a good one. One might as well ask, 'What genre must we write if it is not a spy novel?' or 'What will we play if we stop playing football?' However, we can say something about how educational institutions and practices which are concerned to jettison their technical-realist, rational pretensions might become *more postmodern*, *more textual*; how we might infuse them with new style; how they might become more open to the play of *différance* within their boundaries and how we might become more ironic.

The teacher-deconstructor

Teachers and student teachers will become deconstructive in their readings of educational texts, in their situating of received wisdom, in their creation of values, in their evaluation of courses and of the statements of bureaucrats and politicians. This will require, though in practice may need to precede, the development of institutions in which teachers and students will be encouraged to become ironic in reconciling the foundationless status of their beliefs and commitments – and the commitments of others – with the desire to create, develop and defend them. Possession of this ironic attitude – this unstable, dynamic oscillation of the rhetorical forces of deconstruction and position, or reactivity and creativity – is the signature of the postmodern voice and a central characteristic of emancipation in postmodernity.

Indeed, especially because reflective teaching lacks the ironic attitude, it is difficult to see how its theorizing of educational practices could ever hope consistently to resolve the conflict between the emancipatory and award-bearing imperatives of its courses (Groundwater-Smith 1988: 259). This tension arises because reflective teaching holds *equality* to be an essential component of the ideal speech situation and, in consequence, of the emancipated state; thus precluding entry into that heaven of any situation flawed by hierarchies of power.

To postmoderns, however, it does not seem useful to ask general questions about the possibility of *emancipation-in-situations-of-inequality*, for this would require some general theory of equality and that is precisely what cannot be written, any more than can a general theory of inequality. What can be written – what any putative general theory would *actually* be – are particular stories about this or that situation in which judgements about inequality and equality are made, questioned, discussed, supported, opposed, through the interplay of a common, local cultural and rhetorical currency. *That there will be* descriptions of the situation in which there are inequalities (of power, wealth, status, beauty etc.) is as unsurprising as that there will be descriptions that document characters, roles and events that are non-identical. Just as the relationships between characters can only be understood by engagement with the narrative of which they are characters – the story, among possible stories, in which their lives are emplotted – relations of inequality can be understood only through engagement with the vocabulary within which the relevant distinctions are drawn, and *that vocabulary* is itself meaningful only within the local narrative textile. As far as courses of teacher education are concerned, the supposed inequality in status and power of students and lecturers provides no more a general threat to their emancipatory value than do the differential characterizations and experiences which constitute the situation.

The teacher-deconstructor is the postmodern educationalist. She or he will practice the kind of deconstructive manoeuvres outlined and employed in this book: reading for the way in which a text achieves its effect; unveiling its grounding in contradiction and paradox; highlighting the marginal, the concealed, the suppressed themes and assumptions; strongly mis-reading the text; reading with the intention of causing trouble; seeing all assertions, practices and positions as textual; using the text's assumed rationality against itself; identifying, reversing and displacing its conceptual hierarchies; showing its dependency on bivalence; tracing the play of *différance* in the text's construction of its own origins, the story of its own foundations; exposing the implications of its central metaphors; collapsing its distinctions between the literal and the metaphorical; exhibiting its assumption of the primacy of the metaphor of speech and its commitment to a metaphysics of presence; mapping the adventures of the trace within its narrative; identifying its suppressed need for supplementation; reading-as through intertextuality; placing positions *sous rature.*

Postmodern teaching practices are, in McLaren's (1995: 21) words, 'acts of dissonance and interventions into the ritual inscription of our students into the codes of the dominant culture; into structured refusals to naturalize existing relations of power; into the creation of subaltern counterpublics.' The effect of a deconstructive education will leave students and teachers able to exhibit the textual, political and ideological devices and perspectives inherent in all texts; able to expose the intrinsic metaphors and characters of any example of educational dialogue. They will recognize that each position, each commitment or belief is contingent: its foundations are epiphenomena of its narrative; its truths are symbols which conceal a politics and an ethics; its overt story hides a covert message; it is, in short, a metaphor of a way of life, a view of education.

What the postmodern teacher recognizes is that we have a choice in education; that every decision to teach this way, or assemble that collection of subjects on a curriculum, or organize one's classroom according to this set of principles or anecdotes, is ungrounded in reality, has no ultimate, compelling justification. Every decision involves potentially endless levels of choice which we can contrive to forget or conceal but which deconstruction is always ready to uncloak. We are responsible for those decisions in a most extreme way. We have a responsibility for our decisions that the world cannot excuse since the world is, itself, an outcome of our deciding so to take it.

Creating postmodern educational institutions

In taking up the postmodern style, educational institutions must repudiate bureaucratic imperatives to embrace the literary enterprise and organize for free textual plurality. Intellectual and reflective activity is, as things are, conducted within a framework the values of which are determined by a vocabulary which administrators, managers and bureaucrats can understand. It is a vocabulary that embodies conceptual relations which can be processed in a determinate way to give bureaucratically manageable statements as their outcomes. The concept of effectiveness, for example, becomes, under the descriptions available within that vocabulary, a quantitative measure of the extent to which prespecified outcomes are realized. As such it is an *administrator-friendly* concept but *intellectually and educationally disastrous*. It signals a textually reductive exercise; one in which the literature of human enterprise and struggle, hopes and fears, interests and desires is divorced from its Shakespeare, its Austen, its Tolstoy, to be written in the narrative style of a Haynes manual of motor mechanics. This latter certainly translates readily into a *kind* of practice, but at what cost? As Peter Winch has said,

> Would it be intelligent to try to explain how Romeo's love for Juliet enters into his behaviour in the same terms as we might want to apply to the rat whose sexual excitement makes him run across an electrically charged grid to reach his mate? Does not Shakespeare do this much better?
>
> (Winch 1958: 77)

Using this reductive vocabulary is worse than wrong; it demonstrates an ignorance even of the stylistically appropriate vocabulary. It is, in short, bad mannered; and bad manners are not to be cured by formal, rational argument but by providing the vocabulary appropriate to the context within which good manners become identical with the reasonable thing to do. It involves educating the ignorant into proper ways of speaking and appropriate ways of behaving. But it also requires that we recognize them not as wrong, as making a wrong move within the appropriate context, but as ignorant; as lacking in the vocabulary and manners appropriate to this conversation or this literary dialogue. The ignorant are not yet in a position to be wrong for they have not yet acquired the concepts and stylistic awarenesses about which they might make a mistake.

Qua ignorant, these people ought to command our sympathy. However, the arrogant, swaggering self-importance of the administrative, managerial and bureaucratic voice demands our contempt. When ignorance is abetted by arrogance the result is burlesque; and we should not resist the temptation to ridicule this buffoon at every opportunity. Indeed, it is interesting on this point how the policing of academic and intellectual discourse has traditionally been achieved within the realist, objectivist, positivist, technicist framework by the insistence on its austerity and seriousness – seriousness, here, being the handmaiden to truth. But irony, the recognition of the contingency and language-game parochiality of seriousness, compels us to be reactive upon determinate, austere cant, thus legitimizing the intellectual value of satire, parody, aphorism and ridicule (see Rorty 1980: 369–70).

One of the difficulties in the way of change in respect of the value-setting of an educational institution is that the procedural imperatives of bureaucracy have, over many years, become internalized in the day-to-day practices of academics and intellectuals. 'Working in bureaucratic settings has taught everyone to be compliant, to be rule governed, not to ask questions, seek alternatives or deal with competing values. People are supposed to follow orders from those at the top' (Lieberman cited in Day 1993: 88). Insofar as the values of an institution are the bureaucratic values of the efficient satisfaction of means–ends imperatives under a universalizing standard of conduct there will be a conflict between postmodern, ironic intellectuals and the bureaucrats. The problem we shall have with bureaucrats, and with those academics who have absorbed their vocabulary, is that *they will be unable to see the significance of what we are talking about.* We will satisfy them more easily if we talk about lecturers, teachers and students as if they are rats on a grid; but we might move them if we make them appear ridiculous. We are unlikely to convince the bureaucrats by arguing with them within their own language game.

In regarding this abomination of literary taste we postmoderns find ourselves sympathetic to the exhortations of writers such as Peter McLaren, John White, Carr and Kemmis, that teachers should become political activists. Following re-inscription, the critical dialogue may be exorcised of its mythology of presence and read as a stimulus to become active in writing the vocabularies within which notions of rationality and justice can find characterization. I agree with Giroux and McLaren's (1995: 32) view that a 'critical pedagogy' must reject conservative claims that 'schooling is a politically opaque and value-neutral process' to argue that 'schools operate mainly to reproduce the discourses, values and privilege of existing elites.'

A key question here is how to 'move from a position of criticism to one of substantive vision' (Giroux and McLaren 1995: 32). Deconstruction opens language itself to creative play. Re-inscription places the criteria of rationality and justice up for grabs and the struggle to secure them is the conspiracy to bewitch, seduce, entice, enchant by exhibiting the attractions, glamour, beguilement of a text.

Freed by postmodern re-inscription from the mythologies which infected and inhibited its non-ironic dialogue, reflective teaching is more comfortably able to help schools avoid taking 'the structure of society for granted', assuming 'that our social structure is "natural"' (Carr and Kemmis 1986: 222). This 'taking for granted' of current vocabularies generates formidable rhetorical inertia. Many teachers are like Catholics whose apotheosis of the biblical text compels them to swallow a man-made dogma under a naturalistic disguise. Given a realist, technical-rationalist basis for their traditionally humanitarian, liberal view, teachers are vulnerable to a rhetoric which preserves and employs that rational base while utilizing it to contort and subvert teachers' value commitments. A neat sleight of hand; but ultimately an inevitable working out of the implications of realist rhetoric which was waiting to happen. It is the realization in this world of the mythology of ultimate commensurability; and it serves to explain the relative lack of opposition to the literary dogma involved in such innovations as competency-based teacher education, university staff appraisal systems, National Curriculum testing regimes and programmatic forms of *study*, apprenticeship-based clinical teacher education, systems management approaches to curriculum development and programme evaluation, the imposition of ready-made administrative structures upon and across the educational and intellectual scene, the centralization of political control of education and the de-democratization of educational practice within universities . . . Blind, inarticulate acceptance of this corruption has been the most widespread reaction to its insinuations. Arguing *within* its vocabulary is a possible if inevitably weak strategy of opposition, as the rhetorical high ground has already been captured. Deconstructing the rhetoric is a better response, as it prepares the ground for the best response of all, which is to laugh at the silliness of the emperor in his new clothes. Postmodernist irony provides the appropriate stance – and therapeutic vocabulary – with which to ridicule the puffed up, vulgar gestures of this stylistic grotesque and to begin to treat it with appropriate disdain.

Educating the postmodern teacher

Teacher education courses will need to equip students with the deconstructive man-oeuvres by means of which they will be able to throw off the inhibitions of realism and engage in creative, literary writing. The postmodern deviation from a philosophy of *demonstration* to one of *persuasion* collapses the rigid distinction between reason and rhetoric, truth and consensus. Thus licensed, and in contrast to the plodding realist, the postmodernist will make extravagant leaps, cavalier gestures, resting on nothing more solid than the hope that she or he might entrance through the sheer flourish of style. Realism's measured rationality is replaced with a hodgepodge of manoeuvres and dirty tricks which might become gold if an audience falls for them. There is no secure distinction between rational argument and rhetorical prestidigitation. Our concern may as well be to humiliate our opponent as convince her. Postmodernists probe the limits of persuasion, testing what might prove to be dirty tricks on an audience to see if through winning they can earn the honorific title: *rational*. No general principle inhibits this 'anything goes' abandon; just the domestic inertia of current practice and what its rationality allows its acolytes to swallow. Anything might go; and some things don't, not because they are determinately false or irrational but because they fail to secure a consensus.

In the struggle to persuade, the gap between literature and theory dissolves, for while we may rationally manipulate agreed facts to secure a consensus we might equally create new facts, new ways of being rational. Close reasoning, the hallmark of positivist and reflective practices, is a myth. Deconstruction exposes the concealed leaps and disguised metaphors infesting the weave of any article of persuasion. Prior to persuasion, closeness itself is just a dirty trick. Agreement fills the gaps, enables the narrative to work. But without the rigidity of a technique of close reasoning the distinction between theory and literature collapses. Both present stories that are full of holes.

Students will be initiated into traditional and current literatures to gain experience in the use and deconstruction of their vocabularies. They will be helped to acquire and develop strategies or, more properly, *manoeuvres* to deal with the literary oppression which they are likely to meet from the vocabularies of politics and bureaucracy and traditional educational mythologies of convergence and commensurability. They will be encouraged to remember that the wider strategic theatre is simply a mythology, an epiphenomenon of some local skirmish conjured up to dress it with a purpose within a longest-term narrative. These deconstructive manoeuvres occupy only a self-created rhetorical space, depending only on their effect, taking advantage of weapons provided by the opponent – the demands for sincerity, the character of autonomy, the law-giving of reason – to use these against him. Deconstruction is the process of manoeuvres, the covert incision into the text, the rhetorical act of subversion and sabotage. For postmodern students, no text will remain immune; all texts will provide potential theatres in which to rehearse the manoeuvres of deconstruction.

Students will therefore receive plenty of opportunity to engage in the deconstruction of a wide range of texts from educational theory, principles of pedagogy, political treatise, religious doctrines, government position papers, school and education authority policy statements, research reports etc. Students will interrogate and re-describe the relationship between their classroom practice, pedagogic concerns, knowledge and commitments and the textual setting provided by the socio-political-cultural hinterland.

They will be encouraged to find new ways of re-inscribing these elements and relationships in different stories. Re-inscription imposes a new reading on a text to enable it to be re-contextualized as part of another or as containing and partly explaining others which become its sub-texts or text-fragments. Through the free play of re-inscription that deconstruction opens for us we can 'analyse and unsettle extant power configurations, to defamiliarize and make remarkable what is often passed off as the ordinary, the mundane, the routine, the banal'; an operation which 'ambiguates the complacency of teaching' to exhibit its views of normality and neutrality as inseparable from considerations of value and power (McLaren 1995: 231). It involves students in seeing the claims to truth or knowledge, the principles and recommendations of an educational text as story-items, the value and implications of which may be altered through their re-inscription within other stories or by changing the relations within the story in which they are packaged to see, for example, the assembled facts as the outcome rather than the cause of the recommendations, or taking the universal claims and applying them select-ively to just some situations; that is, recontextualizing facts/truth as recom-mendations of ways of seeing that are optional.

Students will rehearse and practise the rhetorical manoeuvres of logic, assumption-analysis, fallacy detection, philosophy, *phronesis*, deconstruction etc. , and apply these in a range of narrative contexts to work upon a variety of vocabularies. These will form the double gesture of affirmation and decon-struction by providing the strategic materials for the defence, projection, re-inscription, reversal, dis-placement, of texts. The constitutive material, how-ever, will come through literature in its general sense; the dialogical placement of books, magazines, films, TV, events, political manifestoes and so on which will go much wider than the narrow confines of educational textbooks, for *they* are unlikely to provide exciting, unexplored metaphors for the educational enterprise of lifestyle design. Rather than being a curriculum, the experience will be more like a journey through a newspaper or magazine. It will be global, a participation in the world's conversations with itself.

Consequently the students and children of postmodernity will have a more assertive, robust, creative disposition written into them through their education. In contrast to traditionally passive, discovery/acquisition models of learning, in which the learner comes to know the text, postmodern learn-ing involves coming to control the text, to be able to dismantle its rhetorical structure and refashion its themes to a new, preferred purpose. One problem for teachers attempting to engage in reflective practice and revise their rela-tionships with their 'clients' has been the relative weakness of the teacher's position in making claims to expertise; a situation that has arisen out of the academic insouciance of university research together with the absence of a universalistic, technical-rational basis for teachers' professionalism. When the teacher is seen as a 'mere service provider' (Schön 1983: 298), her or his dif-ficulty is that of acquiring enough voice in the professional–client relation to establish an appropriate framework of autonomy for her or his practice. The postmodern remedy is not (*contra* Day 1993: 90) to develop a general theory of how reflection may lead to change, nor even a general theory of change itself. It is, rather, to equip students and teachers with a repertoire of rhetorical manoeuvres and literary devices; the weapons with which they can be em-powered to fight the battle for change, and the achievement of an identity, in the postmodern revolution. Learning, the acquisition of knowledge, becomes the ability to control or manipulate; knowledge itself is not a state but an activity, a strategic intervention in a discourse context, one whose result is to persuade others to speak and act in a certain way or to re-contextualize their own claims to know.

The literary use of theory

Any theory, educational or otherwise, will be seen as a non-convergent literary offering providing a vocabulary with which to describe and create practice. Teachers will use educational theories for their pragmatic purposes and place them in the service of furthering their own deliberations about, and justification of, educational ends. Theory becomes a prime manoeuvre of re-contextualization, an intertextual catalyst for strong mis-reading, providing one more possible story to impose on practice. Simultaneously theory is a protective cloak for an educational vision – or prejudice. It is the textual precipitate of a commitment to a chosen style of education rather than the epistemological foundation for pedagogy.

Postmodern teachers and students will see the irony of employing contradictory theories in different contexts – *or even within a single context* – but will not be tempted to see this situation as requiring therapeutic treatment via a dialectical process of resolution via synthesis and commensuration. They will see that as with artistic creation or the competition for fashion there can be no universal meta-procedural theory of the process, for there is nothing outside of participation in the discourse, the audience-relative game of persuasion. Success here is its own criterion and – though textually liquid – is more secure than any meta-theory could be. Once the unwanted metaphysical baggage of realism has been discarded we can acquiesce in the irony of our postmodern educational relativism with its multiple approaches to creating ways of seeing the world, of constructing new *seeing-as-ifs*, of designing styles of living.

Postmodernist teaching is not a passive discovery of facts about classroom life but an active construction of those facts; a narrative for the class and its characters – the teacher and the students – of where they are going. It employs theory as rhetoric for defence and attack, not as a neutral framework within which to describe truth. The fragmentary use of research statistics or anecdote to persuade an audience bites the bullet of the accusation against action research that it is *just* anecdotal. Are these dirty tricks? Manipulative? Or rational? There is no answer prior to the audience falling one way or the other; there is just winning and losing. Reading of theory is therefore crucial so that the teacher can both use and deconstruct it; though *use* here is more like *mention* – name-dropping theory to employ its image of authority selectively. First comes prejudice – textual commitment – then comes truth. Theory is a building material *selected* for the collective purpose of creating a dialogue with social and rhetorical inertia.

Educational pluralities

Postmodernism issues in a plurality of educational dialogues, practices, ends and values. This will involve education and teacher-education institutions in becoming less like departments of science and more like departments of literature; less like the factory production line, where the singular values of a particular product-interest determine the linearity of a means–end mindframe, and more like a fashion house, where a multiplicity of styles coexist while offering the potential for an endless plurality of *statements* through their cultural and aesthetic currency, their intertextuality and their susceptibility to re-inscription under new stylistic gestures or novel iconographies;

their conversational style becoming less centred on psychology, to borrow vocabularies from philosophy, literary criticism, cultural studies, fashion and art. Alternative interpretations of the practices and dialogues of education will exist side by side without institutional or meta-theoretical pressure to become commensurate.

Every reading is deconstructed within postmodernity. The hegemony of any interpretation is dissevered. The tyrannical story of universalization becomes just another mis-reading. The postmodern person is Gemini multiplied, numerous selves in different contexts, the identity-switcher: unknowable and non-existent except within a relationship. At the same time she or he is committed to a framework of self-chosen, self-created values and realities. The postmodern person is one who lives the deconstructive manoeuvres which enable her to see no *truth* as necessary, *no truth* as necessary, all truth as created, contingent and transiently enshrined in *the role of permanence* within some currently fashionable text-style. She sees no set of values as fixed or intrinsically desirable but some values as contingently assertable.

One consequence of textualist plurality is that universal methods of course organization, assessment and appraisal would come to look like embarrassing, stylistic gaffes rather than confident, expert applications of the true account. Just as one would invite ridicule were one to try to interpret the paintings of Dali as if he were attempting to do just the same thing as Monet (or Jane Austen), so one would look ridiculous were one to attempt to interpret and make judgements about courses by applying universalized criteria independent of the particular case, the particular con/text. To the postmodernist, the brief of teacher *training* accreditation agencies in general has been precisely to read Dali as Monet – or vice versa.

A significant indicator of a postmodern educational culture will be its eagerness to institutionalize the open play of styles, the trace of *différance* which would inhabit its key dialogues. Students and lecturers will come to see realism's commitments, like the tales of another Olympus, as fragments of a mythology which once was useful in the evolution of humankind's self-creation but which is now worn out, passé. In rejecting this mythology they will come to see ways of life, styles of being human, as a matter of choice rather than discovery. For them, teaching will constantly involve a double gesture of affirmation and deconstruction; the positive assertion of a thesis or style combined with the negation of its foundational claims, the denial of its warrant in arguments purporting to show it to be more true than alternatives.

Postmodern institutions will oppose attempts to centralize control of education or to bring its form, content and processes under universalizing criteria. Such logocentric artifacts as a uniform national education system – such as the National Curriculum of England and Wales – and the singular voice of an inspectorate will be seen as manifestations of a literary and cultural tyranny. For these reasons postmodernism stands opposed to a certain kind of multiculturalism, i.e. one which accentuates sameness, universality, smoothing out difference and contradiction, one which attempts to reconcile conflicting narratives and values, one which claims that all institutions should be homogenized. Postmodernism rejects the consensus politics of the left, with its implicit dream of the domination of a universal narrative of identity, in favour of a politics of difference (cf. McLaren 1995: 190–204). Postmodern educational institutions reject the idea that there are experts on lifestyle. There are no experts because the title is fatuous in a world where style is created not found, where what is good is permanently up for grabs.

In acclaiming the plural forms of signification inherent in postmodernity the state must provide schools, and lots of them; smaller schools, providing more choice, more mobility of both pupils and teachers, who can gravitate towards the institutions whose values they share most. This cannot be left to private funding, as commercial control would work to exercise a hegemony over the general educational landscape to reproduce a universalizing, hierarchy of privilege. The state must enable its population – parents, children, teachers – to engage in the dialogue of their own reproduction. *Their* taxes fund *their* state, *their* voice in *their* future. A worry of liberal democrats and socialists at this point concerns the risk of precipitating forms of separatism involving sterile individualism and 'the supremacy of competitive values over communal life' (Best cited in McLaren 1995: 216). This is a risk, a contingent possibility of postmodernity; but it is not a necessity. Indeed, the need to define identity *through* difference presupposes the dependency of the self-identification of a culture upon the narrative proximity or textual counterpoint provided in the representations of others which its vocabulary makes available; a dependency which displaces the traditional relation of self-identification to the universal code.

This postmodern gesture of dedivination, deuniversalization, should not be assumed to be automatically also a denationalizing movement. If it were, the question of why the state should fund it could legitimately be pressed, for the state funds the machinery of its perpetuation. But if that reproduction is of postmodernity then the case for funding it is as good as that for a logo-centric state to fund *its* reproduction. What is reproduced in postmodernity is dynamism rather than stasis; a future intended to be different from the present rather than identical with it; a progressive rather than a conservative reproduction; one for which sameness would be failure.

As for curriculum, get rid of it. Postmodern schools will jettison the model of knowledge which curriculum carries: universally respectable categories of belief and opinion; necessarily worthwhile pursuits independent of situation or local interest; absolute and invariant stepping-stones to citizenship and maturity; the admission ticket, sold from only one box-office, to theatres of activity, reward and privilege to which it is related by only an emaciated narrative; organization around age-range categories which match children to content under universalized age-knowledge imperatives. What postmodernism recognizes is the materiality – the physicality – of coherence: the necessity by which our understanding requires our control, our possession, of the content of our belief and the framework of its significance among other objects in our possession. The disaffected – the alienated children of late modernity – whose cultural identity is untouched by national curricula and remotely controlled values of schooling, recognize the humiliation of living as the distant effects of others' preferences. Postmodern teachers will construct pedagogy out of local interests and concerns where worth and value is set within a narrative in which its players have a stake and a voice.

Postmodern style fashions an educational practice, like any practice, out of conversational settings: philosophical dialogue concerning the values of society and education, literary consideration of the cultural placement of education, consideration of the texts of tradition and the writing of new possibilities. Judgement here is essentially literary-aesthetic; which is simply to say that it presupposes no rules and no ends that it doesn't make up in the process of developing its dialogue. We don't take a checklist to the theatre to discover whether the play was good or to find out whether or not we really enjoyed it. And neither should we take one to the school, the classroom or the student. Assessment or outcomes imperatives make for unhappy theatre and an impoverished story of human relationships, where the possibilities for excitement and surprise are restricted by the conditions of the guarantee specifying precisely what the participants will get. Postmodern modes of learning will no longer require any determinate structure; will crave no guarantee of course identity from one year to the next, no trans-course procedural framework aligning the delivery structures of one school with another or *education* with *engineering, philosophy* with *home economics* within a university. Rather, they will consist of a narrative affiliation of activities, topics, discussions, conversations, canon and novelty. They will give postmodern children, students and teachers an opportunity of self-creation, the end point of which will not be describable through a determinate catalogue of competences or achievements but will instead be what we might prefer to call a cultivated, literate and ironic human being; a citizen of postmodernity.

This, of course, flies in the face of current trends towards universality in curricula, teaching methods and assessment systems. It suggests that when we write programmes of fixed curricula within frameworks of delivery imperatives and entitlement, when we standardize testing procedures across and within courses and institutions, when we prespecify determinate learning outcomes and competences which a course must work to guarantee, when we structure a course around predetermined learning units which are governed by assessment requirements, when, in short, we do all the things that in most educational institutions we currently do, we are simply wrong; *and we are wrong in about as big a way as we possibly can be.*

Postmodernity asserts the literary qualities of judgement; that is, their non-algorithmic, non-bureaucratic nature. Postmodernity requires that judgemental styles are plural, relative to the particular context of enactment. It is simply a nonsense to impose a template of judgements upon textually embedded behaviour. We don't, as a matter of taste, do it with the novels we read and we shouldn't, as a matter of taste, do it with human beings either. Our judgements need to be made within the relevant context – itself a concept which is always *sous rature* – and in collaboration with relevant others; relevance being defined not in algorithmic or bureaucratic terms but with reference to membership of a literary community with shared interests and vocabulary. No set of rules will determine how the correct judgements are to be arrived at. We have, rather, the expectation that when conversation takes place within an atmosphere of common interests and academic freedom something interesting and worthwhile – if unexpected – will result (see Rorty 1980).

Anti-synthetic malevolence

Our postmodern sensitivity to textuality will enable us to see the idea(l) of the ultimate commensurability of dialogues as rhetorical fallout of the myth of convergence; and our irony will enable us to live with the consequences of its re-description and with incommensurability as an expectation. Reflection's dialectical process presupposed the possibility – and the desirability – of synthesis; its process was one of continual synthesis whose grand enterprise was to progress to yet higher levels of rationality and theoretical comprehensiveness. Built into the process was an arrow of rationality and truth which, like the arrow of time, points in only one direction: synthesized theories are better than the binary oppositions which precede them and worse than the future, grander syntheses of which they will – in time – form an element. But once the myth of convergence has been dissolved there is no longer any reason to believe either in the efficacy of dialectic or that the commensurability of all text/styles is a desirable literary ideal. For postmodernists the synthesizing of two literary artifacts seems an odd thing to do; which might turn out to be interesting in its creation of new poetic effects but which has no more of a 'right' to be interesting than does the dismantling of a text to make two new ones. Synthesis, on this view, presents us not with a better realization of the hopes, fears and concerns of the separate texts but produces, through interweaving, a new text; not a *'higher'* text, just *another* text.

This inaugurates at least two novel turns of style which will appear malevolent to the reflective teacher. First, the dialectical synthesis of conversational genres will no longer seem to have any point. Conversations – about, for example, personal autonomy *and* our duty to others; individual freedom *and* communal responsibility; one's own prosperity *and* global suffering; developing creativity and spontaneity in our students *and* initiating them into established patterns of behaviour, rites and traditions; the development of excellence *and* equality of opportunity; running emancipatory courses in our university *and* assessing the students – will no longer appear to be potentially commensurable *if only we can reason them through carefully enough*. They will be seen instead as the incommensurable outcomes of different styles of writing, of writing the literature of the individual or the group, of the avant-garde or the establishment, of the revolutionary or the traditional etc. These narratives may remain separate or may become conjoined. The postmodern twist to their story is that there will be no general desire that the narratives should be so conjoined or any general rule that the results of conjunction will be an improvement or even meaningful.

Indeed, as we saw with stories of autonomy, the only way to conjoin stories is to re-describe them, to re-situate the roles of their story elements to form something different, something novel, something which has a meaning which is not simply the additive effect of its parts. In other words, *synthesis,* if that is what the device can still be called, *destroys meaning*. Instead of preserving the significance of the components of its constituent stories, synthesis re-inscribes their sense to situate them within a new con/text. This is the second malevolent payoff of postmodernism: the effect of forming a new narrative out of existing literary materials is to change the currency of their characterizations, of their emplotment, of their vocabulary; it is to write something different; it is to talk about the situations and events of the stories in a different way, using a new vocabulary; it is to produce yet one more incommensurable artifact of literature. In short, *the necessary result of synthesis is distortion*. In this it mirrors precisely the corrupting effects which I have already shown to be an unwanted yet necessary element in the realist's conception of *rational analysis*.

Nightmares of relativism

What worries people about postmodern relativism is that among the disparate contexts, religions, customs, interests, sexual proclivities etc. lurk such monsters as human sacrifice, cannibalism, child pornography, Nazism. This worry arises, however, out of an erroneous concatenation of two distinct and conflicting stories. One is the relativist story of difference, the other is the liberal story of tolerance. As relativists, we postmoderns define ourselves through our differing; but this does not mean that we *must* rely upon *all* possible differential relations in order to define ourselves. That would be to fall in with a version of the myth of presence. Still less does it mean that we are committed to tolerating *all* differential styles. What is a real and urgent problem at the borders of liberalism is, for us, a triviality.

Fearsome narratives will get thrown up, sometimes by design, sometimes as the unforeseen consequence of a developing lifestyle narrative. Deconstruction takes advantage of their occult presence at the heart of even the most sublime treatise to manipulate them for its mutilatory purposes. They include: the monsters of *différance* which inevitably dismember our attempts to articulate rational foundations; the contradictory traces of oppression and licentiousness in liberal tolerance; the chaos and contrivance propping up the veneer of the ideal speech situation. They gain figurative expression as the id-monsters which came from the subconscious to destroy the hyper-rational civilization of the Krell in *Forbidden Planet*. We cannot eliminate them; for the very possibility of language and thought presupposes them. But we can rule them out. We can recognize the contingent, merely circular justification of our style and rule out the monsters on grounds *we* choose to be decisive. Here argument may not be appropriate. We may try to persuade the Nazi; or we might decide to ridicule him. Postmodernists are not debarred from saying that the artifact of Nazism is wrong; but it is wrong because it offends *our* literary taste and not because ethical reality itself is offended. And that is enough.

While deconstruction exposes the breach of all texts, an opening which postmodernists opportunistically exploit for play and creativity, this is not simply to replace realism's singular universality with a veridical anarchy of narrative islands of truth. *That* would be to fall for a new mythology of a universalized relativity. Postmodernism sires no such thing. While a multiplicity of stories are scribable, only a few will emerge as convincing candidates for truth, as most will fail to engage with the conversations of our time. These conversations have their own rhetorical inertia consequent upon the range of narratives which can form acceptable grounds for action. The readiness of our narratives to dissolve is not equivalent to their being incapable of standing solid for us. The limitations on anarchy, pliable and ephemeral as they are, are the methods, criteria, commitments, assumptions, beliefs and hopes that, for the moment at least, we are unwilling to negotiate. Following the incisions of deconstruction, closure itself becomes a particular kind of opening; one through which we choose not to pass. For our community itself, for the criteria we adopt, there can be no further, community-independent criterion of correctness. Unless we decide to re-describe it, it has no standard to meet.

The retail transaction of a novel fantasy will inevitably take place against the backdrop of accepted practices and discourse-forms whose transient general rightness will, in the initial gesture, not be questioned. The very concept of persuasion is only possible within such a stage-setting. In the initial gesture we must be concerned to honour the setting of our conversation, within whose narrative coherence our words of persuasion can find a meaning. Actual conversation with fellow human beings is our only guide to where we go right or wrong; hence the conversational relativity of persuasion and truth.

Lifestyle design

Teachers will see their role as involving the creation of educational ends, of educational values, through the articulation of new narratives of education, community and human flourishing.

Free of realist metaphysics, postmodern pedagogy constitutes the attempt to articulate a lifestyle; it becomes a fashion house of the textual possibilities for the creative participation in and extension of styles of being human. It attempts to make certain textual closures seem charmed or attractive. This quasi-aesthetic placement of our decisions to favour one conversational style over another is bound to seem criterionless and therefore arbitrary to the metaphysically challenged realist, but this is just a symptom of his conception of reason and truth, which blinds him to the point that the threshold of arbitrariness is itself indefinitely mobile across textual re-inscriptions. His failure to understand is caused by his belief that ultimately he will be able to differentiate good literature from bad through the application of a mathematical algorithm. In the educational conversations and institutions of postmodernity, however, reasons will be situated – affirmed, denied, argued, debated etc. – *in the name of literary coherence*; which has nothing to do with the Philistine desire for absolute, formal coherence.

The ends of education are not arbitrary, but they are not discoverable either.

This is another binary opposition that collapses under deconstruction. The ends of education, its values, commitments, practices and styles, are not objects of reflection but its products. They are created, contrived. They occupy a rhetorical space whose rules are negotiable and whose boundaries are soft to supplementarity; a rhetorical space whose DNA is a metaphorical structure which permeates, informs, grounds and regulates possible activities and self-understandings; which constitutes and inheres in its *characters*; which is manifested at the borderlines of legitimacy where the metaphors combine to exclude or marginalize general opposition. It is a space which constitutes the system's unconscious self-identity and, consequently, its inertia.

In siting her behaviour, consciously or unconsciously, explicitly or implicitly, around a cluster of metaphors, the teacher creates or reproduces a system, a textile, which will inevitably precipitate *characters* and cognitive, social and moral forces channelling descriptions, explanations and teleology this way or that in the narrative construction of an education. Postmodern educators repudiate the image of detachment as providing knowledge. There is no appropriately detached perspective. All they can try to do is create truth, create an audience, as purveyors of a narrative fashion. Detachment collapses with the recognition that in writing or in acting the teacher is always already embedded in the situations her descriptions partially create.

Consequently the postmodern teacher will not worry about indoctrination, for the indoctrination/education opposition is indefinitely mobile across misreadings. Deconstruction, in any case, unfolds an embarrassment of alternatives to the singular closure manifested within any particular reading or chosen pedagogy. All education becomes a special case of indoctrination following the displacement of a system which relied upon the absolute rigidity of a distinction between appeals to reason and appeals to authority. There will be no aim at neutrality, for the neutral will be fabricated within the story of an education. Education becomes the double gesture of indoctrination into a culture which deconstruction simultaneously exhibits as contingent, as a story unjustified by any metanarrative. The forces of closure which circumscribe our choice of one style over another – a commitment to one set of values or pedagogic style while ignoring alternatives – are the traces of the fashion as it contrives to bring us under its spell. They are not imposed as a censorship on style by some style-independent world. The style of the fashionable textile always already contains the suggestion of its own subversion, distortion, modification, transformation, exaggeration in the deconstructive movement of its displacement through the creation of new fashions. It is always, in other words, already inhabited by the disruptive force of *différance*; it contains the blueprint for its overturning in the possibilities for future novelty.

Identity through difference

The worries which reflective teaching has about partiality arise out of its general worry about difference. Despite its pluralism, personal and socio-contextual self-identity are taken as absolute, essential qualities of the normal;

difference, change, irregularity, *the abnormal* is what requires explanation. This, I have argued, shows itself in the presupposition of the stability of language, the identity across contexts of the person and the commitment to independent standards of rationality. It is manifested in the realist's faith in convergence: the idea that sentences ultimately converge around the *truth*; that rationality improves as systems of reasoning free themselves from the distortions of ideology to converge upon the single, true, rational standard; that the world's disparate, contrary moralities can ultimately converge in a morality founded on reason and in which the principles of justice and equality can gain universal assent and universal applicability.

But, *pace* Rorty, difference is only a problem *in general* if convergence is seen to be *generally desirable*. To postmodernists, however, convergence is no more generally desirable than our wearing the same style of dress, having the same sexual preferences or liking the same films is *generally desirable*. Indeed, the result of the homogenization of *haute couture* is not guaranteed facticity but a loss of cachet. For the postmodernist, difference is not viewed as parasitic upon identity but, rather, it is *in differing* that the literary artifact of self-definition – of persons, groups and cultures – becomes available. Intertextuality is the creative presupposition: the textual tools for our self-descriptions are only significant among other signifiers; there is no private construction free of the trace of otherness. Only among differences can we attach a meaning to the story we tell about ourselves. Differing – and *différance* – are the conditions of identity. Unless we can understand and articulate our distinctiveness we cannot conceptualize, assert or defend our identity because, simply, we have none.

It is at precisely this point that postmodern irony is necessary so that one can accept a self-definition while recognizing the foundationless contingency of each option. Postmodernists do not worry about truth, about reasoning within normal limits, for they are interested in seeing how far those limits can be distorted, corrupted, turned inside out, in articulating new style, new taste. Postmodernists do not see foundational problems lurking at the heart of every social practice as universal tensions in the human condition. There are no universal problems; just *ad hoc, ad hominem* rhetorical manoeuvres of persuasion; strategic interventions within the textual structure of actual, living conversations. There is no ideal rational framework to provide a philosophical foundation for educational theory and practice; just style-wars.

None of this entails a *rejection* of the concern for emancipation; but it does require that the literary setting of the concept of emancipation is displaced and that the vocabulary within which the emancipatory conversation is set is changed. Emancipation, given the ironic attitude, is freedom from humiliation (cf. Rorty 1989: 73ff). It is not an overcoming of the 'unseen constraints of assumptions, habit, precedent, coercion and ideology' (Carr and Kemmis 1986: 192). It is the feeling that the narrative placement in which one finds oneself is one's own; the sense that one maintains some capacity to read, and sufficient mastery to ride, the tides of re-description. The most that one can achieve in the creation of a story of emancipation is identical with what Coleridge saw is the most that one can hope to achieve in poetry:

it is to create the taste by which one will be judged (see Rorty 1989: 97). Only at this point can we feel sufficiently emancipated from the mythology of realism.

Thus emancipated, postmodernism's educational metaphysics is the world-making enterprise of the contrived artifact: making stories look sensible or silly by embedding them in further stories, situating plausibility as a move in the text which it does not occur to us to ridicule in respectable company. We write texts in which other texts feature and which hang together along various dramatic dimensions. We overwrite the universalizing *characters* of modernity – the manager *et al.* – to fabricate our own congress within a literature of cultural initiation; *characters* about which our moral discourse and self-descriptions will pivot; *characters* who resist subsumption under a universal, codified ethics but whose names instead, like those of Dickens's characters, replace and embody a moral cornucopia, making moral discourse a matter of name-dropping rather than the recitation of principles (Rorty 1991b: 78). In these narrative inventions some texts win and some lose, not because there is some higher theory of the text but because sometimes we require in our reading that there be winners and losers. Weaving a textile of new metaphors to create possible realizations of human life is the artistic adventure of the postmodern educator.

For the denizens of postmodernity what this creates is identity-through-difference; significance among signifiers. Our identity becomes a precipitate of our identifying our differing; our adoption of a narrative of our difference from others. Up for grabs are disposable lifestyles which shed universalism and naturalism, which define themselves through differing from one another. They are valued by us *because* they are different, reactive, and not in spite of or in tolerance of their differing. Disarming the limitations and restrictiveness of realism, the taboos are de-naturalized and de-nationalized. It is through these negotiable borders where the friction lies; the friction of differing which enables us to define ourselves. The frontiers of permissiveness and restriction are authorized within a technologically situated locality extending beyond the physical limits of speech to make context and community less an accident of geography and more a question of non-spatial textual commonalities.

If the story of education is to be the story of the kind of society in which we want to live then we need the cultural and rhetorical space in which to weave and enact our styles; especially in the face of the homogenizing forces of modern society, politics and educational administration. The institution-alization of *différance* and the opening this creates for the literary enterprise meet this requirement nicely. The hope is that education, textually conceived, can build a sense of community, of fellowship under a common literary style, and write the story of our difference.

Without creativity like this there is no reflective teaching but just oppression under others' narratives. Insinuated within postmodern education is the need to describe and create ways of living which communities can believe in; whose textuality articulates their commitments, beliefs, hopes and fears; whose *characters* and heroes set the moral tone for social intercourse and who are designed to provide a vocabulary constitutive of the building blocks of self-identity. Postmodern education nurtures communities who will create their own style, decide what they want to learn, what practices will characterize their schools, how their teachers will be educated, what standards their children will be judged by, what their literary setting will be. But these are excerpts from the wider story of postmodernity, which is that the narrative of our lives is up for grabs and it is up to us as a community woven together in the forging of a shared reality to take control; up to us to have courage enough to say, 'There is no why . . . This is how I act. My judgments themselves . . . characterize the nature of judgment' (OC p. 22); up to us to see it as possible that we will stamp our impress on millennia through creating ourselves.

Out of deconstruction comes the fashioning of style; from textual incisions and dismemberment comes the building of communal identity. The process from destruction to creation is the education of postmodernity:

> And if your hardness will not flash and cut and cut to pieces: how can you one day – create with me?
> For creators are hard. And it must seem bliss to you to press your hand upon millennia as upon wax.
>
> (Nietzsche, *Thus Spoke Zarathustra*)

BIBLIOGRAPHY

Abbs, P. (1974) *Autobiography in Education: an Introduction to the Subjective Discipline of Autobiography and Its Central Place in the Education of Teachers*. London: Heinemann.

Archambault, R.D. (ed.) (1972) *Philosophical Analysis and Education*. London: Routledge & Kegan Paul.

Arcilla, R.V. (1995) *For the Love of Perfection: Richard Rorty and Liberal Education*. London: Routledge.

Ayala, F.J. and Dobzhanski, T. (eds) (1974) *Studies in the Philosophy of Biology*. New York: Macmillan.

Baker, G. (1981) Following Wittgenstein: some signposts for *Philosophical Investigations* §§143–242, in S.H. Holtzman and C.M. Leich (eds) *Wittgenstein: to Follow a Rule*. London: Routledge & Kegan Paul.

Barnes, B. and Bloor, D. (1982) Relativism, rationalism and the sociology of knowledge, in M. Hollis and S. Lukes (eds) *Rationality and Relativism*. Oxford: Blackwell.

Bennett, J. (1974) *Kant's Dialectic*. Cambridge: Cambridge University Press.

Bennett, N. (1976) *Teaching Styles and Pupil Progress*. London: Open Books.

Bernstein, R.J. (1979) *The Restructuring of Social and Political Theory*. Oxford: Blackwell.

Bernstein, R.J. (1983) *Beyond Objectivism and Relativism*. Oxford: Blackwell.

Best, S. (1989) Jameson, totality, and the post-structuralist critique, in D. Keller (ed.) *Postmodernism/Jameson/Critique*. Washington, DC: Maisonneuve Press.

Beyer, L. (1987) What knowledge is of most worth in teacher education?, in J. Smyth (ed.) *Educating Teachers – Changing the Nature of Pedagogical Knowledge*. Lewes: Falmer.

Bowles, S. and Gintis, H. (1976) *Schooling in Capitalist America*. London: Routledge & Kegan Paul.

Canary, R.H. and Kozicki, H. (eds) (1978) *The Writing of History*. Madison: University of Wisconsin.

Carr, W. (1980) The gap between theory and practice, *Journal of Further and Higher Education*, 4(1), 60–9.

Carr, W. (1982) What is Educational Research?, *Journal of Curriculum Studies*, 14(2), 206–8.

Carr, W. (1985) Philosophy values and educational science, *Journal of Curriculum Studies*, 17(2), 119–32.

Carr, W. (ed.) (1989) *Quality in Teaching: Arguments for a Reflective Profession*. Lewes: Falmer.

Carr, W. and Kemmis, S. (1986) *Becoming Critical: Education, Knowledge and Action Research*. London: Falmer.

Claire, H. (1996) *Reclaiming Our Pasts: Equality and Diversity in the Primary History Curriculum*. Stoke-on-Trent: Trentham.

Connerton, P. (1980) *The Tragedy of Enlightenment: an essay on the Frankfurt School*. Cambridge: Cambridge University Press.

Cooper, D.E. (1983) *Authenticity and Learning*. London: Routledge & Kegan Paul.

Corey, S. (1953) *Action Research to Improve School Practices*. Columbia, NY: Teachers' College Press.

Culler, J. (1983) *On Deconstruction*. London: Routledge & Kegan Paul.

Dadds, M. (1995) *Passionate Enquiry and School Development: a Story about Teacher Action Research*. London: Falmer.

Davidson, D. (1974) On the very idea of a conceptual scheme, in D. Davidson (1984) *Inquiries into Truth and Interpretation*. Oxford: Oxford University Press.

Davidson, D. (1984) *Inquiries into Truth and Interpretation*. Oxford: Oxford University Press.

Davies, B. (1994) *Poststructuralist Theory and Classroom Practice*. Geelong: Deakin University.

Day, C. (1993) Reflection: a necessary but not sufficient condition for professional development, *British Educational Research Journal*, 19 (1): 83–93.

Dearden, R. (1968) *The Philosophy of Primary Education*. London: Routledge & Kegan Paul.

Dearden, R. (1975) Autonomy and Education, in R. Dearden P. Hirst and R.S. Peters (eds) *Education and Reason*. London: Routledge & Kegan Paul.

Derrida, J. (1968) *Différance*, in J. Derrida (1973) *Speech and Phenomena*. Evanston, IL: Northwestern University.

Derrida, J. (1976) *Of Grammatology*. Baltimore: Johns Hopkins University Press.

Derrida, J. (1981a) *Positions*. London: Athlone.

Derrida, J. (1981b) *Writing and Difference*. London: Routledge & Kegan Paul.

Derrida, J. (1982) *Margins of Philosophy*. Chicago: Harvester.

Devitt, M. (1984) *Realism and Truth*. Oxford: Blackwell.

Dewey, J. (1916) *Democracy and Education*. New York: The Free Press.

Dewey, J. (1933) *How We Think: a Restatement of the Relation of Reflective Thinking to the Educative Process*. Chicago: Henry Regenery.

Dummett, M. (1963) Realism, in M. Dummett (1978) *Truth and Other Enigmas*. London: Duckworth.

Dummett, M. (1978) *Truth and Other Enigmas*. London: Duckworth.

Dummett, M. (1981) *The Interpretation of Frege's Philosophy*. London: Duckworth.

Elliott, J. (1989) Teacher evaluation and teaching as a moral science, in M. Holly and C.S. McLoughlin (eds) *Perspectives on Teacher Professional Development*. Lewes: Falmer.

Elliott, J. (1991) *Action Research for Educational Change*. Milton Keynes: Open University.

Ennis, R.H. (1996) *Critical Thinking*. Upper Saddle River, NJ: Prentice Hall.

Feyerabend, P. (1982) *Science in a Free Society*. London: Verso.

Flew, A. (1972) Ends and Means, in P. Edwards (ed.) *The Encyclopedia of Philosophy*. New York: Macmillan.

Freire, P. (1972a) *Cultural Action for Freedom*. Harmondsworth: Penguin.

Freire, P. (1972b) *Pedagogy of the Oppressed*. London: Sheed & Ward.

Galton, M., Simon, B. and Croll, P. (1980) *Inside the Primary Classroom*. London: Routledge & Kegan Paul.

Giroux, H.A. and McLaren, P. (1995) Radical pedagogy as cultural politics: Beyond the discourse of critique and anti-utopianism, in P. McLaren, *Critical Pedagogy and Predatory Culture*. London: Routledge.

Gray, J. (1995) *Liberalism*. Buckingham: Open University Press.

Griffiths, M. and Tann, S. (1991) Ripples in the reflection, in P. Lomax (ed.) *BERA Dialogues*, 5, 82–101.

Groundwater-Smith, S. (1988) Credential bearing enquiry-based courses: paradox or new challenge?, in J. Nias and S. Groundwater-Smith (eds) *The Enquiring Teacher*. Lewes: Falmer.

Habermas, J. (1970) Towards a theory of communicative competence, *Inquiry*, 13, 360–75.

Habermas, J. (1974) *Theory and Practice*. London: Heinemann.

Habermas, J. (1976) *Legitimation Crisis*. London: Heinemann.

Habermas, J. (1978) *Knowledge and Human Interests*, 2nd edn. London: Heinemann.

Habermas, J. (1982) A reply to my critics, in J. Thompson and D. Held (eds) *Habermas: Critical Debates*. London: Macmillan.

Habermas, J. (1984) *The Theory of Communicative Action*. Vol. 1. London: Heinemann.

Hacker, P.M.S. (1972) *Insight and Illusion*. Oxford: Oxford University Press.

Hamlyn, D.W. (1978) *Experience and the Growth of Understanding*. London: Routledge & Kegan Paul.

Handy, C. (1984) *The Empty Raincoat*. London: Random House.

Hirst, P. (1965) Liberal education and the nature of knowledge, in R.D. Archambault (ed.) *Philosophical Analysis and Education*. London: Routledge & Kegan Paul.

Hirst, P. (1974) *Knowledge and the Curriculum*. London: Routledge & Kegan Paul.

Hollis, M. and Lukes, S. (eds) (1982) *Rationality and Relativism*. Oxford: Blackwell.

Holly, M. and McLoughlin, C.S. (eds) (1989) *Perspectives on Teacher Professional Development*. Lewes: Falmer.

Holtzman, S.H. and Leich, C.M. (eds) (1981) *Wittgenstein: to Follow a Rule*. London: Routledge & Kegan Paul.

Hume, D. (1740) *A Treatise of Human Nature*. Oxford: Oxford University Press (1958 edition).

Isaac, J. and Ashcroft, K. (1988) A leap into the practical: a BEd (Hons) programme, in J. Nias and S. Groundwater-Smith (eds) *The Enquiring Teacher*. Lewes: Falmer.

Kant, I. (1781/1787) *Critique of Pure Reason*, 1st and 2nd edns (trans. as *Immanuel Kant's Critique of Pure Reason*). London: Macmillan (1987 edition).

Kant, I. (1788) *Critique of Practical Reason* (trans. as *Kant's Critique of Practical Reason and Other Works on the Theory of Ethics*). London: Longman (1967 edition).

Kerferd, G.B. (1989) *The Sophistic Movement*. Cambridge: Cambridge University Press.

Kielkopf, C.F. (1970) *Strict Finitism*. The Hague: Mouton.

Korner, S. (1967) The impossibility of transcendental deductions, *The Monist*, 51 (3), 317–31.

Krupnick, M. (ed.) (1983) *Displacement: Derrida and After*. Bloomington: Indiana University Press.

Kuhn, T.S. (1970) *The Structure of Scientific Revolutions*. Chicago: Chicago University Press.

Lakoff, G. and Johnson, M. (1980) *Metaphors We Live By*. Chicago: Chicago University Press.

Langford, G. (1985) *Education, Persons and Society: a Philosophical Enquiry*. Basing-stoke: Macmillan.

Lipman, M. (1985) *Harry Stottlemeier's Discovery*. New Jersey: The First Mountain Foundation.

Lukes, S. (1982) Of gods and demons: Habermas and practical reason, in J. Thompson and D. Held (eds) *Habermas: Critical Debates*. London: Macmillan.

MacIntyre, A. (1985) *After Virtue*. London: Duckworth.

McLaren, P. (1995) *Critical Pedagogy and Predatory Culture*. London: Routledge.

McLennan, G. (1995) *Pluralism*. Buckingham: Open University Press.

Martin, J.R. (1994) *Changing the Educational Landscape: Philosophy, Women, and Curriculum*. London: Routledge.

Mink, L.O. (1978) Narrative form as a cognitive instrument, in R.H. Canary and H. Kozicki (eds) *The Writing of History*. Madison: University of Wisconsin.

Mortimore, P., Sammons, P., Stoll, L., Lewis, D. and Ecob, R. (1988) *School Matters: the Junior Years*. London: Open Books

Newton-Smith, W. (1982) Relativism and the possibility of interpretation, in M. Hollis and S. Lukes (eds) *Rationality and Relativism*. Oxford: Blackwell.

Nias, J. and Groundwater-Smith, S. (eds) (1988) *The Enquiring Teacher*. Lewes: Falmer.

Norris, C. (1982) *Deconstruction: Theory and Practice*. London: Methuen.

Nietzsche, F. (1892) *Thus Spoke Zarathustra*. Harmondsworth: Penguin (1969 edition).

Nozick, R. (1974) *Anarchy, State and Utopia*. Oxford: Blackwell.

Parker, S. (1986) Relativism, anti-realism, and the metaphilosophy of education. Unpublished PhD thesis, University of London.

Paul, R.W. (1984) Critical thought essential to the acquisition of rational know-ledge and passions. Paper presented to Connecticut Conference on Thinking.

Peters, R.S. (1966) *Ethics and Education*. London: Routledge & Kegan Paul.

Pollard, A. and Tann, S. (1994) *Reflective Teaching in the Primary School: a Handbook for the Classroom*. London: Cassell.

Popper, K.R. (1959) *The Logic of Scientific Discovery*. London: Hutchinson (1968 edition).

Popper, K.R. (1963) *Conjectures and Refutations*. London: Routledge & Kegan Paul.

Popper, K.R. (1974) Scientific reduction and the essential incompleteness of all science, in F.J. Ayala and T. Dobzhanski (eds) *Studies in the Philosophy of Biology*. New York: Macmillan.

Potter, S. (1947) *The Theory and Practice of Gamesmanship*. Harmondsworth: Penguin (1962 edition).

Putnam, H. (1976) Realism and reason, in H. Putnam (1978) *Meaning and the Moral Sciences*. London: Routledge & Kegan Paul.

Putnam, H. (1981) *Reason, Truth and History*. Cambridge: Cambridge University Press.

Quine, W.V.O. (1948) On what there is, in W.V.O. Quine (1963) *From a Logical Point of View*. New York: Harper and Row.

Quine, W.V.O. (1951) Two dogmas of empiricism, in W.V.O. Quine (1963) *From a Logical Point of View*. New York: Harper and Row.

Quine, W.V.O. (1960) *Word and Object*. Cambridge, MA: MIT.

Quine, W.V.O. (1963) *From a Logical Point of View*. New York: Harper and Row.

Rorty, R. (1971) Verificationism and transcendental arguments, *Nous*, 5, 3–14.

Rorty, R. (1980) *Philosophy and the Mirror of Nature*. Oxford: Blackwell.

Rorty, R. (1982) *Consequences of Pragmatism*. Brighton: Harvester.

Rorty, R. (1989) *Contingency, Irony, and Solidarity*. Cambridge: Cambridge University Press.

Rorty, R. (1991a) *Objectivism, Relativism, and Truth*. Cambridge: Cambridge University Press.

Rorty, R. (1991b) *Essays on Heidegger and Others*. Cambridge: Cambridge University Press.

Ryan, M. (1983) Deconstruction and social theory: the case of liberalism, in M. Krupnick (ed.) *Displacement: Derrida and After*. Bloomington: Indiana University Press.

Ryle, G. (1949) *The Concept of Mind*. Harmondsworth: Penguin.

Sarup, M. (1988) *An Introductory Guide to Post-structuralism and Postmodernism*. Hemel Hempstead: Harvester Wheatsheaf.

Schön, D.A. (1983) *The Reflective Practitioner*. London: Temple Smith.

Siegel, H. (1987) *Relativism Refuted*. Dordrecht: Reidel.

Siegel, H. (1988) *Educating Reason*. London: Routledge & Kegan Paul.

Siegel, H. (1991) Indoctrination and education, in B. Spiecker and R. Straughan (eds) *Freedom and Indoctrination in Education: International Perspectives*. London: Cassell.

Smyth, J. (1987) Transforming teaching through intellectualizing the work of teachers, in J. Smyth (ed.) *Educating Teachers – Changing the Nature of Pedagogical Knowledge*. Lewes: Falmer.

Spiecker, B. and Straughan, R. (eds) (1991) *Freedom and Indoctrination in Education: International Perspectives*. London: Cassell.

Staten, H. (1985) *Wittgenstein and Derrida*. Oxford: Blackwell.

Stenhouse, L. (1975) *Introduction to Curriculum Research and Development*. London: Heinemann.

Sterne, L. (1781) *The Life and Opinions of Tristram Shandy, Gentleman*. London: J.M. Dent & Sons (1961 edition).

Strawson, P.F. (1966) *The Bounds of Sense: an Essay on Kant's Critique of Pure Reason*. London: Methuen (1975 edition).

Stroud, B. (1968) Transcendental arguments, *Journal of Philosophy*, 65, 231–56.

Sturrock, J. (1986) *Structuralism*. London: Paladin.

Taylor, C. (1975) *Hegel*. Cambridge: Cambridge University Press.

Thomas, D. (ed.) (1995) *Teachers' Stories*. Buckingham: Open University Press.

Thompson, J. (1982) Universal pragmatics, in J. Thompson and D. Held (eds) *Habermas: Critical Debates*. London: Macmillan.

Tickle, L. (1992) Professional skills assessment in classroom teaching, *Cambridge Journal of Education*, 22(1), 91–103.

Trigg, R. (1973) *Reason and Commitment*. Cambridge: Cambridge University Press.

Walker, R.C.S. (1978) *Kant*. London: Routledge & Kegan Paul.

Weiner, G. (1989) Professional self-knowledge versus social justice: a critical analysis of the teacher-researcher movement, *British Educational Research Journal*, 15 (1): 41–51.

Weiner, G. (1994) *Feminisms in Education: an introduction*. Buckingham: Open University Press.

White, H. (1978) The historical text as literary artifact, in R.H. Canary and H. Kozicki (eds) *The Writing of History*. Madison: University of Wisconsin.

White, J.P. (1973) *Towards a Compulsory Curriculum*. London: Routledge & Kegan Paul.

White, P. (1983) *Beyond Domination*. London: Routledge & Kegan Paul.

White, S.K. (1988) *The Recent Work of Jurgen Habermas: Reason, Justice and Modernity*. Cambridge: Cambridge University Press.

Williams, B. (1978) *Descartes: the Project of Pure Enquiry*. Brighton: Harvester.

Winch, P. (1958) *The Idea of a Social Science*. London: Routledge & Kegan Paul.

Winter, R. (1988) Fictional-critical writing: an approach to case study research by practitoners and for in-service and pre-service work with teachers, in J. Nias and S. Groundwater-Smith (eds) *The Enquiring Teacher*. Lewes: Falmer.

Winter, R. (1989) *Learning from Experience: Principles and Practice in Action Research*. Lewes: Falmer.

Wittgenstein, L. (1953) *Philosophical Investigations*. Oxford: Blackwell.

Wittgenstein, L. (1969) *On Certainty*. Oxford: Blackwell.

Wittgenstein, L. (1978) *Remarks on the Foundations of Mathematics*, 3rd edn. Oxford: Blackwell.

Wright, C. (1980) *Wittgenstein on the Foundations of Mathematics*. London: Duckworth.

Young, R.E. (1989) *A Critical Theory of Education: Habermas and Our Children's Future*. Hemel Hempstead: Harvester Wheatsheaf.

Young, R.E. (1992) *Critical Theory and Classroom Talk*. Clevedon: Multilingual Matters.

INDEX

FOR EDUCATION
TOWARDS CRITICAL EDUCATIONAL ENQUIRY

Wilfred Carr

A recent review of his work describes Wilfred Carr as 'one of the most brilliant philosophers now working in the rich British tradition of educational philosophy ... His work is rigorous, refreshing and original ... and examines a number of fundamental issues with clarity and penetration.'

In *For Education* Wilfred Carr provides a comprehensive justification for reconstructing educational theory and research as a form of critical inquiry. In doing this, he confronts a number of important philosophical questions. What is educational theory? What is an educational practice? How are theory and practice related? What is the role of values in educational research? Is a genuinely educational science possible? By appealing to developments in critical theory, the philosophy of science and the philosophy of the social sciences, Wilfred Carr provides answers to these questions which vindicate the idea of an educational science that is not 'on' or 'about' education but 'for education' – a science genuinely committed to promoting educational values and ideals.

Contents

Introduction: Becoming an educational philosopher – Part 1: Theorizing education – The gap between theory and practice – Theories of theory and practice – Adopting an educational philosophy – What is an educational practice? – Part 2: Towards a critical educational science – Can educational research be scientific? – Philosophy, values and an educational science – Whatever happened to action research? – The idea of an educational science – Epilogue: Confronting the postmodernist challenge – Notes – References – Bibliography – Index.

160pp   0 335 19186 X (paperback)   0 335 19187 8 (hardback)

TEACHERS' STORIES
David Thomas (ed.)

In *Teachers' Stories* David Thomas and his contributors present an argument for the content and process of teacher training to be enriched by the inclusion of educational biography, both general (grounded Life Histories) and subject specific accounts, as significant ingredients to be stirred in with more formal theoretic and practical aspects of training. Creating educational biographies is one way of introducing students to critical reflection on their 'taken-for-granted' educational beliefs and values, and their origins.

Though not a training manual, *Teachers' Stories* will be of interest to all teacher trainers including the new cohort of trainers – the teacher mentors. Students will also find support for their attempts to introduce, through journals, diaries or logs, their individual experiences as alternative voices to the pre-eminent discourses of the training institution. It is suggested that such opportunities are especially valuable for students and tutors where the student's background and culture provide unusually distinctive experiences with possibilities for course enrichment as well as personal development.

Contents
Introduction – Treasonable or trustworthy text: Reflection on teacher narrative studies – My language experience – The pupil experience: A view from both sides – An education biography and commentary – What do I do next? – Autobiography, feminism and the practice of action research – Making the private public – Crossing borders for professional development: Narratives of exchange teachers – Breaking tradition: The experiences of an alternative teacher in a rural school – Empirical authors, liminal texts and model readers – Keys to the past – and to the future – 'Composing a life': Women's stories of their careers – Index.

Contributors
Kath Aspinwall, Waltraud Boxall, Arda L. Cole, Florence Gersten, Morwenna Griffiths, Mary Jean Ronan Herzog, J. Gary Knowles, Doreen Littlewood, Anne Murray, Jennifer Nias, David Thomas, Elizabeth Thomas, Peter J. Woods.

240pp   0 335 19254 8 (Paperback)   0 335 19255 6 (Hardback)

EDUCATION REFORM
A CRITICAL AND POST-STRUCTURAL APPROACH

Stephen J. Ball

This book builds upon Stephen J. Ball's previous work in the field of education policy analysis. It subjects the ongoing reforms in UK education to a rigorous critical interrogation. It takes as its main concerns the introduction of market forces, managerialism and the national curriculum into the organization of schools and the work of teachers. The author argues that these reforms are combining to fundamentally reconstruct the work of teaching, to generate and ramify multiple inequalities and to destroy civic virtue in education. The effects of the market and management are not technical and neutral but are essentially political and moral. The reforms taking place in the UK are both a form of cultural and social engineering and an attempt to recreate a fantasy education based upon myths of national identity, consensus and glory. The analysis is funded within policy sociology and employs both ethnographic and post-structuralist methods.

Contents
Preface – Glossary – Post-structuralism, ethnography and the critical analysis of education reform – What is policy? Texts, trajectories and toolboxes – Education, Majorism and the curriculum of the dead – Education policy, power relations and teachers' work – Cost, culture and control: self-management and entrepreneurial schooling – 'New headship' and school leadership: new relationships and new tensions – Education markets, choice and social class: the market as a class strategy in the UK and USA – Competitive schooling: values, ethics and cultural engineering – References – Index.

176pp   0 335 19272 6 (Paperback)   0 335 19273 4 (Hardback)